POWERED ULTRALIGHT FLYING

Dennis Pagen

ILLUSTRATIONS BY THE AUTHOR

POWERED ULTRALIGHT FLYING
A COMPLETE INSTRUCTION MANUAL

First Printing: September, 1983
Printed in the United States of America

Published by Dennis Pagen
P.O. Box 601, State College, PA 16801

Books by the Author
Powered Ultralight Flying Course
Flying Conditions
Hang Gliding Flying Skills
Hang Gliding Techniques

Library of Congress Catalog Card No.: 79-93224

ISBN 0-936310-06-5

The Bird-Like Nighthawk

CONTENTS

FORWARD vii
CHAPTER I - PREPARING FOR FLIGHT 1
    What is an Ultralight 1
    The Ultralight Story 2
    Ultralight Types 4
    Choosing Your Wings 6
    Buying A Used Ultralight 12
    Additional Equipment 15
    Commonly Asked Questions 19
CHAPTER II — LEARNING TO FLY 23
    Types of Training 23
    The Site and the Air 26
    Learning Procedures 27
    The First Flight 28
    Stalls 30
    Basic Turns 31
    Flying the Pattern 32
    Further Practice 34
CHAPTER III — THE AIR 37
    Weather Patterns 37
    Frontal and Pressure Systems 38
    Clouds 40
    Local Effects 43
    The Sea Breeze 44
    Turbulence 44
    Winds at Altitude 48
    Lift Sources 50
    Thunderstorms and Dust Devils 51
CHAPTER IV — THE THEORY OF FLIGHT 54
    Lift and Drag 54
    Speed Variation 57
    Stalls 60
    Flight Control 62
    Turning Flight 66
    Tip Vortices 69
    Power Considerations 70
CHAPTER V — AIRMANSHIP 73
    Set Up 73
    Preflight and Routine Inspection 74
    Care and Cleaning 75
    Ground Handling 77
    Ultralight Trimming 78
    Weather Conditions 79
    Ultralight Instruments 80

Cockpit Check 84
Take Off Procedures 85
Density Altitude 87
Flying in Wind 90
Cross Country 93
Navigation 97
Air Traffic Rules 101
Airport Operations 104
Flying at Altitude 106
Stall Control 109
Using Controls 110
Landing Procedures 112
The End of the Day 118
CHAPTER VI — THE FLYING MACHINE 119
The Structure 119
The Engines 123
Engine Mounting 124
Fuel Systems 125
Care of the Engine 126
Engine Additions 129
Tuning the Carburetor .131
The Propeller 134
Propeller Mounting 137
CHAPTER VII — MORE ADVENTURES .141
Using a Parachute 141
Canards 144
Trike Systems 145
Float Flying 148
Flying on Skis 154
Aerobatics 154
Soaring Ultralights 155
Competition Flying 161
CHAPTER VIII — MEDICAL CONSIDERATIONS 165
Vision 165
Vertigo 167
Hypoxia 167
Physical Fitness 168
Fatigue 169
Hypothermia 170
Decompression 170
Miscellaneous Factors .170
Drugs and Alcohol 171
APPENDIX I — PART 103 173
APPENDIX II — ULTRALIGHT SAFETY 177
GLOSSARY 178
ABOUT THE AUTHOR 183

FORWARD

We live in an amazing time. Not only are we reaching for the stars, but we have brought space-age technology to every facet of life on this planet. All this progress is a product of large-budget scientific teams. Sometimes the accomplishments of the man on the street are overshadowed by the projects of government and big business. It's nice to know that the sport of flying powered ultralight aircraft is a grass roots movement, brought about by tinkers and geniuses in their backyards.

Our sport is in its infancy. We have just begun to spread our wings. There will be many changes and developments as the years progress, but the fact remains that it is now possible for mankind to fly a convenient, safe and exciting personal airplane. And that's amazing.

As with any active endeavor, there is a great need for learning safe techniques. This book covers the many areas of knowledge that all good pilots must master. The ideas are presented in an easy to understand manner. It is my intention to remain as non-technical as possible, yet include all the material necessary for safe flying.

This book is not meant to take the place of an instructor, but rather to provide guidance both during and after a pilot completes a regular instruction course. For detailed step-by-step instruction in powered ultralights, purchase the Powered Ultralight Training Course Manual by this author. The Training Course consists of eleven ground schools and eleven lessons for the uninitiated beginner.

A book cannot take the place of experience. You must practice flying to become an expert. On the other hand, you cannot learn everything by experience—it takes too long and it is senseless to repeat mistakes that have proven dangerous. Use the information provided to broaden your experience and keep your flying safe and enjoyable.

This book was originally written in 1979 and was the only book available at the time. Since then, much has changed in the sport and new ideas abound. For that reason, this revised edition is a complete reworking of the originial, with all sections updated and a great deal of additional material. Have fun reading this book and developing your flying skills.

Dennis Pagen

The Lazair

The Goldwing

CHAPTER I

PREPARING FOR FLIGHT

Why do we want to become pilots? Perhaps it's the urge to swoop and arc through the sky with the freedom of a bird. Perhaps it's due to an inborn desire to leave the humdrum cares of the earthbound world behind. Often, the thrill of seeing things in a new perspective is reason enough to "acquire our wings."

Most of us have dreamed of flying since we were young. Flying an ultralight aircraft is the best way to fulfill that dream. However, we must be willing to do a little work and preparation in order to learn quickly and continue to fly safely. With this in mind, we'll begin the enjoyable task of exploring ultralight flight.

WHAT IS AN ULTRALIGHT?

When we speak of ultralight craft, we can be referring to anything from a small, single-place airplane to a hang glider. For the purpose of this book, we will accept the current Federal Aviation Administration (FAA) definition (see below). In most countries, the term "microlight" is used in place of ultralight. For the record, a hang glider is generally understood to be a portable, foot-launched sailplane. Hang gliders are now classified as unpowered ultralights by the FAA. A sailplane is an airplane designed to stay aloft and soar on the air currents without the use of auxiliary power. A motorglider is simply a sailplane equipped with a small engine to carry it aloft until thermals and other updrafts can be found. Many ultralights with engines can be classified as motorgliders since they can be soared with the engine off.

All of these aircraft are actually airplanes of various sizes and performance ranges. In fact, at this time, these are designs available running the spectrum from general aircraft all the way down to light hang gliders with an engine as well as from large sailplanes all the way down to hang gliders without engines. There is no way to make a distinction between these different airplanes unless we use wing loading, horsepower, total weight or some equally arbitrary criteria. This is exactly what the FAA did when issuing Part 103, the ruling that governs ultralights, (A complete copy of this ruling is found in

1

Appendix I.)

The FAA definition of a powered ultralight is: a single occupant vehicle intended to be used for recreational purposes only, weighing less than 254 pounds (empty weight), with a fuel capacity less than 5 gallons, a 55 knot (63 mph) top speed in level flight and a power-off stall speed of less than 24 knots (27.5 mph). The idea behind the ruling was to limit weight, top speed and fuel capacity so as to reduce the danger an ultralight poses to the pilot, persons on the ground and other aircraft. Pilots and manufacturers appear to be satisfied with the provisions of Part 103, so here we have the definition of an ultralight.

THE ULTRALIGHT STORY

This history of ultralight aircraft is the history of flight itself. Practical aviation began at the end of the last century with the design of a few successful hang gliders. Men like Otto Lillienthal, Percy Pilcher, Octave Chanute and the Wright brothers launched their light wood and cloth gliders from slopes and balloons just like modern hang glider pilots. The success of these gliders inspired the pioneer aviators to add power to overcome the limits of gravity. However, there was a distinct lack of suitable engines at the time. Part of the achievement of the Wright brothers was due to the fact that they designed and developed their own engine.

Sailplane

Hang Glider

Now here was something to excite even the most conservative deacon of the time. A generation accustomed to horse and buggy transportation was suddenly startled to see plucky pilots motoring through the air! Within a few short years, aviation had captured the imagination of the world as powered airplanes grew in size, efficiency and reliability.

Hang gliding had no practical application, so it was soon forgotten. World War I sparked the design of fast, maneuverable biplanes as well as large airships and Zeppelins. The postwar years saw the development of the first sailplanes, helicopters and gyrocopters—all with a limited degree of military application. The airline industry and mail carriers blossomed in this era. Unfortunately, the average individual could no longer afford to fly due to the economics of the time.

Aviation received another boost from World War II. The use of jet engines, metal construction and other improvements assured the airplane a foremost role in military operations. When the war ended, there were two interesting residual effects. The first was the large number of pilots trained in combat created a demand for civilian aircraft. Postwar affluence as well as surplus aircraft and technology allowed many of these airmen to pursue their passion for flying. Private aircraft took to the sky in flocks. Regulation of airspace became a necessity and the Federal Aviation Administration (FAA) grew like an overfed child.

The second postwar boon occurred in Germany. The occupying countries would not allow the Germans to operate powered aircraft after the war. Consequently, frustrated German pilots and designers turned their efforts to developing gliders or sailplanes. The performance of the ships and skill of the pilots improved dramatically. Soaring (the art of staying aloft in a sailplane) turned men into eagles.

In the late 1960's, a rebirth of the original form of aviation occurred. As an offshoot of the American space program, the standard "Rogallo" hang glider appeared. The use of Dacron and modern aluminum alloy allowed the construction of a small portable glider that could be foot-launched like the early aircraft of the last century. Within a decade, these personal wings grew in sophistication and performance while still maintaining their basic ease of transportation and control. The appeal of hang gliding is the low cost (compared to any other form of aviation) and the relative degree of freedom from regulation. Flying is now available for everyone.

Hang Glider With Gemini Engine

The last chapter in this story is the application of power to hang gliders and other small sailplanes. A few pilots living in the flat lands overcame their handicap by adapting small chainsaw engines to mount on their gliders. This was viewed as reinventing the airplane by some, but the Wright brothers never had it so good! The pilots of such craft could set their wings up next to their house, motor up to a few thousand feet, hook a thermal and float around for an hour or so. Thus, the sport of powered ultralight flying was born. Many pilots consider this form of aviation to be the only way to fly.

To be sure, ultralight aircraft were around before the surge of hang gliding, but most were heavy, inconvenient and costly. It took the innovative technology of hang gliding as well as the large batch of eager pilots to guarantee the popularity of powered ultralight flying. Today, a new application of old ideas continues to spring forth and light aircraft designed specifically for motorizing are abundant. We can all fulfull our desire to become a pilot.

The Early Footlaunching Days

ULTRALIGHT TYPES

As indicated above, powered ultralight aircraft come in almost as much variety as the birds in the sky. Let's look at a few general types. Beginning on the light side we have the flex wing hang gliders adapted to powered flight with the addition of a small strap-on engine and landing gear system. These systems are known as "trikes" due to their three point stance. The hang glider consists of an aluminum frame supporting a Dacron sail shaped like a bird's wing. They typically weigh between 60 and 80 pounds (23 to 36 kg) while the engine system weighs less than 100 pounds (45 kg). The cost of these hang gliders continues to rise, but used ones will always be available for under $1,000, while the cost of the engine/gear system is typically under $2,000.

The performance of a flex wing powered ultralight is not as good as a
hang glider due to extra drag and weight, but their maneuverability
and reasonable sink rate makes them a good choice for soaring. Climb
rates up to 1000 feet per minute (fpm) are possible (depending on pilot
weight and engine size). Speed ranges typically run from 20 to 50 mph.
All controls are effected by the pilot shifting his weight forward and
back, or side to side (some designs combine weight shift with control
surfaces). Easy folding of flex wings assures their popularity as
powered ultralight aircrafts. Trike systems are very common in
Europe.

A Hang Glider/Trike System

The next type of ultralights takes a step up in cost, weight, and
usually complexity. These are the fixed wing designs. A fixed wing is a
flying surface that doesn't change shape in flight. The wing consists of
an aluminum frame covered with cloth, plastic, wood or metal. Dacron
is the material most often used.

We can further divide the fixed wing ultralights into subcategories.
One distinction would be whether or not the ultralight had a tail, a
canard (a small wing up front) or neither. We discuss the implications
of these design factors in Chapters IV and VI.

Another major difference in ultralight types is the method of control. Those ultralights that originated as hang gliders may be totally
or partially controlled with weight shift. Other designs have two-axis
contol (the third axis of rotation being controlled automatically by the
ultralight built-in stability). Finally, we have the true three-axis controlled ultralights with control systems similar to a conventional
airplane (usually a stick and pedal hook-up). Pilots in conventional aircraft find learning to fly ultralights is easiest on this latter type.

The cost of a fixed wing ultralight is from $3,000 on up. Usually the more complex and better performing, the more expensive. We cannot generalize on the performance of these ultralights, for they range from downright dismal to virtually awesome. Of course, they all supposedly remain within the FAA weight and speed limits. Engine size is extremely variable and is a big factor determining performance and cost.

Many other factors such as engine-off performance control sensitivity, cross-wind capability, rough field capability, take off and landing distance requirements, portability and quietness vary as well from design to design. The next section tackles the problem of sorting out these details.

A Weight Shift And Rudder Controlled Pterodactyl

CHOOSING YOUR WINGS

One of the hardest jobs that faces a pilot of powered ultralights is selecting the right aircraft. This is because there are so many designs available with widely different characteristics. Choosing an aircraft is like choosing a mate. A hasty decision will often lead to disappointment concerning performance or construction details. Dealers cannot provide much useful guidance since they are usually only interested in selling their own products. To help clear this cloud of confusion, let us look at various criteria upon which a choice should be based. The reader should weigh each point carefully, then choose the aircraft most suited to his situation and desires.

I. The first, and most important, consideration is the goal that each pilot has in mind when learning ultralight flight. The ultimate reason for flying a powered ultralight is for enjoyable recreation—in a word, fun. Of couse, we all have our own idea of what fun is.

The notion that powered ultralights can be a consistent form of

6

transportation should be dispelled. Aviation is more dependent on the whims of the weather than automobiles, motorcycles or even boats. Thus, the vision of masses of commuters winging to work is a pipe dream unless the vehicle is used in the sunny southwest. However, weekend excursions of a hundred miles or more are a reality. With a sleeping bag strapped to the airframe, a pilot can take an extended trip and relive the early barnstorming days.

Another definite reality is climbing to a couple thousand feet, shutting off the power and searching for thermals. Ultralight pilots have gained many thousands of feet in thermals and have logged some impressive cross-country flights. This is what true soaring is all about. Thermaling (and other forms of soaring) requires considerable skill and experience, but is one of the most rewarding forms of flight.

A Canard Equipped Eagle

Some pilots simply want the convenience of toting a portable airplane to the nearest field and cruising around to enjoy the scenery. This "Sunday drive" form of flying is quite a worthwhile pastime as long as the pilot takes care not to disturb the privacy or peace of those on the ground.

The final possible factor in determining which ultralight to buy in terms of desired goals, is competition. As ultralight competitions proliferate, the rewards of being an "ace" pilot will be many. Experience has shown that choice of aircraft is probably the biggest factor in a pilot's competition performance.

What ultralight is best suited for the different goals outlined? The perfect ship to cover everything isn't yet available, so we will look at each criteria in turn.

If your interest lies in touring the country by air, you'll need a fuel efficient machine. We mean fuel efficiency in terms of miles per gallon, not gallons per hour since a slow, efficient craft will be no better than a fast gas guzzler. The manufacturer's published data providing consumption (in gallons per hour) at a given cruise speed will allow you to figure out the miles you can get out of a tank of fuel. This factor is directly related to how suitable a given design is for long trips. Remember some ultralights do not have a full 5 gallon fuel capacity.

Another factor you should consider is the ability to carry extra weight in the form of gear (remember that sleeping bag). Tools and spare parts are almost essential unless you have a ground crew trailing along.

Finally, ease of control is important since you will be flying for hours at a stretch and should avoid fatigue.

All the above items indicate a fast, well-powered, three-axis controlled ship. There are many ultralights on the market meeting this description. Look at the specifications of each ultralight and find the best all-around design for the items listed. Remember you'll be landing in various fields when traveling afar, so look at rough field capability and takeoff requirements as well.

A Two-Axis Controlled Quicksilver

If your interest is in soaring (see Chapter VII), your best bet is a good handling (responsive controls), good performing ultralight with a small engine. By good performing, we mean a slow sink rate and good glide ratio when the engine is shut down. The reason we indicated a small engine is so that is doesn't add excess weight and drag once it is idled back or switched off.

The type of ultralights indicated here are the hang glider/trike systems (the engine packs are fairly light and the glider turns very well) or fixed wing types with efficient wing design. Pilots, dealers and manufacturers can give you some ideas as to which ultralights best meet the bill for soaring.

Finally we have the weekend warrior type of pilot who just wants to cruise around the neighborhood and open a few eyes (there's some of that in all of us). For this type of flying, almost every ultralight is suitable. In fact, that's what ultralights do best. However, be aware that enjoyment in an ultralight is directly proportional to the amount of maintainance required. The more work you have to do on your engine, the less time you'll have to explore the sky. The conclusion is obvious: buy a reliable craft. Ask pilots (not manufacturers) about a given design's reliability, and chances are you'll find out what's best on the market.

A Three-Axis Controlled BI-RD

One more point to consider when purchasing an ultralight is the noise it produces. Not only can this noise have debilitating effects on the pilot, but it disturbs the peace as well. Ultralights tend to produce an annoying high pitched whine and they don't move by an area as quickly as say a motorcycle or airplane. The neighbors and farmers around the country side may run out and gape at your first few flights, but soon the annoying bra-a-a-at of your engine will disturb your neighbor's sleep and the farmer's cows. Your fun will be their bother.

The solution is to select as quiet a power system as possible. A reduction system is in order since this allows the propeller to turn much slower so that the tips don't reach the speed of sound (a major source of noise). Also, a good muffler system is a must. Remember, the less disturbance we make, the more smiles we'll see on the faces of pilots and ground dwellers alike.

II. The second matter to consider when choosing a powered ultralight is your physical condition. If you are a professional football player or a confirmed heavyweight over 200 pounds, shop around for a type that carries a large payload. This is usually a function of powerplant thrust. The manufacturers specifications will aid you here.

An unavoidable relationship is: climb rate decreases as the pilots' weight increases. The heavier your wing loading (ratio of weight to wing area), the less performance (except for speed) you get. Leave yourself plenty of performance margin for those hot, humid days when climb rate diminishes (see Density Altitude in Chapter V).

III. Another factor affecting your choice is cost. This may be the most important criteria for some pilots. As mentioned previously, the cost of an ultralight increases with the complexity and weight. However, it should be noted that some designs come in kits that are cheaper than the assembled price of a less complex design.

Shop around and you can find used ultralights. Classified ads in the publications listed at the end of this chapter are the best source. Also, contacting a local dealer will probably put you in touch with all the used ultralight aircraft in your area. Guidelines for buying a used ultralight are presented in the next section.

Besides the initial costs, you should consider the cost of storage, transportation, fuel and maintenance. If you don't have a roomy garage, you may have to rent hangar space at an airport or in a barn. This can cost $20 a month or more. Obviously, the smaller and more collapsible your ultralight is, the less you'll probably have to pay for storage. You might want to look into this before you make a purchase.

If you have a field by your house, and your ultralight is in your garage, you are in luck. The rest of us will have to consider the costs of transportation to and from the hangar or airfield. This can be a significant cost in view of today's fuel prices. Of course, the cost of actual operating fuel must be considered. Most powered ultralights get exceptional gas milage — anywhere from 20 to 50 miles per gallon — compared to other aircraft, but will never be able to compete with motorcycles and some automobiles for economy.

Two additional expenses that may be encountered are the costs of making a car rack or trailer for your ultralight aircraft as well as the cost of instruments. Larger ultralights will require a trailer for all but the shortest trips. These trailers are usually custom made from boat trailers and can cost as much as $600. Car-top racks can be as elaborate as your creative genius allows. A functional rack can be made for foldable ultralights for much less than $50.

It should be obvious that the smaller and more compact your ultralight folds, the cheaper the transportation arrangements will be. It is up to you to decide whether you want to fly with relative simplicity or pay the price to enjoy the air in comfort. Either way you choose, flying powered ultralights will certainly cost you much less than flying conventional aircraft.

IV. The next thing to consider when choosing your wings is convenience. The availability of parts should be a major concern. It's nice to have a dealer nearby when you lose those elusive safety pins. Indeed, the presence of a nearby dealer may be the biggest reason to buy a particular ultralight, as long as it meets the other criteria to a reasonable degree.

All the items mentioned before, such as weight, portability and collapsibility, as well as take off or landing field requirements, are matters of convenience. Before you buy an ultralight, think about how easy it will be to store, how you will transport it and how far you'll have to drive to find a suitable flying area. Each of these points will contribute to the difficulty or simplicity of getting airborne.

In general, the smaller and lighter an ultralight is, the more convenient it will be. Of course, performance can be considered to be a matter of convenience also, since climbing to a given altitude or flying a given distance will take a lot longer in a poorer performing ship. The larger ultralights would be the choice here. Each pilot must consider the specifics of his or her situation. Remember, the easier it is for you to get to your take-off area, unfold your wings, start your engine and climb out, the more airtime you will get. Floating through the sky is the fun part, not fumbling with bolts and nuts down on the ground.

V. Safety is the last selection criteria we will consider here. The structural integrity and stability of your aircraft is most important since your body will be the valuable cargo. Despite any exhaustive analysis or test flying, there is only one sure way to tell if an aircraft is safe. That is, to accumulate countless hours of flying time in a wide variety of conditions. For this reason, it is recommended that a prospective pilot purchase only those ultralights that have been in production for at least a year and enjoy a good safety record.

The Hummer

New designs are constantly entering the market. Unless a pilot has the experience of a designer along with the insight of a wizard, he cannot be sure that a new ultralight is totally airworthy. There are still a few unknowns relating to ultralight design. Most ultralights have seen the inside of a wind tunnel. Even aircraft that have passed rigid FAA testing requirements can sometimes exhibit dangerous flaws after continual use. Again, the test of time is the ultimate test.

Stability depends on a number of aerodynamic effects (see Chapter IV for more details). Whether a design employs a tail, canard or neither, there are many subtle factors that affect stability. Each individual design must stand on its own merit. Again, check the safety record of the ultralight you buy before you commit yourself. Old copies of ultralight publications are a good source of this type of information.

The above five criteria will give the powered ultralight enthusiast plenty to think about when shopping around for the "perfect" ship. Take your time; there are over a hundred designs to choose from. Visit areas of ultralight activity and ask plenty of questions. Your best source of information is pilots actually flying the aircraft you are interested in.

Beware of manufacturer's claims. You can imagine how enthusiastic they get after working on a project for a year and suddenly seeing it pass flying tests like a graceful butterfly. Their enthusiasm carries over to their performance spec sheets. It's hard to test for performance, so at times vigorous (not rigorous) "guestimates" are put down. This won't help you; you want facts. Let your own two eyes see and compare the performance of different ultralights at fly-ins, meets and shows. Don't rush your choice. The sky will be there when you are ready.

BUYING A USED ULTRALIGHT

Besides getting your money's worth, the main thing to beware of when buying a used aircraft is damaged components. Remember, the original owner is selling for some reason. It is best to find out why. If the aircraft has been crashed, you must make a thorough inspection. Also, expect to do some repair work.

There are few government officials who know anything about ultralight design, so you cannot expect a used ship to have a safety certificate like a conventional aircraft. You must know what to look for yourself. Inspection of airframe and structural integrity will be discussed in Chapter V. Read the section on safety inspection before you attempt to negotiate for a used ultralight.

Additional factors such as proper shaping of the wings, adequate washout, balance of controls, smooth wing covering and flying trim must be considered. The wings must be formed exactly the same on both sides. Furthermore, each wing must have an adequate and equal amounts of twist (washout). The controls should be set the same on both sides and activate with the same pressure.

A poorly covered wing will exhibit wrinkles, or sag between the ribs. This leads to poor performance and possibly stability problems. Finally, the shape of the wings, the dihedral balance and center of gravity placement (see Chapter IV) must be proper to assure the correct "hands-off" trim speed.

Obviously, if you are just becoming acquainted with powered ultralights, you can't be expected to understand all the items mentioned above. However, you have an excellent recourse. Simply ask the individual selling the aircraft to demonstrate a flight or two. Specific things to watch for are: how easy it takes off and lands, how fast it climbs, how smooth it turns (in both directions) and whether or not it will continue in straight flight at a constant speed when the pilot lets go of the controls. If the seller of an ultralight is unwilling to demonstrate it for you, it may be because he built it from a kit and found it wouldn't fly. Be especially wary of aircraft built from kits as there is no assurance of quality control.

If an aircraft is built from a kit, an elaborate set of plans should be available. Get these from the builder or manufacturer and go over every detail of construction to see that dimensions and assembly procedures have been followed to the letter. Occasionally, an enthusiast buys an ultralight kit and finds that he doesn't have the time or incentive to complete it. These items can be a real good buy. Be sure to recheck any work already completed.

There are, of course, instances where an individual is selling a wing in perfect shape but he is unable to demonstrate it due to his inadequate flying experience. In this case, you can enlist the aid of an experienced pilot to see if the aircraft flies properly. Expect to pay the pilot a bit since you are taking his time and asking him to be a test pilot.

The Mitchell Wing

In addition, a call to the manufacturer of the aircraft you are looking at can provide you with a lot of information concerning what construction details to look for. Most ultralights have a serial number which you can use to find out how old the aircraft is and what a reasonable price should be. A pilot may have the aircraft sitting in his garage unused for a couple of years and expect to sell it for a new price. Despite the fact that prices are constantly increasing, the rapid advancements in design make many ultralights obsolete after a few years. Again, the manufacturer can advise you as to what changes have been made since the aircraft was built. If the changes are many, don't pay top dollar for the ship.

Be sure to start the engine and check its performance. Look for ease of starting (good engines start with one or two pulls in most cases), smoothness of idle and transition up to full power with no misses or flat spots. A hard starting engine or one that doesn't run smoothly may only need a tune-up—or a major overhaul.

Tune-ups for ultralight engines are relatively inexpensive (less than $100, usually). However, a rough engine may need more than an overhaul if a broken piston, ring or crankcase is the cause of the problem. Bring along a friend with knowledge of small engines to help guide you if you suspect trouble with the engine on a used ultralight.

Take a close look at the propeller. You don't want one with any cracks or major nicks. Of course, props can be replaced for $100 or so, but you should figure this in with your bargaining.

Look at the fabric or covering on the wings. Most often this is Dacron cloth. If it appears faded, abraded or wrinkled, chances are the craft was handled poorly. Storing ultralights outside in most areas is very hard on the wing covering material. Sunlight deteriorates Dacron readily (ultraviolet radiation is the culprit), so if the ultralight in question was stored outside without wing covers, be very suspicious of the strength of the fabric. You might ask the owner to poke it hard with his finger. If he's reluctant to do so, be wary (a new wing will easily withstand poking and pulling). This deterioration factor is not often understood by pilots and is hard to check for on a regular basis, so try to find an ultralight that appears well cared for.

One of the best indicators of the type of care an owner gives to his or her ultralight is whether or not a log is kept detailing the number of hours on the engine and airframe. Most designs have an inspection and replacement schedule. A conscientious owner will keep track of the flying hours and attend to such necessary maintainance.

Of course, the more hours on the ultralight in question, the less you should pay for it. Most engines and airframes need considerable maintainance after 200 hours.

When you do purchase a used ultralight, be sure to get the original owner's manual. This document will be invaluable in teaching you how to store, ground handle and fly your particular ultralight. Also, get on the manufacturer's mailing list. This will provide you with updated information about your particular aircraft as well as keep you abreast of fly-ins and meets pertinent to your aircraft type. The more you learn about an ultralight from other pilots and the manufacturer, the better you will be able to judge what it is worth. We still operate under that old Roman admonition: caveat emptor—let the buyer beware.

ADDITIONAL EQUIPMENT

Besides your set of wings, you may need a few other items. Some of these items are necessary for safety or efficient operation of your ultralight. Start with the basics such as instruments and parachutes then add other items as you deem necessary.

INSTRUMENTS – Small powered ultralight aircraft can be flown without instruments. However, during certain types of opertion and for certain ships, some instrumentation is necesary. For example, when flying in or around controlled airspace, an altimeter is needed to determine flight altitudes.

An altimeter is a device for telling you how high you are. It works by detecting absolute air pressure and can be set to measure altitude above sea level or above a designated area such as a landing field. There are many types of altimeters available, from heavy airplane models to small wrist types. They all seem to work with about the same accuracy. The smallest models are the best choice, but they are expensive – over $100. Cheaper altimeters are available.

Variometer And Altimeter

Airspeed indicators are as useful as the speedometer on your car and are recommended always. Although hang glider pilots do very well without airspeed indicators, ultralight pilots cannot detect airspeed as well due to the effects of the engine and propeller. Again, there is a choice of instruments. Fortunately, some of the cheapest ones turn out to be the lightest and most accurate. You can also use your airspeed indicator to measure the wind velocity on the ground. This is important since high winds increase the chance of strong turbulence.

Other useful instruments are variometers (vertical speed indicators) and compasses. A variometer tells you how fast you are going up or down. This device works by measuring the change in air pressure and is a great aid for detecting lift when soaring. A compass is necessary when navigating over unknown areas. Without a compass, you may set out for your girlfriend's house and end up lost in the wilderness.

A few instruments useful for monitoring the performance and state of the engine operation are a tachometer (to measure RPM), exhuast temperature gauge and head temperature gauge. These instruments are more important on the larger aircraft since engine failures are more critical when larger landing fields are required. However, all engines should be tuned with a tachometer and fitted with temperature gauges for long life. See Chapter VI for more details.

All of these instruments can be purchased from ultralight dealers or through the ultralight media. Whatever instruments you ultimately acquire, be sure not to become overly dependent on the dials, balls and numbers. You should be able to maintain proper flight control and engine settings by using your senses. The instruments should be used for fine tuning your sensual data. You'll miss a lot of nice views if you fly with your eyes constantly glued to the instrument faces.

Ultralight Instruments

EARPLUGS—Noise is always a problem with ultralights. Well designed muffler systems have helped, however, a large part of the noise from small powerplants comes from the propeller. In fact, the first solar powered ultralight produced a noise level only slightly below that of other ultralights with gasoline engines. This demonstrates the large noise contribution of the propeller.

A constant low level noise may cause hearing loss as much as a louder noise of short duration. For this reason, the importance of earplugs shouldn't be underestimated. Use them at all times when flying your powered ultralight or you will suffer hearing loss.

The best earplugs by far according to independent testing are E-A-R disposable foam plugs from E-A-R Corp., 7911 Zionsville Rd., Indianapolis, IN 46268. You may be able to find these at drugstores, hardware or sporting goods stores. They are convenient to use and reduce the noise level more than any other type of earplug.

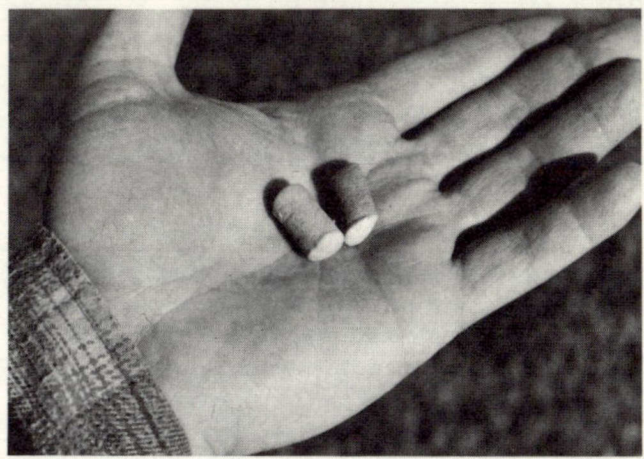

Earplugs

PARACHUTES—Since 1977, many small and light (ca. 10 lbs.) parachutes have become available. These chutes were developed for hang gliding, and sized up are quite appropriate for powered ultralights. The only problem with these chutes is the possibility of entanglement in the propeller. For this reason, all ultralight chutes should have a kevlar or steel cable bridle.

Most of these parachutes require the pilot to throw the inner envelope away from the aircraft for proper deployment. This requires at least one free hand. You must keep the parachute attached to your body or harness in an easy to grab position. Practice throwing the chute while on the ground so you don't have to think about each step if an emergency occurs.

Other types of parachutes, called ballistic parachutes, are deployed by pulling a line or pressing a switch that explodes a capsule to shoot the chute away from the entangling ultralight. These ballistic chutes tend to deploy more rapidly (thus saving the day at a lower altitude than the hand deployed type). Ballistic chutes are heavier and much more expensive than the hand deployed ones, but probably more reliable.

Your dealer can supply you with a good parachute system. Expect to pay $300 to $500 for a hand deploy and as much as $1000 or more for a ballistic chute. We strongly recommend a parachute for all ultralight flying over 100 feet above the ground. The parachutes bring both the ultralight and pilot to ground reasonably slowly (the pilot doesn't have to bail out), and have certainly proven their worth. In Chapter VII we discuss parachute use in more detail.

HELMETS—All ultralight pilots should wear protective headgear. This sweeping statement is made on the basis of irrefutable data from the analysis of accidents in all action sports. The brain cavity is very fragile. Of all parts of the body, the head needs the most protection to survive a severe blow. Nobody plans to have an accident. However, just as we wear parachutes in recognition of our human nature, we also wear helmets. Again, they have shown their value by saving lives.

If you are going to wear a helmet, wear a good one. Don't fool yourself by thinking that bicycle, rock climbing, hockey or some other soft shell or unlined helmet is adequate. It isn't. Use only a hard shell helmet with a foam liner. These are the type of helmets that have proven necessary for accidents occuring at our flying speeds.

The helmet shells are generally made of fiberglass or polycarbonate (Lexan is an example of the latter) while the liners are high density foam. An adequate strap system is an integral part of any helmet. The strap must hold the helmet on comfortably and not let it slip during impact. Be sure to select a helmet with a proper (snug) fit for both comfort and safety reasons.

You may choose a helmet with a full face gaurd or the "half helmet" type that only covers the upper part of the head. The full-face helmet certainly affords more protection, however, they are heavier and they cut down on peripheral vision. Of course, ultralight pilots need to have as wide a field of view as possible in traffic. Consequently the ultimate safety of one design over the other is debatable.

Various organizations set standards for helmets. Generally, the safer a helmet is, the heavier and more expensive it is. The standards in order of their rigor (easiest to toughest) are: FMVSS-218 (set by the Department of Transportation or DOT); Z-90 (by the American National Standards Institute); and Snell-1980 (the Snell Foundation). If your helmet meets any or all of these qualifications, it will be permanently displayed in the helmet. If it does not, be suspicious of its adequacy. Remember, you need your head to do all that dreaming of those great flights.

MISCELLANEOUS EQUIPMENT—There are many additional items you should consider. One such item is a trailer. If your ultralight is too large to lug on your car and doesn't have road worthy wheels, you will have to pull it on a trailer. As mentioned, converted boat trailers work best. Expect to sink several hundred dollars in this project.

A cover for your aircraft is the next item. This is essential to protect all surfaces during transport and storage. Of course, an enclosed trailer will serve both purposes. Most manufacturers supply a cover with their aircraft. Tie downs for holding the ship in a wind also come in handy. Spiral stakes for holding pets work good here.

Floats for your ultralight will allow you to fly from lakes and rivers, while skis are necessary for snow. Flying with floats and skis will be covered in Chapter VII. Another add-on is a fairing which shields the pilot from wind (a great idea in cold weather) and helps reduce drag. Of course, you should expect to have a supply of good warm clothing including boots and gloves for all but those warm summer days. Remember wind chill effects.

Other useful items are: FM radios for communicating with ground crew or other pilots. This may be essential when traveling cross country. Sectional maps (available at airports) are necessary for indicating air traffic areas to avoid. Strobe lights are mandatory for flying at dusk. Water bottles are a relief for those long, hot flights. Additional fuel tanks will extend your range considerably. Be sure to use tanks comparable to the manufacturer's original. A 5 gallon gas can is necessary for mixing fuel. Remember, you are flying an airplane, so keep your equipment first rate.

The Goldwing - Note Canard and Winglets

COMMONLY ASKED QUESTIONS

The preceding sections covered a lot of material basic to understanding and preparing for powered ultralight flight. In this section we will answer a few more common questions before we start the actual practice of flight.

I. HOW HIGH CAN I FLY? This depends on a number of factors including the performance of your ship, the amount of fuel you carry and the atmospheric conditions. If you have an ultralight that roars through the sky with plenty of excess power, you can climb fast and high. The more fuel you take, the longer you can climb. (Remember the 5 gallon legal limit.)

The density of the air has a big effect on climb rate. The warmer and more humid the air is, as well as the higher you go, the thinner or less dense the air is. This affects engine performance (less oxygen) and the "bite" the propeller can get per revolution. Consequently, every airplane has a design ceiling no matter how much fuel is carried. The measurement of the air density in relation to a standard case (sea level at 59 °F) is called density altitude. In Chapter V we will see how density altitude determines not only climb rate, but take off ability as well.

Another atmospheric condition that affects performance is the amount of lift or sink in the air. If the air is moving upward, climbing will be greatly facilitated. On the other hand, there have been times when an ultralight with a very good climb rate could not take off because of massive widespread sinking of the air.

Most powered ultralights achieve a climb rate of well over 500 feet per minute depending on the weight of the pilot and the atmospheric condition. Larger ultralights have powered up to well above the legal limit of flight without oxygen—12,500 ft. It should be apparent that the current ships are perfectly capable of delivering practically unlimited flight capabilities.

II. HOW FAR CAN I FLY? The answer to this question is very similar to the preceding. It depends on many factors such as wing loading, performance, fuel capacity and air movement. If you fly downwind, you can go further than you can flying into the wind. Generally speaking, most ultralights can fly up to 40 miles on one tank of fuel, while many ultralights can reach over 100 miles in good conditions. Of course, it's pretty easy to spot a gas station along the route, circle down and fuel up when traveling across the country in a powered ultralight.

III. ARE THERE POWERED ULTRALIGHT COMPETITIONS? Not only are there competitions, but fun fly-ins, exhibitions and cross country regattas as well. Competitions involve all-out challenges and tasks such as speed to a distant goal, climb rate contests, distance achieved on a measured amount of fuel, duration tasks, spot landing and precision flying events. Fly-ins can include all of the above, plus pattern flying, target bombing, formation flying and time accuracy through a prescribed course, similar to a road rally. To locate this exciting activity, keep your eye on the calendar of events listed in the publications noted below.

If there's no activity of this sort near you, start it up. Half the fun of ultralight flying is getting together with other pilots and sharing stories or comparing skills and equipment. Also, think about joining a club in your area or forming one with your fellow pilots if there's none around.

IV. WHAT GOVERNMENT REGULATIONS MUST I OBEY? Congress has given the FAA the duty and the power to control all forms of aviation in the United States. There is no doubt about it, the regulation of powered ultralights is one of their concerns. Look at this: There are tens of thousands of private airplanes and thousands of commercial craft in use. The number of powered ultralights could easily reach these figures. Although there seems to be an unlimited amount of airspace available, much of it is heavily traveled, especially around populated areas. Consequently, some regulations and traffic control must be in effect.

Now, guess who has the most clout in Congress. Certainly not the private owners, the experimenters or ultralight pilots. It's the airline companies, of course. They pay the bills and they call the game. When a crisis occurs, it's the small plane pilot who gets the blame. Consequently, pressure for increased regulation moves right on down the line to the ultralight pilot.

The FAA has issued Part 103 which states the rules for ultralight flying. The rules are fairly simple and straightforward. It's up to each pilot to obey these rules in order to preserve the freedom to fly with as little hassle as possible for everyone. Note that fines may be levied if the FAA determines that a pilot violates Part 103.

In addition to Part 103, each pilot must pass a simple flying test and register his or her aircraft. As of this writing these latter requirements are purely voluntary, but expect to see them made mandatory in the future. All flight rules are covered in Chapter V and Appendix I.

V. HOW SAFE IS POWERED ULTRALIGHT FLYING? All aviation contains an element of danger, as does travel in any moving vehicle such as an automobile, bicycle or horse. The fact is, when we choose to progress at speeds faster than a leisurely jog, we entertain the possibility of coming in contact with an object not inclined to move at our chosen pace, for example, a tree, a house, a hill. Ultralight flying is no different from any other form of aviation in this respect. However, since ultralights fly at such a slow speed, crashes tend to be less lethal than with conventional aircraft.

Of course, ultralights are more susceptible to the vagarities of the air than larger aircraft. Consequently, much more time must be spent learning to judge conditions and the way of the wind in the same manner you judge the elements of danger on the highway when you drive. This can be enjoyable callenge in itself.

Another matter important to safe ultralight flying is the actual skill of the pilot. If you learn to fly in gradual steps with a conservative approach, you will learn safely. If you continue this conservative philosophy throughout your flying career, you will get nothing but enjoyment from this great aerial sport.

VI. WHERE CAN I FIND MORE INFORMATION? Pilots often get initiated to powered ultralights either through seeing an ultralight fly by or through the media. If you can find pilots in your area, offer to help in some manner. Most pilots are receptive to assistance and downright eager to promote their sport. After a few outings with the locals, you'll pick up a lot of information and begin to feel like an old pro. Be careful to respect the pilot's need to attend to detail during preflight inspection. Don't make a nuisance of yourself by asking too many detailed questions, but show your enthusiasm for ultralighting and it will be returned.

Of course, dealers are a valuable source of information. Best of all are publications such as this book and magazines covering the sport. Some of these are (in alphabetical order): *GLIDER RIDER,* Box 6009,

Chattanooga, TN 37401; *ULTRALIGHT* (published by the Experimental Aviation Assn.), P.O. Box 229, Hales Corners, WI 53130; *ULTRALIGHT AIRCRAFT*, 16200 Ventura Blvd, Encino, CA. 91346; *ULTRALIGHT PILOT* (published by the Aircraft Owners and Pilots Assn.), 421 Aviation Way, Fredrick, MD. 21701.

VII. HOW HARD IS IT TO LEARN TO FLY? You can't learn to fly in a day, but you can experience flight early in your training. The process is a gradual one, but each step is enjoyable. In other words, it's not too hard as long as you have a true desire to fly.

Don't fly for friends or appearances. Take up ultralight flying because you want to. Both males and females with a wide variety of backgrounds and physical types have made this choice. Turn the page and the learning process will begin.

The Quicksilver Mx · Note Fairing

CHAPTER II

LEARNING TO FLY

Man is not born with wings. He notices little in his everyday earth-bound existance to prepare him for flight. Consequently, learning to fly offers a unique and exciting experience. You will find a whole new world in the air. When you become a pilot you see things from a different viewpoint.

The above sentiments are never more true than when flying small aircraft. There is a personal feeling to the sky when you are exposed to the airstream and your wings weigh only a bit more than you do. There is one problem however. By the very nature of ultralight aircraft, every flight must be solo. This adds difficult to the learning process but also provides a real sense of self accomplishment once you become a proficient pilot.

The method for learning powered ultralight flight, by necessity, consists of making gradual progress in small, safe steps. This book will outline that progress. However, an instructor is imperative for learning to fly safely. Contact dealers or manufacturers for a source of instructors near you. For detailed guidelines in learning to fly powered ultralights, purchase the Powered Ultralight Training Course by this author (see the address in the front of this book). The training course manual consists of eleven ground schools and eleven lessons that take you from an uninitiated enthusiast to an intermediate level ultralight pilot. This manual is used by most professional schools.

TYPES OF TRAINING

Methods of training in powered ultralights vary somewhat according to the school's equipment and background. Some schools use ultralights made to carry two passengers. Note, these don't fit the regular FAA definition, but an exemption is made for instructional purposes. Certain pilot requirements are also mandatory, over and above an ultralight instructor's normal qualifications. Unfortunately, the added expense of qualifying and purchasing these dual ultralights mean that many schools do not use them.

Dual instruction provides the quickest and most controlled method of learning to fly, but other alternatives are viable. One method involves using flight simulators and giving a student a certain number of hours in a conventional airplane. Another method is to use radios and progress the pilot very gradually. Obviously, the best method is to use all of the above, but only certain schools can afford this, so the ultimate determinant of a school's success is its attention to safety. As a prospective student, ask about a school's safety record before you sign up. A positive response and a good conservative attitude on the part of the instructors will let you know that you are in good hands.

A Dual Equipped Quicksilver

Ask about a school's total program. How much ground school is provided? Do they use up to date books and materials? Do they have well organized classroom and flying sessions? Is their equipment well maintained? All of these items are factors that determine the quality of a school. Be wary of the school that promises to get you flying in no time at all. Learning to fly safely takes time and a little effort. If matters are rushed, you'll end up being a less adept pilot or worse, be headed for a mishap due to the bits of knowledge that you missed. Remember, the slower you go on the basics, the better you will be later on.

The type of ultralight a school uses will be a factor in the safety and ease of learning. Generally, if you are uninitiated to flight, a weight shift or two-axis controlled trainer will be easiest. If you are a licensed pilot, the three-axis controlled ultralights will be easiest to learn in. If you have a choice of schools, consider this point.

If a school uses simulators, they may be static (that is, not moving) or they may be a platform pulled or pushed by a vehicle. Another type of flight simulation is towing the ultralight at a slow speed. In all cases, the object is for the student to get a feel for the controls in a safe manner. You'll be surprised at how quickly you feel comfortable providing up and down, left and right input and feeling the changes. Even learning is great fun.

Before we leave this topic of types of training, we should say a few words about the student. Whereas ultralight flying doesn't require great physical effort, the learning process can be very taxing as adrenaline flows and new concepts are absorbed. Be sure your body systems are on go (heart attack sufferers should certainly consult a physician before considering learning to fly) and you are mentally prepared. The latter item means you should have nothing on your mind but flying. A stressful or emotional situation that you bring with you to the training field will certainly affect your learning in an adverse manner. Let your instructor know if something is bothering you and he or she will make a wise decision whether or not you can handle the day's lesson. Again we remind you that ultralights will be around for a good long time and there's no rush.

One more point while we're on the subject of preparedness: be sure to eat a proper breakfast before your morning lesson, for you need all your energy and who wants to be distracted by a growling stomach? In all seriousness, a well balanced meal will keep your blood sugar at its proper level so you will be less affected by the demands of learning to fly. Fatigue is a factor in many accidents and improper nutrition enhances the onset of fatigue. Remember this point in your day to day flying when you are an official experienced pilot as well.

There are generally three types of students learning to fly ultralights. The first is totally inexperienced with any type of flight. This student will take the longest time to learn, but can learn safely with the proper instruction. The second is a student with previous hang gliding experience. This person probably has all the judgement necessary and can learn very quickly once he or she learns the use of the engine and the flight controls if different than the weight-shift control of a hang glider. The third type of student is the person with experience in regular airplanes. This individual will probably feel very comfortable in the air (although the open cockpit of an ultralight may take some getting used to) and be quite familiar with the use of the engine and controls (especially if learning on a conventional three-axis ultralight). However, an ultralight is different enough from a regular airplane that caution must be observed.

Some of the matters a licensed pilot should be aware of are wind gradient effects (they can be very dramatic in an ultralight since the change in wind velocity can be a large percentage of stall speed), differences in flying velocities, differences in control response, differences in pattern positioning and landing set up (with an ultralight, aim for a point ⅓ of the way down the runway, not for the "numbers" at the beginning as with an airplane). Just as driving a car doesn't qualify one to drive a motorcycle, so a pilot of conventional airplanes shouldn't expect to be qualified to fly ultralights without some training. Severe accidents have occured due to such a supposition.

No matter what a student's background, or what type of training program a school uses, a gradual, safe approach should be used. Most schools use a close facsimile of the outline given in the remainder of this chapter. Remember, this is a guideline to prepare the student for the actual training course. First we will describe the ideal training site and conditions.

THE SITE AND THE AIR

An ideal training site would be a perfectly flat plain without a single obstruction for miles around with a barely noticeable breeze constantly blowing. A site meeting this description is about as rare as a poor banker, so let's get down to reality. From our above fantasy site, we can guess that two big problems in learning to fly are obstructions and wind. Lets take obstructions first.

We'll consider an obstruction to be any solid object rising above the ground. A solid object in the path of our less solid ultralight is obviously a grave hinderence to our progress if not our continued health. Thus, we want to avoid obstructions. The best way to avoid them, especially when we are inexperienced on the controls is to not have any around. What this boils down to is much more open space is required for instruction than for recreational flying as an experienced pilot.

Although we can get by with smaller areas, at least 2,000 ft. long by 200 ft. wide is the preferred dimensions for a training field. The higher the obstructions (hills, trees, power lines, buildings, etc.) around the field, the larger the training field should be.

A good training site will be flat and smooth. It is hard enough to judge height above the terrain as a beginner that we don't want the added complications of having the terrain change as well. A smooth field is necessary to minimize the abuse to the ultralight, let alone the pilot. The better all these factors are, the easier a student will learn.

It is very possible that more than one site will be necessary for proper training. For example, one field may be large and ample for the early days of flying up and down the field or around the pattern, but be unsuitable for initial cross-countries due to a lack of additional landing areas for miles around. As a student, you can rely on your instructor to make a wise choice in field. However, eventually you will be making these choices yourself in terms of your own flying, so be aware of the necessary criteria.

The condition of the air when learning to fly is of utmost importance. The desired wind when at the early stages of learning is none. Wind complicates all flying and we are working on the KISS principle (keep it simple, stupid) as beginners. Wind can cause turning problems, judgement problems and control problems if turbulence is present. Wind socks and streamers are very important at a training site (or any flying field for that matter) so that pilots and instructors can monitor the wind at all times.

As an ultralight pilot, you must become very aware of the ways of the wind. It will become second nature to you to sense the wind direction and velocity as well as the turbulence and density. All these factors affect flying in one way or another. In the next chapter we tell the full story of the air and all its secrets. For now, remember for learning, no wind is good wind.

LEARNING PROCEDURES

The general process of learning to fly consists of studying the basics in ground school followed by some hands-on practice, then more ground school, more practice and so forth. Schools will vary this process somewhat to accomodate their equipment and conditions. However, a student should be aware that much learning of new skills and concepts must take place which requires a period of days, weeks or months. Again, the following outline is intended to let a student know generally what to expect. The complete course is provided in the Powered Ultralight Training Course manual.

Before we start, sit back and try to imagine yourself cruising high above the countryside on a warm summer day. The blue sky and breeze in your face fills your senses so that you feel more alive than ever before. That is the feeling you get when flying ultralights.

Now that you're properly motivated, read on and put yourself in each situation described so that you start learning before the actual practice.

You will begin your learning to fly with a familiarization with the aircraft. The various parts of an ultralight are explained in Chapter V of this book. Of course, some ultralights have unique design features, so your instructor will fill you in on the necessary details. You should, however, learn as many terms as you can before your first lesson so that you can communicate more readily with your instructor.

On your first outing you will walk around the craft and learn to do a careful preflight inspection. This is a necessary procedure and is described in Chapter V. Next you will probably sit in the craft and become familiar with the controls: throttle, choke and kill switch on the engine, stick, pedals, steering bar and brakes on the airframe itself. Also, your instructor may introduce you to the instruments at this point.

The next step is to become familiar with the operation of the engine. You'll learn the proper choke and throttle setting for starting and operating as well as the power limits for your initial runs. At this time earplugs or a muffling helmet are a necessary part of your equipment.

Always remember to yell "CLEAR PROP" and wait for the response "PROP CLEAR" from others nearby. This is to remind you and your assistants that you will be turning on a dangerous whirling object and everyone must remain clear from that point on. Do not neglect this important procedure, for many pilots have injured themselves by becoming nonchalant about the propeller dangers. It can easily sever a hand.

When your instructor feels you are ready you will begin learning how to taxi under control in a slow manner. At such slow speeds, most steering input takes place through the landing gear. Later, when you learn to fast taxi, the in-flight controls become more effective as ground steering devices since more air is moving over the control surfaces.

You will learn to taxi faster and faster while remaining under takeoff speed. The object here is to learn to use the throttle smoothly as well as steering and braking control. Also this is the time to start feeling airspeed (watch the indicator), judging distances and being aware of air movement by watching the streamers.

The matter of where you look as you control the aircraft needs some mention. Humans have an ingrained habit to go where they are looking. Consequently, if a student is intent on missing a large tree, in the middle of the field, he may watch it carefully, all the while heading right for it. Many instructors, have learned the hard way not to emphasize the places to avoid, but the places they wish the student to go. You should do the same. Look where your instructor tells you to go, and go there. Do not concentrate on obstructions you are trying to miss—they deserve only a glance or two, for you are now controlling the ultralight and can go where you wish.

After taxi practice (the amount of time taxiing depends on the instruction program and your experience), certain training ultralights lend themselves to "wheel walking" (these are the tricycle gear designs). In this practice, the nose wheel of the craft is lifted off the ground with a nose up control at an airspeed below that necessary for takeoff. This practice requires a very precise throttle and nose up (pitch) control to run along with the nose wheel off. This is excellent practice for the next step: the first lift off.

THE FIRST FLIGHT

Any takeoff requires a bit of level flight and a landing as well to be considered a safe endeavor. Consequently, we learn a method to control all three phases from the onset. By now you should feel confident in your ability to control the ultralight in pitch and power.

Once you have been briefed you will line up at the end of your runway heading into any trickle of wind that may be present (remember, you want as calm conditions as possible). Is your helmet on, seatbelt secured and your earplugs in? Alright, when your instructor gives you the nod, begin your fast taxi and reach takeoff speed. For most ultralights, this is between 18 and 25 mph (29 to 40 kph) airspeed. Once the proper airspeed is achieved, produce a slight nose up control to lift off. As soon as you feel (and see) the main wheels leave the ground, lower the nose a bit and reduce power. Just before you touch down, raise the nose a bit to slow your descent.

Now this is very important: make all controls *gradual* and *smooth*. Do not jerk the control stick or bar to raise the nose. Turn the throttle off gradually so the nose doesn't drop rapidly. A smooth nose up control on landing will "spread" the ultralight on the runway like soft butter. The thing to learn here is gradual light controls. Finesse, not gorilla control.

Your instructor will guide your control movements while you are sitting still so that you can practice them over and over in the right sequence with the right amount of travel for your particular trainer. Remember, we lower the nose before we cut power in most craft so that we aren't caught with no power in a nose-high position.

The Mitchell Wing

Practice this lift-off and touch-down continuously until you can perform it flawlessly (without an uncontrolled climb or hard landing). Then you can progress to what are known as crow hops. These are takeoffs followed by level flight a couple of feet off the ground and landing. The length of these flights can be from practically nothing to the length of your training field. Obviously, you must leave lots of room to come down if you gain too much altutude. A training site with plenty of runout is absolutely necessary for any long low level flights. In case you get higher then you expect, it is always better to reduce power gradually and land straight ahead if possible. The same is true if an engine failure occurs during a crow hop or on any takeoff. In the case of an engine failure, lower the nose and maintain airspeed. Your instructor will tell you the proper engine-off airspeed for your craft. Generally it is about 10 mph (16 kph) above stall speed.

This is a good point to initiate engine off landing practice. Once your crow hops are high enough so that you can stabilize in level flight, try reducing power more and more so that you eventually are on idle while still a few feet above the terrain. The object is to experience the change in nose position (attitude) as power is reduced. Note this very well: the less power you are using, the more nose down your craft must be in order to maintain a given airspeed. With the engine completely off, you may feel that you are diving quite a bit at your normal lift off airspeed. This is true, for without power a dive must occur for the wings to have flying airspeed. This airspeed represents control, so maintain the airspeed and flare (pull the nose up smoothly) a few feet above the ground in order to land lightly.

Along with this engine off practice, you can gradually be flying higher and higher. An ideal plan would be to take ten flights less than 10 feet (3 meters) above the ground. After that, increase your height in 5 foot (1½ meters) increments until you reach 50 feet (15 meters). Then add 10 ft (3 meters) per flight to 100 feet (30 meters) and after that add bigger bites of altitude. Of course, you can't get nearly so high as even 50 feet if you don't have a long runway. Also, before you get much more than 10 feet off the ground you should learn the basics of turn control so that you can correct for small inadvertant heading changes.

Here we introduce the concept of ground effect. This is an apparent cushioning of an aircraft as it nears the ground. The craft seems to float along further than expected. For this reason you must leave extra room when landing so that you don't float off the end of your field.

Ground effect is caused mainly by the interaction of the ground with the wing (the ground reduces drag losses by blocking tip vorticies – see Chapter IV). Ground effect can help an aircraft get off the ground before enough power to climb has been applied. This is why we keep the nose down while taxiing.

STALLS

Throughout this whole learning process we are taking precautions to avoid a stall. What is a stall? A stall occurs in any aircraft when the nose is raised too high (angle of attack too great) so that airspeed diminishes and the flow separates from the wing. The result is a sudden dropping of the wing and usually a nose-down. Of course, dropping rapidly in a nose down position is not good for the nerves, so we avoid a stall by maintaining airspeed which means avoiding too much nose up control. This is why we preach gradual, smooth control actions. This is also the reason we emphasize careful attention to airspeed.

Certain ultralights are very resistant to stalling. Most notable in this respect are the canard designs although many others are docile in stall as well. This is one of the attributes of a good trainer. It should be noted that any ultralight will stall if radical enough handling takes place. Of course, in the training situation we progress carefully enough, so with the proper awareness, stalls shouldn't occur.

Stall recognition, understanding and avoidance is very important to safe flying, so we cover this topic several times. In Chapter IV we learn more details about what causes a stall and in Chapter V we learn how to detect, correct and avoid stalls. Most stalls occur because the pilot isn't paying attention to airspeed or the control inputs. Awareness is the key to stall avoidance.

BASIC TURNS

An ultralight (or any aircraft) turns by banking to one side to produce an arcing flight path and thus the intended heading change. We shall explore the intricacies of more involved turns in Chapter IV, but for our purposes here, we should mainly be concerned with gradual, low-banked turns.

The turn control generally consists of moving the stick in the direction of the desired turn. For example, if you want to go left, move the stick left. Simple, huh? With a weight-shift ultralight, you move the bar away from the intended direction to tilt the wing. This soon becomes second nature too. Some ultralights require depressing a rudder pedal on the side which you intend to turn.

No matter what the controls are for the particular craft on which you are training, you can practice them on the ground while taxiing so that they become second nature by the time you actually get airborne. Once in the air, try a very gradual control movement and note its effect. This, of course, should occur on a calm day so you don't have extraneous inputs from the air. Be sure to hold the control long enough so that the craft has time to respond. There is a lag with some designs. Don't hold the turn control too long or a steeper bank than intended will occur.

To stop a turn, simply move the control to the other side, then center it once you have leveled out. Remember the lag and stop the turn before you reach your desired heading or you may turn past the intended point.

The Rotec Rally

An outline of a proper turn follows: check your airspeed then move the control in the proper direction slowly. As your wings reach the desired bank angle, center the control. Once your heading has changed the desired amount, level out by moving the control in the opposite direction then back to center once you are level. Check your airspeed at all times. This should generally be best maneuvering airspeed (about 10 mph above stall speed). Your instructor will give you a more definite airspeed for your ultralight.

Once you are comfortable and proficient at basic turns, you can go down the runway turning more and more until you can accomplish almost a 90° change in heading. This is shown in figure 1. Obviously, you need a reasonably wide field for this practice. Also, we want to always land into the wind, so if possible, land in the original direction you took off as shown, even though you are flying in calm.

The essence of this practice is to prepare you for the next section in a safe, well-controlled manner.

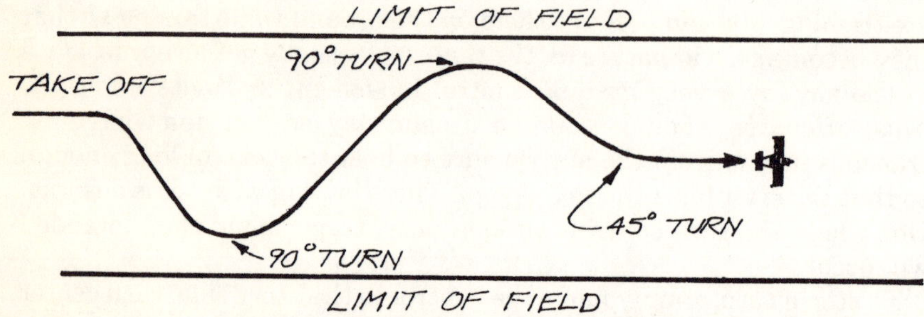

Figure 1 · 90° Turns Down the Runway

FLYING THE PATTERN

There is a standard pattern around all airports that airplanes (and ultralights) generally adhere to. This is shown in figure 2. Note that we have drawn a counterclockwise pattern, known as a left hand pattern since all turns are to the left. Often ultralights operating at an airport will use a right hand pattern away from the airplanes. In any case we are going to learn to fly the pattern in both directions to gain proficiency in judging turns, altitude, position and landing set up from both sides.

Once you have mastered turns in the field, your instructor will guide you around the pattern by pointing out landmarks at your turn points. You should climb 30 to 100 feet (depending on obstructions around the field) and begin the pattern. Watch your airspeed and produce the identical turn you did down low. Once around the pattern, reduce power, and land. After debriefing, try it again. Aim to perfect your turns, altitude control and landing set up. You should have a spot or a line which you try to land near every time. This line should be in the first half of your field.

As you practice flight in the pattern you will learn many new skills.

Steeper and steeper turns may be tried. Note that steeper turns may require added power in order to avoid losing altitude. You will learn to fly higher and higher by making multiple circuits of the pattern while climbing. Oval patterns requiring 180° turns at either end and figure 8s (left pattern followed by right pattern) are great practice. As you get higher you may widen the pattern (always remaining within gliding distance of the field in case of engine failure). Finally, you'll learn to fly the pattern in increasing wind.

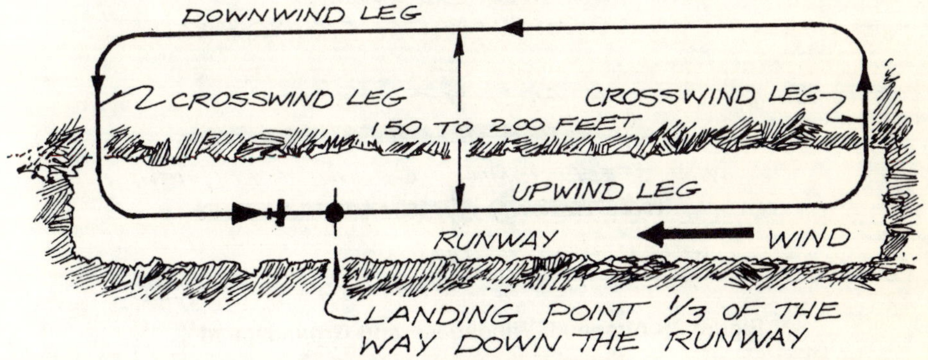

Figure 2 · Flying The Pattern

Once complication wind adds to flying is the perceptual differences when flying upwind and downwind. Here we will point out the changes while we go into more detail in Chapter V. Just like a boat in the river traveling upstream, an ultralight's progress over the ground will be slowed by a headwind. Similarly, when a boat or ultralight turns downstream or downwind, the speed in relation to the ground increases dramatically. The stronger the flow, the greater the upwind and downwind difference.

The simple relation is: airspeed and windspeed combine to give groundspeed. If we are heading into the wind, we must subtract the windspeed from our airspeed to get groundspeed. If we are heading downwind, we add the windspeed to our airspeed to get our groundspeed. Remember airspeed is the speed of the air over our wing which is the most important matter concerning the ability to control our craft. Windspeed is the speed of the wind in relation to the ground. Groundspeed is the speed at which we move in relation to the ground and is only important if we are trying to go someplace or when we are near the ground trying to land (we land into the wind to minimize our groundspeed at touchdown).

Figure 3 shows the relationship between airspeed and groundspeed. From this we can see that the difference in what we perceive in the upwind and downwind leg (as labeled in figure 2) will be quite noticeable in a significant wind (above 5 mph) The downwind leg will be covered in less time and it may appear that we are flying too fast. Don't be fooled—check your airspeed. If you use groundspeed as a judge of airspeed, you will slow down on the downwind leg and possibly stall. Again: *watch thy airspeed.*

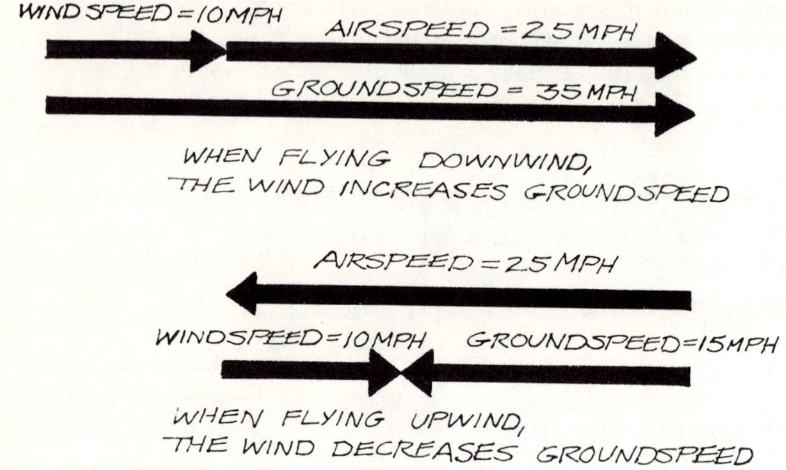

Figure 3 · Airspeed, Windspeed and Groundspeed

FURTHER PRACTICE

There are many more things we can learn while flying the pattern. One of the most important is landing set up with the power off. These are referred to as dead stick landings. We learn this important skill so that we can perform a safe landing any time we suffer an engine failure. This practice cannot be emphasized enough. Learn dead stick landings by cutting the engine at various points in the pattern, starting with the final approach leg and progressing backwards. Remember, ultralights were originally designed as gliders and they fly very well with the engine off.

You will want to learn to do 360° turns and a variety of maneuvers allowing you to fly anywhere within the safe gliding range of your field. Eventually you will be prepared for your first cross-country. These more advanced skills are covered in later chapters.

You are now a full-fledged pilot. You are a long way from being an expert, however. There is a lot more material to learn as can be seen in the following chapters. You must acquire a sixth sense to read the conditions in flight and avoid possible dangers. You must learn to perform flawless, conservative maneuvers.

Two matters you should be constantly on guard against are fatigue and ego. When exciting things happen our adrenaline pumps which leads to fatigue more readily once we calm back down. Be conscious of your energy and attention level, for 90% of flying is judgement. Random errors occur more readily when you are tired. Ask yourself often: "How do I feel?" "Fine," should be the only answer that leads to the decision to fly. Here's a little tip: If you gaze at the horizon and objects seem to fade back or move you are probably suffering from fatigue. That one last flight isn't worth the risk.

Ego is a killer. The most dangerous pilot by far is the one flying for cameras, friends or relatives. Fly for yourself only, not to impress the folks. When others are present, resist the urge to show-off and fly one step below the limits of your ability. Ultralights certainly attract attention, but if that's the reason why you are flying, then the chances of you flying safely for long are greatly reduced. The rewards of flight are not dependent on the oohs and aahs of others.

Remember, there are three factors that make up a safe flying situation: the pilot, the equipment and the conditions. You have control over all three of these and must carefully consider each item in order to insure safety.

Knowledge and practice comes gradually. Only hours of airtime will allow you to advance to an expert level. Fly carefully, observe and ask plenty of questions. With such a sensible approach, the pleasure of the sky is yours to enjoy for a long time.

The Eagle

CHAPTER III

THE AIR

The air is like the ocean—sometimes it is calm, sometimes it swells and rolls, then at times it howls and pounds. A pilot must learn to read the air like a sailor reads the sea. The only problem is, the air is invisible, so its motion must be deduced from its action on visible objects such as windsocks, trees, smoke and clouds. Learning to assess the nature of the air in this manner requires a bit of study, a bit of experience and a lot of imagination. One of the enjoyable facets of flying is learning to scope out the conditions.

Why do we need to learn the ways of the wind and weather? First, we must be able to recognize areas of danger such as turbulence, rotors or high winds. Secondly, we should be aware of areas of useful lift or favorable winds. Finally, we can plan flying days or excursions in advance if we can predict the weather or interpret the reports.

Pilots of ultralight aircraft rarely fly more than a few hours or more than tens of miles at a time. Thus, the interest in large-scale weather effects is secondary to that of small-scale or local effects. The study of local conditions is called micrometeorology. This chapter covers the aspects of meteorology and micrometeorology necessary for safe and enjoyable flying. For a complete coverage of micrometeorology pertinent to all forms of ultralight flying, the reader is referred to the book *Flying Conditions* by the author.

WEATHER PATTERNS

All of the changing atmospheric conditions we experience as weather are caused by the heating effects of the sun. The surface of our terrestial globe is not heated uniformly due to the concentration of the sun's rays at the equator, the different heat absorption properties of land and sea masses and the daily rotation. Since the air is heated by the surface below it, the atmosphere also receives unequal heating.

The net effect of all this unequal distribution of heat in the atmosphere is a world-wide circulation of air. This circulation is complex and not totally understood by scientists; however, the general patterns are well established.

The air warmed at the equator rises and heads towards the poles in the upper atmosphere. The air tends to pile up at about 30° latitude due to the Coriolis effect (explained later) and also at the poles. Now, the result of this pile up of air in the upper levels is the formation of high pressure areas in the lower atmosphere. This is easily understood since the air pressure we detect is due to the weight of air above us. The more air above us, the higher the pressure.

In the northern hemisphere, the high pressure system in the north and those at the mid-latitudes oppose each other in a continual battle. At times, the northern highs win and a mass of cold air breaks to the south in what is known as a cold front or polar wave. When the mid-latitude highs prevail, they push warm air northward in the form of a warm front. This movement of cold and warm fronts as well as the passage of pressure systems is what causes the changes in weather.

Figure 4 illustrates a typical weather pattern on the globe. The weatherman on TV presents a small section of this picture. Since the weather travels from west to east in the mid-latitudes, we can predict the weather from large-scale studies of this nature. However, more useful to the pilot is a study of air movement around pressure systems and fronts.

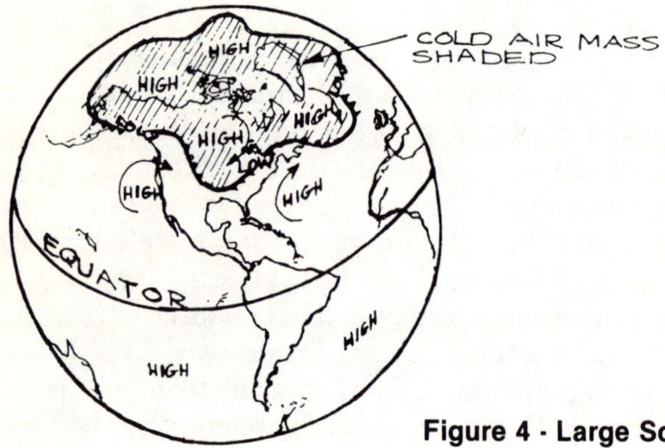

Figure 4 - Large Scale Weather Patterns

FRONTAL AND PRESSURE SYSTEMS

We have already noted how high pressure areas or cells are formed at the surface by air converging or piling up aloft. Since air (or any gas) tends to flow from high to low pressure, we find the air around a high pressure cell flowing away from the cell as it is formed (see figure 5[a]). However, any object in motion experiences an apparent force to the right (in the northern hemisphere—the force is to the left south of the equator) due to the rotation of the earth. This apparent force is called the Coriolis force. As a result of the Coriolis force, the wind gradually changes its direction and begins flowing around the high pressure cell as in figure 5(b). The wind *always* follows a clockwise path around a high.

Low pressure systems are usually formed over heated land areas or along cold fronts. The wind flowing towards a low is also turned to the right, so the air eventually flows counterclockwise around a low. This is opposite the direction of flow around a high pressure cell.

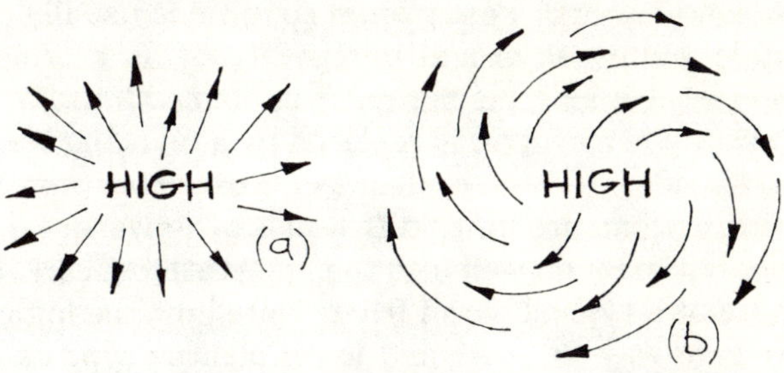

Figure 5 · Air Flow Around a High

The natural laws relating to the flow around pressure cells can be used to predict wind direction. Simply locate the high and low pressure systems on a weather map, then draw the clockwise flow around the highs and the counterclockwise flow around the lows. From this over-all flow pattern we can observe the general wind direction at any position on the map. In addition, some idea of the wind speed can be deduced from the knowledge that winds are usually lighter the closer we are to the center of a high and stronger near a low. Finally, some idea of future weather conditions can be gained by noting that pressure cells as well as cold and warm fronts gradually progress from west to east.

A cold front condition exists when cold air is moving into an area of warmer air. The cold front is located at the interface of the cold and warm air. Since warm air is less dense than cold air, the warm air is lifted as the cold air plows forward. If the warm air contains any moisture, clouds will form as the lifted air cools and the water vapor condenses. Figure 6 illustrates a typical cold front.

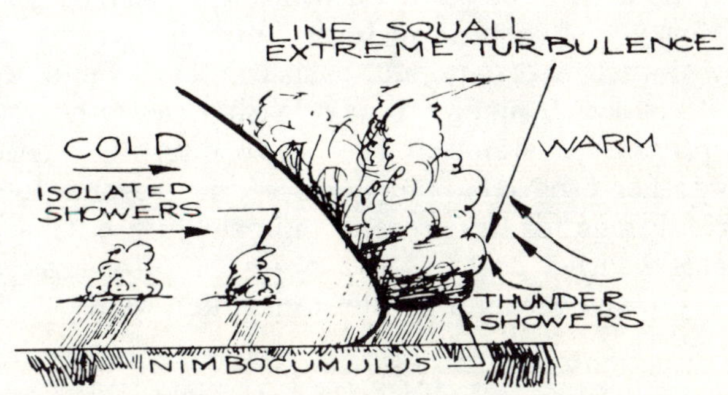

Figure 6 · Typical Cold Front Cross Section

Cold fronts are very often accompanied by towering cumulus (cotton ball-like) clouds, squall lines or thunderstorms. The front can travel over 20 mph (32 kph) in extreme cases. Faster moving fronts tend to be accompanied by more severe weather conditions. When a cold front passes, wind direction changes up to 180 degrees and large temperature drops are normal. Post frontal conditions usually consist of northerly winds, sunny skys and bumpy flying as thermals are generated in the unstable air (this matter is explained later).

Warm fronts occur when cool air is replaced by advancing warm air. Again, the warm air rides over the cool air as it pushes forward. In this case, the cloud formations are quite different as the warm air is not lifted so abruptly, but extends well into the upper atmosphere. Figure 7 shows the nature of a typical warm front. Note how the high cirrus clouds gradually give way to lower and lower stratus type clouds as the front approaches. This phenomena can be readily used to predict the coming of a warm front. If high cirrus (mare's tails) are gradually replaced by lower and lower layer type clouds, expect the presence of a warm front within a day or so.

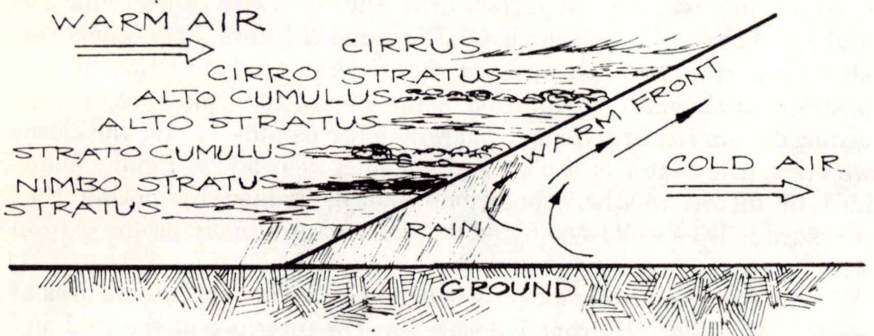

Figure 7 - Typical Warm Front Cross Section

A warm front is usually accompanied by a good deal of rain extending over hundreds of miles and lasting for a day or more. Warm fronts advance much slower than cold fronts (15 mph or less) and cause a wind shift of about 45°. After a warm front passes, the air is warm, smooth and hazy with a southwesterly flow.

The study of weather on a regular basis can teach a pilot a great deal about what to expect from day to day. With a basic understanding of fronts and pressure systems, it is easy to interpret weather maps, television weather programs and flight service reports to determine the flying conditions for the present and near future. Observation of the large scale weather patterns is the first step towards understanding the ways of the ocean of air through which we fly.

CLOUDS

One of the best aids to weather recognition for pilots is clouds. These misty masses are formed when water vapor condenses into small visible droplets. Condensation occurs usually when the air is cooled through lifting. Some of the ways the air is lifted are: by the action of advancing fronts (cold or warm), by mountains in the path of the wind and by cold air flowing under warmer air in a valley. In short, whenever a cloud exists, some form of upward motion is occurring or has occurred.

There are almost as many varieties of clouds in the sky as there are birds. However, it is instructive to point out some general types and their related conditions. The first type are the high cirrus. These clouds are composed mainly of ice crystals and look like wisps of angel's hair. They are commonly called mare's tails. Cirrus clouds are too high to relate to conditions in the realm of powered ultralights, but they often foreshadow the approach of a warm front as mentioned previously, as well as steady high winds at midday.

Goldwing Under Cumulus Clouds

Stratus clouds are the second general type. They consist of large extensive layers of cloud with fairly uniform appearance. Stratus clouds are formed when a whole layer is lifted uniformly. These clouds are associated with steady rain and also light smooth winds. The only turbulence expected under stratus clouds occurs if a warm layer is moving over a cool layer. This action is termed shear and will be explained later.

The next category is cumulus clouds. These are the clouds that look like giant puffs of wool or cotton. They are formed by small areas of lifting air rising like a bubble or column until condensation forms the cloud. Cumulus clouds can be small and isolated or huge towering masses consisting of many areas of lift feeding one cloud (see figure 8). In the former case, good weather is in the offing. The latter case often means thunderstorms. In either case, some turbulence is expected since the rising bubbles or thermals disturb the air as they pass. Since these thermals usually originate at ground level, we can learn to judge the turbulence in the air by observing the gustiness on the ground.

Figure 8 · Cumulus Cloud Types

The last form of clouds worth mentioning are orographic clouds. These are formed by irregularities on the earth's surface. A cap cloud is formed when air striking a mountain is forced upward. Many western mountains are adorned by cap clouds by midday. A banner cloud forms behind a mountain in a high wind. The reduced pressure in the lee of a mountain cools the air and forms the cloud. Finally, lenticular clouds are formed when a row of mountains create waves in the air similar to those behind a submerged log in a river. The clouds are formed at the crest of the wave and tend to line up downwind as in figure 9.

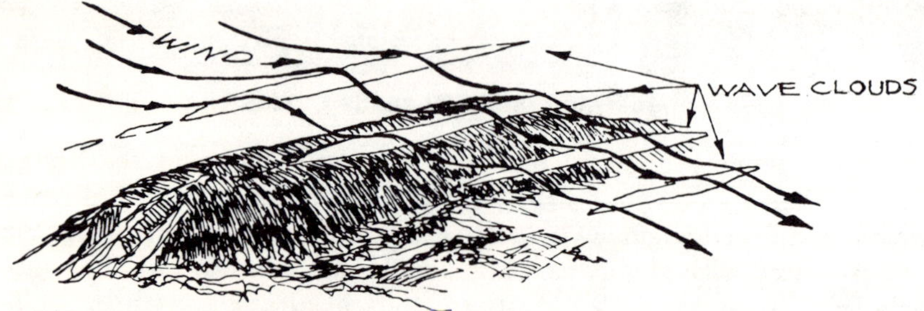

Figure 9 · Formation of Wave Clouds

The last three clouds tend to be stationary in relation to the ground, whereas all other clouds move with the wind. Thus, by recognizing the cloud types and watching their movements, a good idea of the wind velocity at the level of the cloud can be acquired. Develop the habit of observing clouds whenever possible. Experience at watching these aerial banners is an important part of interpreting the conditions.

LOCAL EFFECTS

Local effects refer to weather conditions unique to small area—say from tens of miles to a few hundred yards. These small-scale phenomena are caused mainly by the sun's interaction with terrain irregularities. Local effects are very important to the ultralight pilot since they very often overpower large scale effects (general weather).

The most common small scale effect experienced in hilly or mountainous terrain is the daytime upslope winds and the evening downslope breeze. In the morning when the sun begins heating the valleys, the different pressures created in the air causes a light breeze to begin drifting up the slopes of the mountains. This breeze reaches a peak velocity of up to 10 mph (16 kph) or more during the early afternoon. The upslope wind is known as a valley or anabatic wind. Valley winds are strongest in summer when the sun's heating is greatest. Also, slopes facing the sun will produce the strongest valley winds. Since the upward moving air can exist in a layer up to 300 ft. (100m) thick, a pilot may find it much easier to maintain altitude above a slope than in the middle of a valley where the air is sinking on a bright sunny day, unless thermals are rising in the valley.

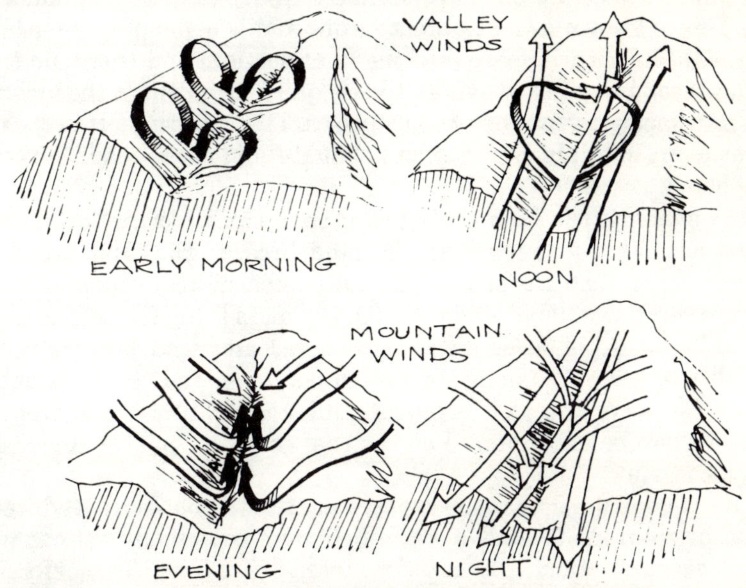

Figure 10 - Circulation Due to Solar Heating

Downslope winds are termed catabatic or mountain winds. They occur in the evening when the valleys begin to cool. The air lying over the surface of the slope cools and slips downward, filling in the valley. As the valley fills, the air in the center is lifted so that a pilot flying in the evening usually finds a better climb rate in the middle of the valley than above the slope (in the absence of ridge lift). Mountain winds are generally confined to a layer less than 20 ft. (7m) and are usually lighter than valley winds.

Figure 10 illustrates the cyclical behavior of valley and mountain winds. Note the lift in the middle of the valley in the early evening. Of particular importance is the indication of strong downhill winds as evening wears on. In high mountains and at the end of a clear day, the sudden cooling can cause flow from valleys and canyons that disturb the main flow on the plain, causing turbulence and wind direction changes.

THE SEA BREEZE

Another familiar local effect is the sea breeze that occurs near the ocean or other large bodies of water. During the day, the land heats much more rapidly than the water. This results in a gradual flow of air from the sea to the shore. As the day progresses, this flow gets stronger and stronger and reaches further inland—sometimes as much as 30 miles (48km).

Occassionally, the sea breeze sets in so strongly (as in the case of desert areas next to the ocean) that the cool moist air from the sea acts like a miniature cold front and advances under the hot, dry land air mass. This is known as a sea breeze front and is common in Southern California. Shear turbulence (see the next section) and thermals triggered by a sea breeze front render the air quite turbulent in the vicinity of the interface between the two airmasses. There is great lift in the rising warm air, but only expert pilots should fly in these conditions due to the heavy turbulence.

In the evening, the land cools faster than the water so the reverse flow occurs. This is known as the land breeze. The land breeze is usually weaker than the sea breeze unless nearby mountains add the effect of their downslope winds. Again, the main thing for an ultralight pilot to be aware of in connection with sea and land breezes is the possibility of a sudden change in direction as evening falls. Also, at the front of the sea breeze as it is pushing inland, turbulence and areas of strong lift can be encountered as the cool ocean air pushes under the warm air inland.

In the same manner that the cool sea next to the hot land produces a circulation from sea to land, a warm field next to a cool forest can produce a local circulation. A light breeze often drifts from the cool forests to the warm field. This breeze will rise above the field and drift back to the forest a couple hundred feet up. This type of circulation is simply convection and is present everywhere.

TURBULENCE

Many other local effects are related to turbulence and will be discussed in this section. Turbulence is simply a random swirling motion of the air. These swirls are sometimes called eddies or vorticies. The eddies can be any size or strength. Since turbulence can cause severe control problems, it is the greatest single threat to safe ultralight flying. We will do well to learn the nature of turbulence.

To simplify matters, we will separate turbulence into three categories according to their cause. The first cause of turbulence is the interruption of the wind by ground objects and terrain irregularities. To visualize how this occurs, watch a stream flowing over and around boulders or sticks. You'll notice swirls or eddies downstream from the obstructions. In a similar manner, turbulence in the air is created downwind from trees, buildings, hills, mountains or any other solid object in the path of the wind. This is illustrated in figure 11.

Figure 11 - Turbulence Formation

It should be clear that turbulence occurs in this case only if there is wind. Wind tends to be a complicating factor in all flying. Put that statement in an accessible part of your mind for review on every flying day. The stronger the wind and the larger the obstruction the stronger the turbulence and the further downwind from the obstruction the turbulence extends. To avoid this type of turbulence, simply do not fly on the lee side (downwind) of solid objects and avoid strong winds. A good rule of thumb is to stay about seven times the height of an object away from the downwind side. Of course, this distance diminishes in lighter winds. You can often get a feeling for the strength of this type of turbulence by noting the variations of the wind on the ground, in trees and windsocks.

Downwind from trees, turbulence tends to be smaller and less severe than downwind from a solid object since trees allow some of the air to pass through. However, this varies greatly with the thickness of the group of trees so you cannot be sure of the degree of turbulence. For the sake of safety, avoid the downwind side of any solid object, including trees.

An ultralight pilot must learn to judge the wind by looking at his or her surroundings. Gradually you will learn to access the windspeed and turbulence by watching the terrain and the sky. The chart below provides guidelines for you to look for. Try to relate these cues to what you feel as you go flying.

Terms Used by U.S. Weather Service	Velocity mph	Estimating Velocities on Land	Estimating Velocities on Water
Calm	Less than 1	Smoke rises vertically	Sea like a mirror
Light air	1 - 3	Smoke drifts; wind vanes unmoved.	Ripples with the appearance of scales are formed but without foam crests.
Light Breeze	4 - 7	Wind felt on face; leaves rustle; ordinary vane moved by wind.	Small wavelets, still short but more pronounced; crests have a glassy appearance and do not break.
Gentle Breeze	8 - 12	Leaves and small twigs in constant motion; wind extends light flag	Large wavelets; crests begin to break. Foam of glassy appearance. (Perhaps scattered whitecaps.)
Moderate Breeze	13 - 18	Dust and loose paper raised; small branches are moved.	Small waves, becoming longer; fairly frequent whitecaps.
Fresh Breeze	19 - 24	Small trees in leaf begin to sway; crested wavelets form in inland water.	Moderate waves; taking a more pronounced long form; many whitecaps are formed. (Chance of some spray.)
Strong Breeze	25 - 31	Large branches in motion; whistling hear in telegraph wires; umbrellas used with difficulty.	Large waves begin to form; many whitecaps are more extensive everywhere (Probably some spray.)
Moderate Gale	32 - 38	Whole trees in motion; inconvenience felt in walking against the wind.	Sea heaps up and white foam from breaking waves begins to be blown in streaks along the direction of the wind.

Wind Force Table

The second cause of turbulence is thermals. A thermal is a warm bubble or column of air that is formed on the surface by the sun's heating. This bubble breaks away and rises similar to the bubbles of air formed at the bottom of a pan of boiling water. As the bubble rises it pushes the surrounding air away and leaves a trail of swirling air behind. A continuous column thermal will be formed when the solar heating isn't too great and a large layer of air is heated that can feed the thermal over a period of time. Bubble thermals form when the sun heats the surface readily (as at midday) and differential heating occurs (as when dry fields lie next to green areas). In strong conditions a thermal rises rapidly, sucking cool air from surrounding green areas under it which shuts off the warm air feeding the thermal, thus forming a bubble. On a given day, thermals may start out as columns then begin to form as bubbles as the solar radiation gets more intense, then change back to columns as the sun starts dropping, just as water in a heated pan exhibits convection columns changing to bubbles. Experienced thermal pilots will fly both types of thermals throughout the course of a day.

When flying through a thermal, a pilot may feel a few bumps, then a sudden surge of lift, then a few more bumps as he leaves the thermal. This "textured air" is what conventional pilots commonly call air pockets. Sailplane and hang glider pilots as well as hawks commonly use thermals to climb many thousands of feet (See Chapter VII).

The problem thermals represent to the powered ultralight pilot is occasional very strong turbulence. When wind is present, this turbulence is even worse. Powered ultralight pilots are cautioned to fly *ONLY* in calm or very light winds when thermals are present. Large weak thermals are the only safe thermals for this type of aircraft since the organized rolling air can seriously hamper control (see figure 12).

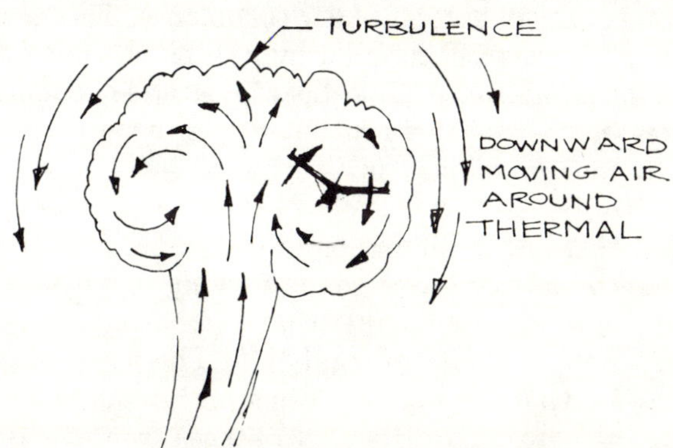

Figure 12 - Thermal Cross Section

Since thermals are usually produced by the sun's heating, it should be apparent that flying only in the early morning hours (usually before 10:00 AM) and in the evening is the best way to avoid thermal turbulence. Remember, the strongest thermals occur just after midday. Also, since thermals usually originate at the ground, you can get a feeling for how strong thermal turbulence will be by noting the gustiness on the ground away from buildings or other obstructions that create mechanical turbulence. Since thermals take time to build, you should observe for at least a half hour if there's any doubt.

Thermals and the associated turbulence can extend many thousands of feet. They occur most often on a clear, cold day after the passage of a cold front. The presence of hawks circling, the occurrence of isolated cumulus clouds, the appearance of dust devils and sudden gusts of wind all indicate thermals are rising. Approach these type of conditions cautiously, and gradually you will learn to predict the condition of the air before you enter it.

The third cause of turbulence is wind shear. Shear occurs when two layers of air move at different velocities and rub each other the wrong way. Turbulence occurs at the interface between the two layers. The most common incident of shear turbulence is where the warm and cool air meet in cold or warm fronts. Generally the layers that cause shear turbulence are of quite different temperatures.

One good way to avoid shear turbulence is to avoid flying when fronts are near. Other incidences of shear do arise, however. In mountainous regions, cool air can flow into a valley and replace warmer air. As it flows under the warmer air, a layer of shear can be formed at the top of the cool layer. In a similar manner, cool air can settle in a valley in the night, then form a shear layer as warm air flows across the top in the morning.

Often at the end of a hot day, the lower layer of air will cool rapidly as the sun goes down. This layer will be very stable and sit still while the warmer air a couple hundred feet up may be moving. The level where these layers rub will exhibit shear turbulence. This occurs even over flat ground. An unsuspecting pilot may think he's out for an easy glassy ride when he climbs up to this shear layer and encounters a few unfriendly shakes. Recognize shear turbulence for what it is and power back to return to your previously non-turbulent level.

The problem with the latter two types of shear (and shear conditions in general) is that there is no indication of the presence of turbulence. The best policy is to look for lower winds moving in a different direction from the upper winds. Remember that even though it is calm on the ground, there may be plenty of wind aloft. The powered ultralight pilot should be aware that his engine gives him the capability to climb up to conditions that are very difficult to assess from the ground. A careful approach is the only safe and sane policy.

WINDS AT ALTITUDE

We spend most of our life on the ground and consequently are quite at ease judging the wind at lower levels. However, most of us don't have a clue as to the nature of the air at higher altitudes. The first thing to note is that the upper winds drive the lower winds so, if it's windy on the ground you can bet there's wind aloft (unless local effects are strong). The winds generally increase as altitude is gained then taper off at about 25,000 ft. (8,000m) or more. However, the greatest rise in wind velocity occurs in the lower 1,500 to 3,000 ft. (500 to 1,000m). This lower layer is the so-called friction layer.

When the wind moves across the ground it is slowed by the ground objects. This slowing of the wind as the ground is approached is known as "wind gradient." The wind gradient can be sudden or gradual, according to the nature of the terrain, the stability of the air and the wind velocity. When the wind gradient is strong, it is important to maintain extra speed when landing since an approach through a gradient causes a reduction in airspeed as the aircraft descends. This matter is covered in Chapter V.

Another effect of the wind gradient is the change in wind direction as altitude is gained. The Coriolis effect turns all wind to the right with an apparent force proportional to the wind velocity. Since the lower wind is moving slower than the upper wind, it is turned less. The net result is that the wind direction veers in a clockwise direction as altitude is gained. An illustration of the wind gradient and direction change appears in figure 13. Note that the presence of fronts can change the winds aloft picture considerably. One point to note is that the upper winds in the mid-latitudes are almost always westerly (northwest to southwest) so that if we experience an easterly wind at the surface (southeast to northeast) we should expect a greater change with altitude than if the surface winds were westerly.

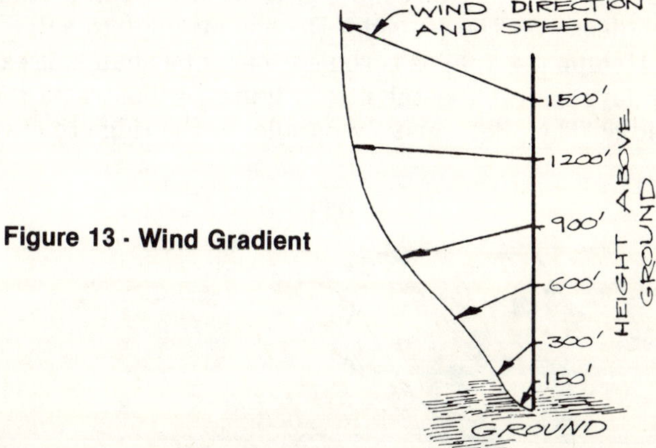

Figure 13 - Wind Gradient

Have you ever noticed how calm it is in the early morning, then how windy it gets at mid afternoon only to return to calm at night? This is the normal daily progression of the surface winds. You may have guessed that the cause is the sun's heating. The mechanism is simply this: as the sun warms the lower air layers, vertical currents are formed, causing mixing. This brings the upper air down to the surface. This upper air is moving quite fast, so a surface wind is created. In the evening, when the sun's heating terminates, the wind turns to calm since surface drag stops it and the upper winds are no longer circulating downward. The upper winds are moving day and night, but the sun only circulates them during the day.

In general, there is nothing of great danger to be encountered at altitude that is not present on the ground. A pilot should be aware of the possibility of shear turbulence, especially near fronts. Thermals usually get weaker as altitude is gained unless they are joined by others in the vicinity, or the air is either very moist or very unstable. Be aware that wind can get considerably stronger at altitude and will change direction. Don't get caught aloft drifting way off course.

LIFT SOURCES

Glider pilots use natural sources of lift to fly great distances for long periods of time. A powered ultralight pilot can use the same sources to aid his craft to achieve overwhelming performance or even stay aloft with his engine shut down. Of course, the normal caution must be paid to high winds and turbulence.

The most common source of lift is ridge or orographic lift. When the wind hits a mountain, hill or ridge, it is deflected upward. The upward component of the air is often strong enough to sustain an aircraft. To utilize this source of lift, a pilot must fly in front of the ridge or mountain. If he positions himself too far in front, he will be out of the lift band and will sink rapidly. If he ventures too far behind the top of the ridge he may encounter strong horizontal winds and find himself facing the turbulence on the lee side. Do not attempt to ridge soar in winds over 15 mph (24 kph) as turbulence may be abundant except on very stable days and at coastal sites. Figure 14 illustrates the lift in front of a ridge. The pilot must fly parallel to the ridge to stay in the lift band.

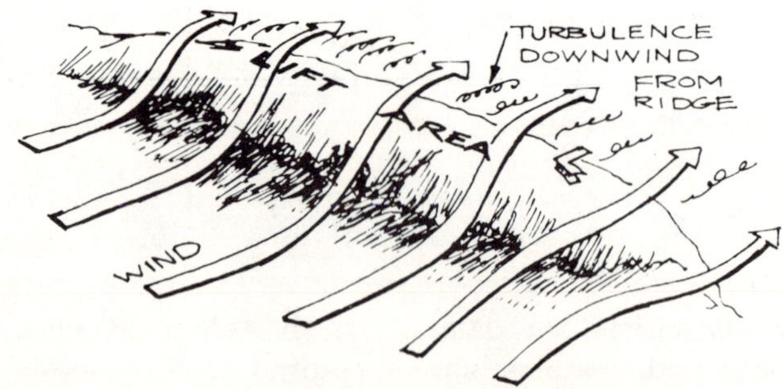

Figure 14 · Ridge Lift

The next source of lift is thermals. As indicated above, these warm rising bubbles originate at the ground and float aloft whenever strong heating of the surface occurs. Areas that are heated readily such as dry fields, parking lots or bare ground are good thermal sources. The art of thermaling consists of circling to stay in the confines of the rising bubble. This skill takes many hours of practice, but can reward the plucky pilot with several thousands of feet gained and a real sense of accomplishment. A powered ultralight suffers a loss of performance due to the engine weight and drag, but successful thermal flights are common. Remember, in thermal conditions use the engine only to climb aloft, then shut down or idle back and try your luck. We will explore ridge and thermal soaring in Chapter VII.

A third source of usable lift is convergence. When airflows from different directions meet, an upwelling will occur. For example, in calm air, the upslope wind on both sides of a mountain will meet at the top and combine to form an area of very bouyant lift. This is known as a convergence zone. Also, air meeting after flowing around a group of mountains will form convergence lift.

Another source of convergence is downslope winds at the end of the day. In this case, the mountain winds from both sides of the valley will meet in the middle and rise as shown in figure 10. There are many sources of convergence. However, most of them are difficult to predict and are only happened into. When you find yourself in light wind magical lift, you can bet it's convergence.

Another source of lift is wave activity. These conditions occur often but are not recommended conditions for powered ultralights. The reason for this is that strong winds, radical turbulence and over-powering lift occasionally occur in association with waves. Certainly gentle waves exist, but a powered ultralight craft is not a good wave exploratory vehicle. Frontal lift is another source of upward moving air. However, as cautioned earlier, fronts of all types are loaded with nasty turbulence.

THUNDERSTORMS AND DUST DEVILS

Two particularly dangerous phenomena related to thermals are thunderstorms and dust devils. Thunderstorms form when the air is moist and good solar heating is present. Sounds like the typical midwest summer day, doesn't it? Moisture is carried aloft along with thermals that develop into vast convention currents. Eventually towering cumulus clouds grow from the tons of moisture carried aloft.

The top of a towering cumulus may reach well over 50,000 feet and form an anvil cloud in the high winds aloft. At some point the moisture in the upper layers may suddenly change to water droplets, or more commonly, ice crystals that fall as rain or hail. Powerful updrafts may sweep this falling moisture back up until the whole thunderstorm cell gets "top heavy" and suddenly collapses in a torrent of rain and hail. The downpour eventually exhausts the cloud's supply of moisure and carries cool air down to the surface which effectively shuts off the warm air supply and the thunderstorm dissipates.

Certainly, a thunderstorm is an awesome creature and interesting to watch. However, you do not want to be caught flying anywhere near one. Here's why: Lightning is produced by the tremendous amount of friction within the thunderstorm. Needless to say, an ultralight is an ideal lightning rod and a fried pilot can't fly too well.

Furthermore, the lift below a thunderstorm may be so great that an ultralight climbs no matter what the pilot does. It is very possible to get sucked up into the cloud where violent turbulence abounds, lightning strikes, hailstones pound and freezing temperatures exist, to say nothing of the frightful disorientation of total whiteout. Pilots who have lived through a thunderstorm encounter (many have not) tell some incredibly scary tales.

Even when you are flying well away from a thunderstorm you are not safe. In very unstable conditions, thunderstorms can suddenly spread out to cover a wide area. And then there's the matter of a gust front. When all those tons of water droplets fall to earth, they drag tons of air along for the ride. This creates strong downdrafts that hit the ground and spread out like a tomato hitting a wall. Often the air will rush miles ahead (downwind) of a thunderstorm in what is known as a gust front. The wind can shift 180° in front of a thunderstorm and reach up to 100 mph (160 kph) although 40 mph (64 kph) is more normal. There is great turbulence as this gust front plows ahead like a miniature cold front. Needless to say, an ultralight pilot should always keep an eye out for massive cloud build-up and zip back to the hangar

Figure 15 · Thunderstorm Anatomy

at the first sign of approaching thunderstorms. Remember, a gust front can reach over 10 miles (16 km) in front of a thunderstorm. Figure 15 shows a typical mature thunderstorm.

Dust devils are formed when thermals lift off in very unstable days, especially over desert areas where the ground is heated intensely. As the air rushes in below the thermal, it starts spinning in the same manner as the water rushing down your bathtub spins as it draws together. This is due to the slight rotation in a large volume being concentrated in a small area as it contracts.

The spinning air forms a column under the thermal, often reaching thousands of feet in ideal conditions. Dust is sucked up (leaves and other debris go along for the ride too) in the lower pressure inside the column and give the system its visiblity as well as its name.

Very strong rotating air currents exist near a dust devil and ultralight pilots are advised to steer well clear of such a threat. Sailplane pilots exploit dust devils for the lift around their outside perimeter, but lightly loaded ultralights (as well as hang gliders) are no match for a dust devil. By the FAA determination of ultralights, they will probably always be lightly loaded and slow, so we doubt if it will ever be safe to fly near a dust devil with such a ship. Deaths have occurred due to pilots failing to heed this simple warning.

It should be obvious that there is much to learn about the weather and flying conditions in general. The best policy to follow until experience and knowledge is acquired is to fly only in gentle conditions. Talk to other pilots as much as possible to learn from their experience—it makes yours come much quicker. Remember, you will only be at home in the air when it becomes as familiar as your living room. Take the time to observe and learn and your flying pleasure will be enhanced.

The Solar Riser

CHAPTER IV

THE THEORY OF FLIGHT

If we were born with the instinct to fly like the birds, we would not find it necessary to learn how our wings work in the wind. Unfortunately, no matter how great our desire to fly, we cannot do so safely without study and practice. The study of the motion of a solid body through the air is called aerodynamics. In this chapter we will cover practical aerodynamics relating to the control of our little wings. With enough work, perhaps we can equal the birds in flying ability.

LIFT AND DRAG

Birds, bugs and airplanes are all heavier than air. This means they must produce lift to stay aloft. Everyone knows the lift comes from the wing. Just how is this accomplished? The secret is in the shape of the wing.

Let's look at a cross section of a wing. This cross section is called an airfoil and appears in figure 16(a). Note how the upper surface is curved more than the lower surface. As this wing section moves through the air, the flow separates at A and rejoins at B. The air moving over the top surface is deflected from its original path greatly while the air moving past the lower surface is deflected to a lesser amount. The reaction of the air with the surfaces results in a lower pressure on the top surface and a higher pressure on the bottom surface compared to the normal pressure of the air at rest. The result is a pressure distribution around the airfoil as shown in figure 16(b). If we add all the little forces on the wing we will come up with a net force indicated by the arrow L. This is the lift that holds us suspended in space. Note: About ⅔ of this lift comes from the top surface and ⅓ comes from the lower surface.

We have to pay for this lift. "You can't get something for nothing" is as true in physics as it is in business. The price we pay is drag. Drag represents energy lost to the air in the form of turbulence. There are two sources of drag on our aircraft. The first is due to the fact that some of the small lift forces shown in figure 16(b) are actually pointing somewhat towards the rear of the wing. These forces must be overcome by the thrust of the engine to maintain flight speed. This type of drag is called induced drag.

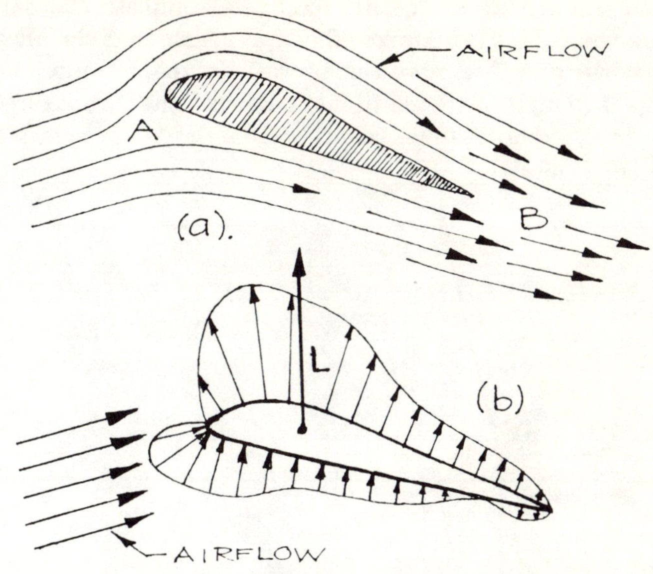

Figure 16 - Production of Lift on an Airfoil

The second type of drag is due to the solid parts of the aircraft pushing through the air. The nature of this "form" drag, as it is called, can be experienced by simply sticking your hand out the window of a moving car. (Form drag can be broken down into profile drag due to the wing's friction with the air and parasitic drag due to all other parts on the aircraft.)

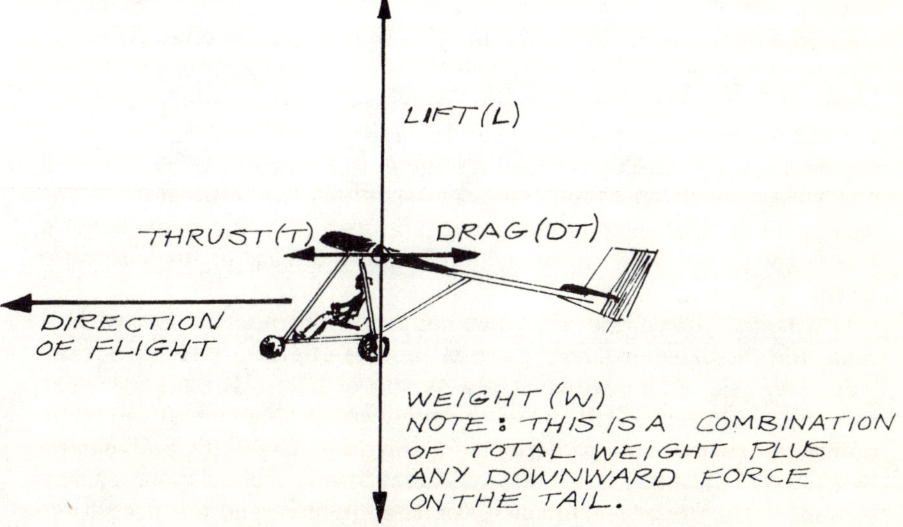

Figure 17 - Balance of Forces in Level Flight

If we combine the induced and form drag into the total drag DT, then add the thrust of the engine T and the weight of the aircraft and pilot W to the picture of the lift force, we complete the balance of forces on a wing. This is shown in figure 17. Note that the lift directly opposes the weight. The more the aircraft weighs, the more lift must be developed to maintain level flight. Likewise, the thrust directly opposes the drag, so thrust must be increased if drag increases in order to maintain level flight.

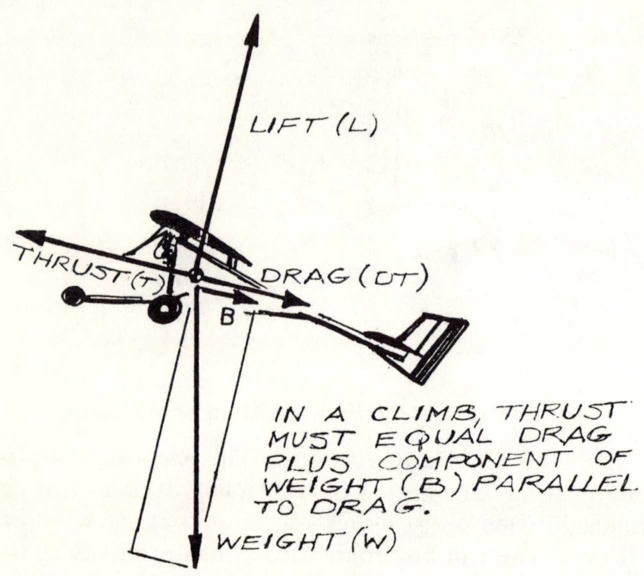

Figure 18 · Balance of Forces in Climbing Flight

In steady climbing flight, the lift and weight are no longer working in exactly opposite directions. The thrust of the engine begins to lift some of the weight, so the lift produced by the wings actually decreases. (In a steady vertical climb, no lift is produced by the wings, as the engine/propeller thrust lifts the entire weight of the aircraft.) The thrust must overcome the drag as well as the component of the weight directed to the rear as shown in figure 18. Drag is dependent on the airspeed and angle of attack so it may increase or decrease in a climb.

If we shut the engine off, what happens? The aircraft is now in a glide and the balance of forces are as shown in figure 19. Note that the weight W still acts downward (gravity never fails). However, there is no thrust, so we must tilt the wing downward so that the lift force L is pointing forward enough to overcome the drag. The flight path can no longer be maintained level since we must lose altitude to gain energy to oppose the drag DT. In this case, the lift force and the drag force combine to hold up the weight. This is represented by the arrow R.

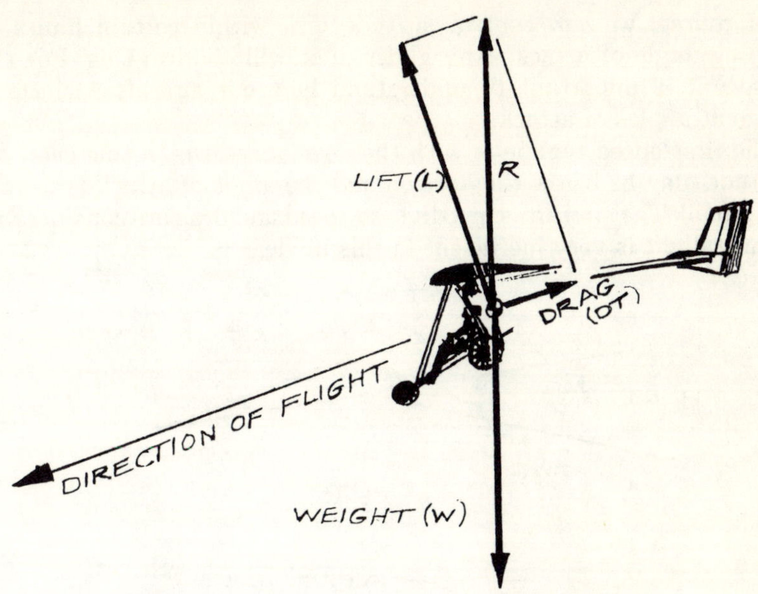

Figure 19 · Balance of Forces in Gliding Flight

SPEED VARIATION

The angle the wing makes with the wind is called angle of attack. The angle the wing makes with the horizon (that is, with a level plane) is called attitude. These angles are illustrated in figure 20. In 20(a), the aircraft is unpowered. Note how the angle of attack is greater than the attitude. Also note that the relative wind direction is always exactly opposite the direction of travel.

In 20(b) the aircraft is climbing under power. In this case, the attitude is greater than the angle of attack. Note that if the aircraft were experiencing level flight, the angle of attack and attitude would be the same. The point to learn from these illustrations is that angle of attack is not totally dependent on how the wing is angled to the horizon, but is also determined by how much thrust or power (and thus speed) is applied.

One important rule in powered flight is that we vary the amount of climb by varying the power, while the airspeed of the craft is varied by changing the angle of attack. This can be seen by looking again at figure 17. If we increase the thrust by opening up the throttle, we speed up a little, but drag and lift quickly increase also. The greater drag prohibits any great increase in speed while the greater lift causes the aircraft to climb. Once the climb path is established, the weight begins to oppose the thrust (as shown in figure 18) and the aircraft slows down to the airspeed appropriate to the angle of attack being held. To speed up permanently, we need to lower the angle of attack to reduce the drag.

Of course, we can control altitude loss within certain limits by varying angle of attack. Any glider pilot will confirm this. For this reason, it is important to understand how our aircraft perform at different angles of attack.

The first speed regime is with the nose very low. In this case, the attitude may be below the horizon and the angle of attack is usually very small. The aircraft is in a dive, so speed and drag are considerable. An ultralight is very inefficient in this mode.

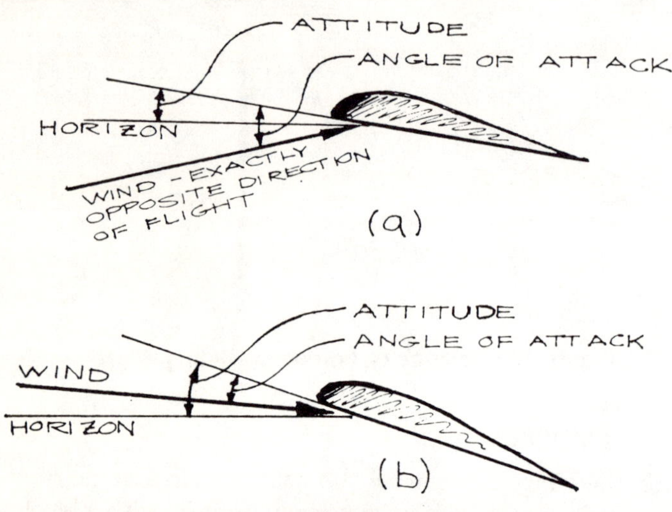

Figure 20 · Angle of Attack Changes

The next important angle of attack is the specific one that yields the best glide speed. For every wing design there is an angle of attack that allows the aircraft to fly the furthest for a given altitude loss. Since this angle of attack also is where the ratio of lift to drag is the greatest, we often call this the speed for maximum L/D. For an ultralight burdened with the weight of an engine, this speed usually falls between 25 and 30 mph (40-48 kph).

As the nose is raised and the aircraft slows even more, we come to the minimum sink angle of attack. In this case, an aircraft flying at minimum sink is descending as slowly as possible with the engine off. This is an important speed to know when trying to utilize lift, since minimizing your sink rate will make the most efficient use of that lift. However, at minimum sink speeds, the aircraft will not reach nearly as far for a given altitude loss as it will at best glide speed. Minimum sink speed are typically 20 to 25 mph (32-40 kph) for a powered ultralight.

The most important concept to acquire from all this speed talk is the variation of climb paths with angle of attack. As shown in figure 21, flying the best glide angle of attack yields the best climb rate. That means the pilot gets the highest in a given time period. On the other hand, flying at the minimum sink angle of attack yields the best angle of climb as shown. Generally, we should not use the best angle of climb speed as it is too near our stall speed. Fields that require such "close to the wire" flying should not be used. Remember, the most efficient airspeed for climb is best rate of climb.

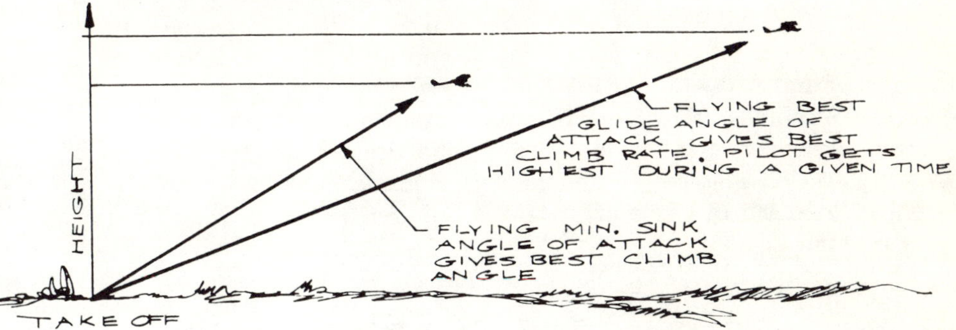

Figure 21 · Best Climb Speeds

Note that all these speeds vary with wing loading so even the manufacturer can't tell you exactly where these speeds occur. As you put on more weight your best rate of climb and best angle of climb speeds increase. Also, the actual sink rate increases although your angle of best glide does not since lift is increased along with drag as you speed up. There is one other speed that also increases with weight. It is so important that it gets special attention in the next section.

For convenience, the cardinal flying speeds are listed (in order of magnitude from slowest to fastest) below. Again, exact figures cannot be given here for they vary with aircraft design and wing loading. You should determine these speeds for your ultralight through experience and the manufacturer's recommendations.

V_S - Stalling speed. The minimum steady flight speed at which the aircraft is controllable.

V_{MS} - Minimum sink airspeed. This is the airspeed which produces the slowest descent rate with the power off.

V_X - Best angle of climb speed. This is the speed at which the aircraft will climb highest in a given distance. It occurs at the same angle of attack as V_{MS} but a slightly higher airspeed.

V_R - Rotation speed. This is the normal lift-off airspeed.

$V_{L/D}$ - Best glide speed. This is the speed which provides the best horizontal distance gain for a given altitude drop in the power off configuration.

V_Y - Best rate of climb speed. This is the airspeed at which the aircraft will climb the highest per unit of time.

V_A - Maneuvering speed. This is the speed above which gust loading may produce structural damage. Fly a little below this speed in turbulence so that V_A is not exceeded in turbulence induced dives.

V_{NE} - Never exceed speed. This is the speed which you should never exceed due to the possibility of breaking the aircraft. This speed should only be approached in smooth conditions.

STALLS

As the nose of the aircraft is raised, the angle of attack is increased, the airspeed is decreased and the path of the airflow above the wing is more curved. At some point, the air can no longer abide by such a demanding change in its path, so it separates from the rear of the wing. At some critical angle of attack, there is a sudden severe separation of airflow and the wing is said to be "stalled." Figure 22 shows a wing section just before and just after stall. Note that only a very small increase in angle of attack is required to create a quick stall separation.

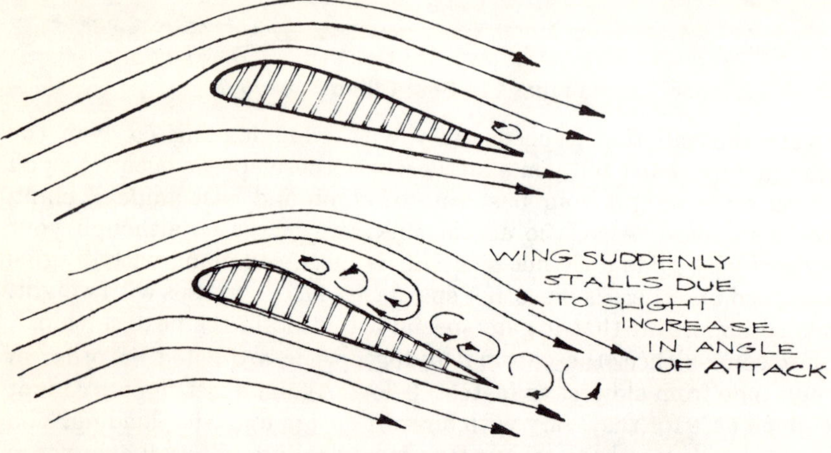

Figure 22 · Stalls

Stalls can be very dangerous for the following reasons: when a wing stalls, it is no longer producing lift. However, gravity never sleeps, so the weight starts pulling the aircraft earthward. Now the wing begins acting like a parachute—a very inefficient one. In normal flight, the center of mass of the aircraft is towards the front of the wing, since that is where most lift is produced. When a stall occurs and lift is destroyed, an imbalance occurs since there is more wing area behind the center of mass than in front. The result is, the aircraft drops its nose and dives. If there is enough altitude, the aircraft will pick up speed, the flow will reattach, lift will resume and the aircraft will pull out of the dive by itself.

However, if a stall occurs at a low altitude, there may not be enough room to dive to flying speed. For this reason, great caution must be taken to avoid stalls when flying near the ground (and all times). To do this, simply keep ample flying speed. That is, avoid too high an angle of attack. This is especially important when flying in turbulence and making a landing approach.

In turbulence, random gusts vary the angle of attack the wing "sees," so a wing flying close to stall angle of attack can be easily stalled by an upward or rearward gust. When approaching to land, very often the wind dies a considerable amount as the ground is neared. This is called a wind gradient and is explained in Chapter III. As the wing descends through the wind gradient, it meets less and less headwind which relates to a greater relative angle of attack. Normally, when the angle of attack changes on a wing due to a variation in the air, the wing adjusts by speeding up or slowing down until the trim angle of attack is again achieved. This happens due to the aircraft's carefully designed stability. However, if a headwind decreases suddenly, airspeed is reduced suddenly (the wing sees a diminished relative wind) and the angle of attack is increased abruptly. A stall will occur before the wing can react if the change of headwind is strong enough. A stall occurs when descending through a wind gradient if the gradient is severe enough for this reason. See figure 23.

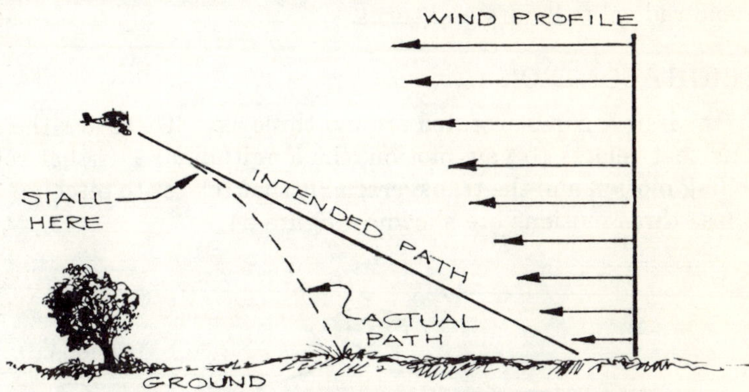

Figure 23 · Stalls Due to Wind Gradient

Ultralights are very susceptible to wind gradient effects due to their slow flying speeds. An ultralight pilot should expect a wind gradient of some degree on every landing. It might not be there, but then neither will the surprises. To avoid wind gradient stalls, lower the nose and gain airspeed *before* you reach the ground. About 10 mph (16 kph) should do it. Remember, it is usually too late to correct for wind gradient stalls once you are stalled, so add your speed at least 30 feet (10 m) up.

The severity of a stall is determined by the attitude at which the aircraft stalls. If you have an excess of speed, and raise the nose suddenly, the aircraft will climb then stall with the nose quite high. On the other hand, if you are flying level and raise the nose slowly, the stall will occur with a much lower nose attitude. In the first case, the fall-through of the nose and the subsequent dive will be much more abrupt and dramatic than in the latter case. It is good practice to experience your aircraft's stall characteristics to learn where the beast lurks and

61

the nature of the recovery. However, try them slow and gentle with plenty of altitude and power at idle.

As mentioned earlier, stall speed increases with wing loading. There are other ways to increasing wing loading besides eating spaghetti. One way is through centrifugal force. Remember that hair raising ride on a roller coaster when you were a kid? At the bottom of the long downhill run the track curved upward and you felt like you weighed a long ton. Whenever you follow a curved path in any vehicle you increase your apparent weight.

In an aircraft, pulling out of a dive or turning increases the wing loading through centrifugal force. The quicker the pull out and the tighter the circle, the greater the apparent wing loading, so the higher the stall speed. For example, a coordinated 45° bank turn increases the stall speed 1.4 times, while a 60° bank turn doubles the stall speed! As we shall see later, there are other problems with stalls in turns. The point to remember is don't get too heavy handed on the controls and avoid radical pull outs and turns.

FLIGHT CONTROL

An aircraft can be rotated around three axis. These are: the vertical axis that relates to yaw motion, the longitudinal axis that relates to rolling motion and the transverse axis that relates to pitching motion. These three motions are shown in figure 24.

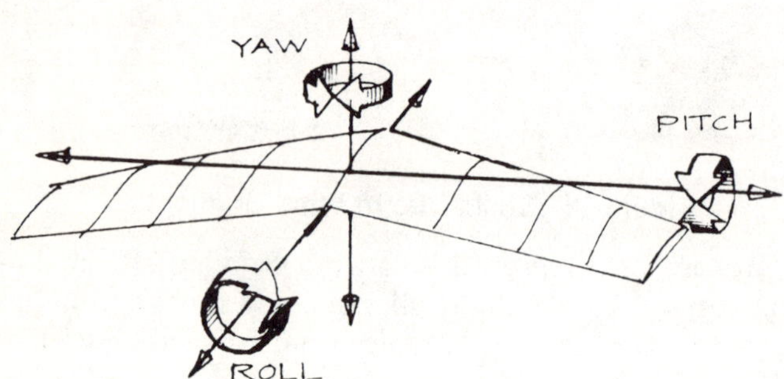

Figure 24 · Control Axis

Conventional aircraft can control motion around all three axes by use of a combination of ailerons, elevator and rudder. These control surfaces work by deflecting air and thus creating more lift or drag force at their location. Common control surfaces are identified in Chapter VI.

Many ultralights don't have all these control surfaces in the interest of simplicity. Indeed, most flex wings have no control surfaces at all, but rely on weight shift to roll and pitch the craft. Moving forward and back controls the pitch while roll is controlled by side movements. Fixed wing ultralights usually have control surfaces to affect motion

Weedhopper Elevator and Rudder

around one or more of the three axes. For example, some ultralights utilize wingtip drag rudders that yaw the aircraft, while pitch is controlled through weight shift. A few ultralights employ both drag rudders and elevons to control both yaw and pitch.

The reader may have noticed in the above cases the pilot only controls motion around two axes. How does he yaw the flex wing around or roll the fixed wings? The answer is that the thoughtful designer constructs the wing so that a roll action creates a yaw in the proper direction to produce a smooth turn. Likewise, a yaw control also produces the proper roll action.

The Lazair Control Surfaces

The secret to this cunning ploy is sweepback and dihedral. If an aircraft with sweepback or dihedral is made to yaw, one wing moves forward in relation to the other, so it meets the air more directly. This creates greater lift on the forward moving side so a roll is induced (see figure 25). In a similar manner an aircraft with the proper anhedral (downward slant) in the wings will yaw when a roll is induced. A flex wing falls in the latter category.

Now, the very thing that leads to good handling characteristics can lead to poor stability characteristics. Stability is the tendency for an aircraft to return to straight and level flight when it is disturbed. This can be seen to be a good property especially in rowdy air.

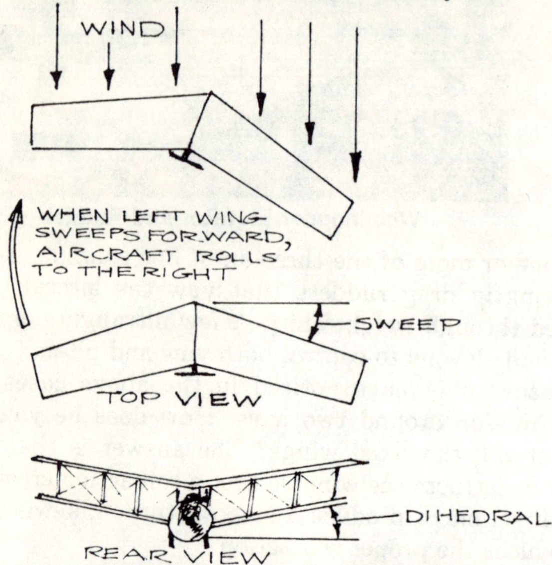

Figure 25 · Sweep and Dihedral

Dihedral produces roll stability: if one wing is lowered, it will produce more upward component of lift than the other wing. This imbalance of lift will return the wings to level as shown in figure 26. Because of this property, a dihedral aircraft of any type cannot be

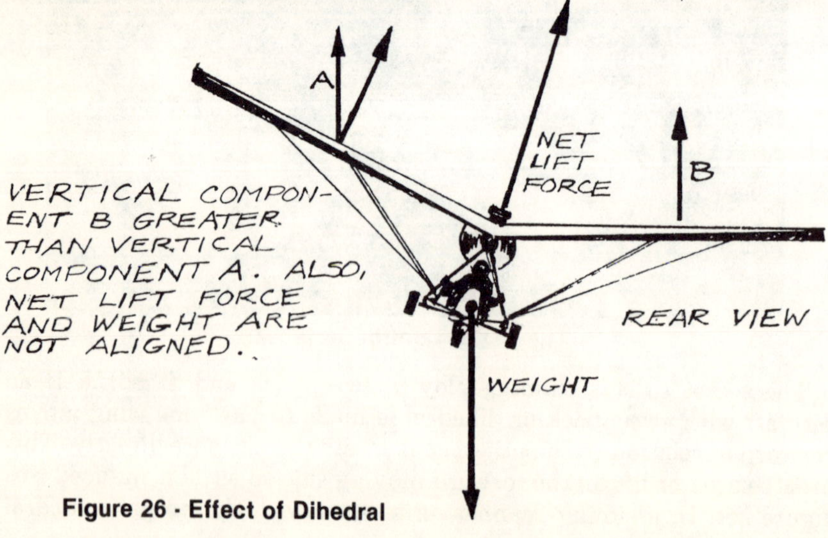

Figure 26 · Effect of Dihedral

rolled by weight shift.

Pitch stability is a complex affair, being determined mainly by the distribution of lift and drag along the wing at different angles of attack. Stability around the pitch axis is the most critical, since poor designs will not pull out of a dive or recover from a stall properly. One factor that leads to stability in pitch as well as stall control is wing twist or washout. Practically all aircraft have this washout in their wings. Washout can be seen by looking down a wing from the tip and noting that the tip is angled down compared to the center or root of the wing (see figure 27). As a result of this twist, the root section is always flying at a higher angle of attack then the wing tip. Thus, when a stall occurs it occurs at the center of the wings first. This helps prevent a spin (see the next section), keeps the wingtip controls working and produces a correcting nose down force if the tips are swept backwards.

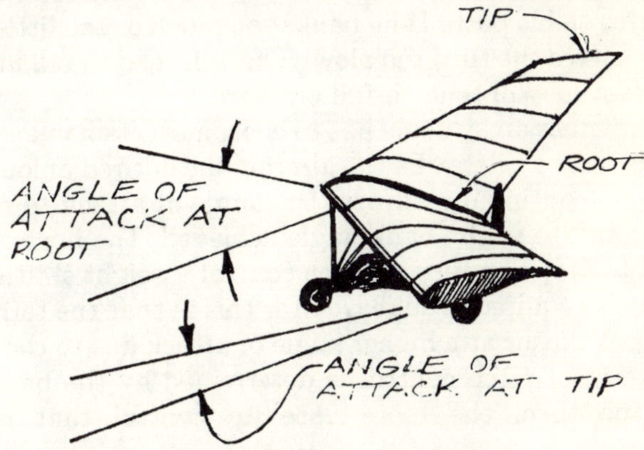

Figure 27 · Washout

Another factor in pitch stability is the angle of the horizontal tail or stabilizer with respect to the rest of the aircraft. This is called the incidence angle. A net downward force should occur at the tail as shown in figure 28. If the front of the stabilizer is set too high reducing the

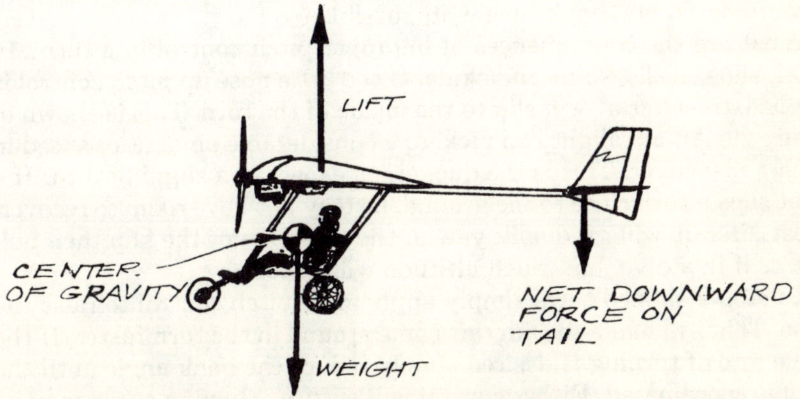

Figure 28 · Pitch Stability

downward force, the craft will not recover from a dive and the craft is unstable. An ultralight pilot should not alter the incidence of his aircraft's tail surface outside of the manufacturers specifications.

The pilot cannot do much about the stability of his aircraft other than obey the manufacturer's recommendations on engine and center of gravity (of the pilot) placement. Remember, a center of gravity placed too far aft results in pitch instability. A wise pilot will choose an ultralight that has a reputation for good pitch stability.

TURNING FLIGHT

We have already mentioned coordinated turns. What do we mean by these terms? Imagine a bicyclist riding around an oval track. When he comes to the sharp curves at the ends of the oval he banks (leans) and easily progresses around the turn. He must maintain the speed and bank that relates to his path. If he banks too much or too little, he will fall over. If he enters the turn too slowly, he will tend to fall inward. If he enters too fast he will tend to fall outward.

In the same manner an airplane has to coordinate its bank and speed in a turn. To do this, a pilot rolls the aircraft the desired amount while at the same time continually adjusts the angle of attack to maintain the speed appropriate to the bank angle achieved. The nose of an aircraft will want to drop in a turn so pitch control — weight shifting back, or up elevator — is required. The reason for this is that the tail or trailing surfaces meet the air at a higher angle of attack due to the curving path. The amount of pitch control is determined by the bank angle. The steeper the turn, the more nose up control that must be administered.

In a coordinated turn, the loading on the aircraft increases due to centrifugal force. This is called G loading and is given in the chart below for all angles of bank. As indicated, in a 45° bank the aircraft and pilot experience 1.4 Gs. The chart shows 2 Gs in a 60° bank. The G loading goes to infinity at a 90° bank angle. This reflects the fact that a coordinated 90° bank turn is impossible.

What are the consequences of improper pitch control in a turn? In brief, slips, stalls, spins and skids. If too little nose up pitch control is applied, the aircraft will slip to the inside of the turn. This is shown in figure 29. An ultralight can pick up a considerable amount of speed in such a maneuver. This is the dangerous aspect of a slipping turn. If a pilot slips a turn close to the ground, he may not have room to recover. Most aircraft will gradually yaw in the direction of the slip then pull out as if in a dive, but much altitude will be lost.

To stop a slipped turn, simply apply more pitch control to raise the nose. This will make the aircraft come around in the turn faster. If the same rate of turning is desired simply reduce the bank angle until the turn is coordinated. Either control will suffice. Slipping turns may be practiced at sufficient height (several hundred feet) as a means of losing altitude quickly. However, get a feel for them gradually and don't use them too close to the ground since speed can build up rapidly.

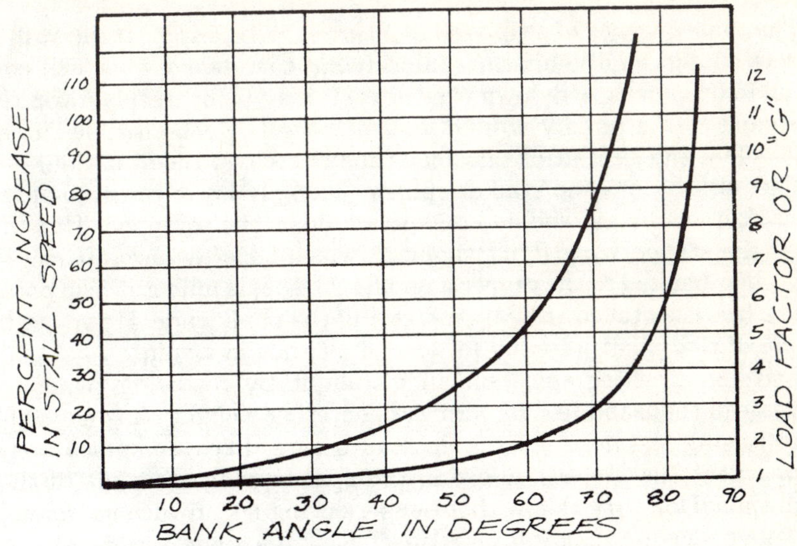

Increase in Stall Speed and Load Factor

If too much nose-up control is used in a turn, the result is a stall. However, the stall does not occur in the entire wing as in straight ahead flight. Only the inside wing tip area stalls. The reason for this is the inside wing is traveling at a much slower speed than the outside wing and thus, has a greater angle of attack. In a turn, a wing stalls at a higher airspeed due to the increased wing loading. The increased stall speeds are shown in the G loading chart.

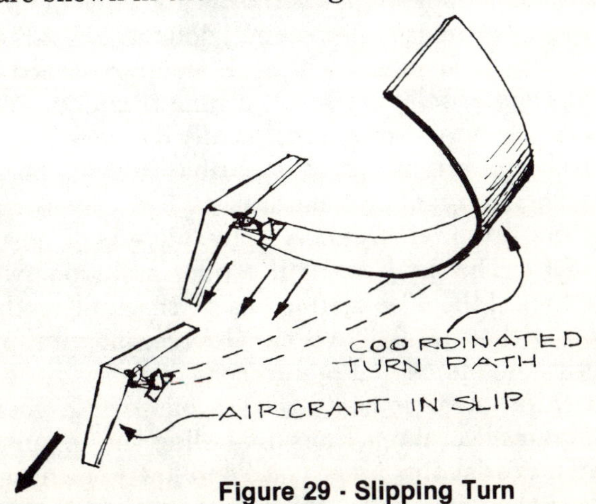

Figure 29 · Slipping Turn

When the inside wing stalls in a turn it wants to retard due to the increased drag, and drop due to the reduced lift. You can often detect when you are near a stall in a turn as the inside wing feels "sticky" or reluctant to fly smoothly. This is a sign to back off on the pitch control.

The consequences of a tip stall in a turn may be a spin. If the stall is severe enough or the aircraft unforgiving, the stalled wing will continue to drop back and down. The aircraft may bank steeply, drop the nose and rotate rapidly around, out of control. Much altitude can be lost before the aircraft or pilot has time to recover the situation.

The remedy for a tip stall or spin is to simply lower the nose of the aircraft immediately and add opposite rudder if so equipped. This will start the stalled wing flying again at which time the aircraft can be leveled or banked to the proper angle. If the spin is mild it is also possible to free the stalled wing by increasing the bank angle. However, be aware of the great potential for loss of altitude in a spin.

You can practice spins on an ultralight by reserving plenty of altitude (a thousand feet for starters), entering a slight bank (say 30°) then raising the nose until a tip stall occurs. Recover immediately, then repeat the process, allowing the spin to progress a bit further each time. Don't try this without experiencing a spin with an instructor in a conventional airplane. Also, consult the manufacturer of your aircraft before trying such advanced maneuvers. Some ultralights are characteristically unspinable. In addition, some designs may suffer damage to the control surfaces in hard slips and spins.

At this point we should mention a hint that is a great aid in coordinating turns on an ultralight. Once you have banked in a turn, watch your airspeed. If it gradually slows, you have added too much nose up control for the amount of bank you have established. If your airspeed gradually increases, you haven't added enough nose up control. Practice turns of varying bank angles with this guideline in mind, and they will soon become automatic. Remember, don't let the airspeed increase or diminish too much or you will be in a slip or stalled mode.

Two other actions can be related to bad turning technique. The first is skids or sliding to the outside of a turn, usually due to too much yaw control. Most ultralights are not too susceptible to skids because of their ample dihedral, so no real problem here.

The other problem is spiral dives. A spiral dive is a nose down continuous 360° turn. This may occur if a pilot stalls one wing tip severely and tries to pull the nose up (increasing the stall) as the wing drops. The problem with a spiral dive is the G forces mount rapidly on the aircraft structure due to centrifugal force.

If you are in a spiral dive, your airspeed is increasing, your body feels massive and your natural reactions are telling you to pull up out of the dive. You must resist this inner voice and lower the nose at the same time you level the wings. You will then end up in a steep dive which will level out quickly with a little nose up control. As you begin to pull out of the dive, add a nose down control to avoid stalling abruptly as you rise rapidly. Level out and think about what you did so you can avoid it next time. Spiral dives can end up in a severe crash or a broken wing in the air due to the high loading. Avoid such maneuvers by avoiding severe stalls and slips.

TIP VORTICIES

We mentioned earlier that the losses that we call drag end up producing turbulence in the air as the wing passes. The quantity we call induced drag is lost in the production of tip vorticies. These are steady swirls that trail out behind the wings of all aircraft. The higher the angle of attack the aircraft flies at, the stronger these vorticies are. Figure 30 shows the typical orientation and movement of tip vorticies after an aircraft passes.

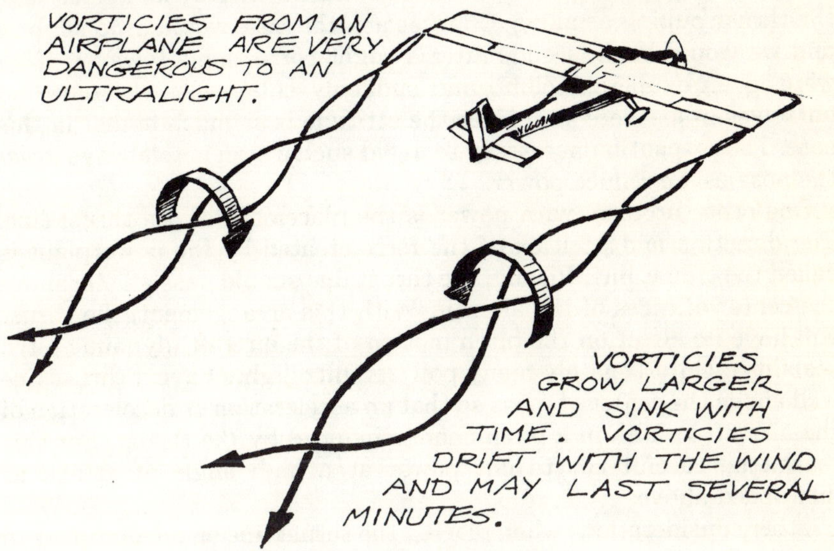

Figure 30 - Wing Tip Vorticies

Tip vorticies are of interest to powered ultralight pilots for two reasons. First, when our aircraft approach the ground, part of the vortex is blocked so that the wing actually performs better. This phenomenon is enhanced as we get closer and closer to the ground. The wing can pick up quite a bit of performance a few feet above the terrain.

Pilots refer to this action as "ground effect." As a result of ground effect, an aircraft will seem to float along the runway quite a bit beyond where one would expect it to touch down. It appears as if it were floating on a cushion of air. For this reason, a pilot must leave himself plenty of runout room when landing, especially if the runway is sloped.

The second reason to understand the behavior of vorticies is that they represent severe turbulence. If you fly through the vorticies of another ultralight, you may only notice a few sharp bumps. However, the vorticies of larger aircraft are dangerous and must be avoided at all times. This is covered in greater detail in Chapter V under Air Traffic Rules. A pilot will do well to pay heed to this warning since tip vorticies tend to be very organized forms of swirling air and thus, very powerful.

POWER CONSIDERATIONS

The use of power results in some complications, in all aircraft. The first consideration is stalls. Under power, the attitude of the aircraft is higher for the same angle of attack when unpowered. As explained earlier, this is because the thrust raises the angle of the flight path (see figures 18 and 20). Now, if we are flying near stall under power, and suddenly stop the engine, we would be stalled since we no longer have the thrust pulling us along. Chances are, the nose would drop slightly and we would begin a glide after a slight correction. However, if we were in an exuberant climb and suddenly cut power, we may find ourselves in a severe stall since the attitude is so much higher in this case. The precaution necessary to avoid such a stall is to always lower the nose as we reduce power.

One other problem with power is the placement of the thrust line. The direction and position of the force created by the powerplant is called the thrust line. Ideally, the thrust line should pass a little above the center of mass of the aircraft. With this arrangement, the thrust will have no effect on the pitch motion of the aircraft (dynamic pitch stability). Unfortunately many powered ultralights have a thrust line well above the center of mass so that an acceleration or deceleration of the aircraft results in a pitch change induced by the thrust. For this reason be careful not to cut power at a high angle of attack as mentioned above.

Other considerations when placing the thrust line on an aircraft is to have it pass through the center of drag and angle it properly. If the thrust line is not through the center of drag, it will require a slight change in pitch control everytime the throttle is changed. This is a very common phenomenon with ultralights. It can be noted by flying close to the ground at cruise power then adding full power. Usually the ultralight will drop several feet before it begins climbing. Be aware of this factor for it can cause an unwanted contact with the ground at high speed to the dismay of the pilot and delight of the spectators as you bounce off the ground.

In addition to the above, a thrust line angled so as to point directly into the onrushing air at best glide angle of attack will result in the best performance. Of course, we can't do much to alter the manufacturer's design, but a pilot should be aware of the problems involved with thrust line placement so he can detect improper engine placement or at least knows enough not to tinker with the approved set up.

There are several other factors that occur when we power an aircraft. We are referring to torque, P-factor and gyroscopic effects.

The torque effect is simply the tendency for the aircraft to roll in the direction opposite the propeller. For example, if the propeller rotates clockwise, the aircraft would tend to roll to the left since the propeller pushes against the air. See figure 31. The pilot may experience this effect as a sluggishness of the aircraft when turning right, but a snappy response to the left.

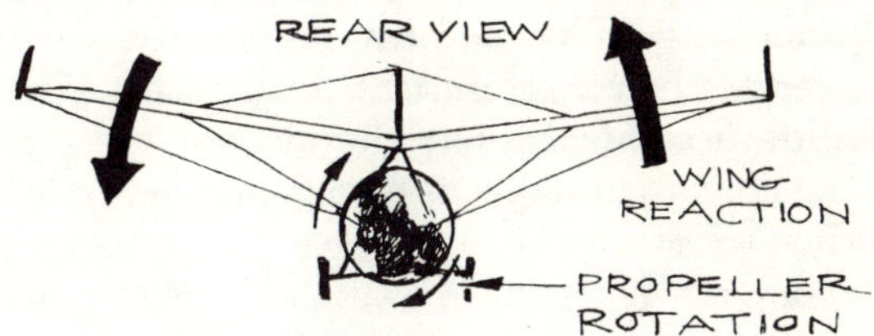

Figure 31 · Torque Effect

P-factor occurs in conjunction with pitch controls. As shown in figure 32, when an aircraft changes angle of attack, the flight path changes with respect to the thrust line. Thus, in 32(a) the two blades of the propeller are meeting the air at an equal angle since the flight path and thrust line are coincidental. However, in 32(b), the flight path (and thus relative wind) intercepts the two blades at very different angles. This means more force is exerted on one side of the propeller, since like a wing it is sensitive to angle of attack. Again, for a clockwise rotating prop, the aircraft will tend to yaw to the left as we increase the angle of attack. The opposite yaw occurs as we decrease angle of attack.

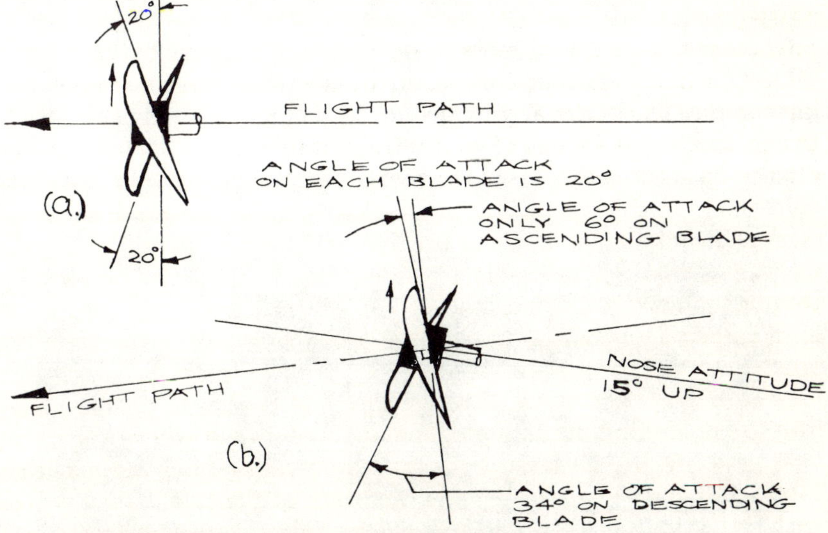

Figure 32 · P-Factor

The final oddity, gyroscopic effect, is the most perplexing. Just like the toy gyroscopes, a propeller wants to do strange things. When a force is applied to rotate it in one direction, it rotates around an axis 90° from the intended axis. Thus, when an aircraft with a clock-wise moving propeller drops its nose, the propeller tends to yaw the aircraft to the right. When the nose is raised, the yaw force is left.

In summary, we see the torque of the engine rolling the aircraft left while a sudden pitch increase causes a left yaw force both from P-factor and the gyroscopic effect. These combined forces can be quite surprising if an uninitiated pilot performs sudden control movements. A stall under power can be very upsetting due to these effects. Not only does the nose drop suddenly, but the aircraft yaws to the right sharply due to the change in angle of attack and attitude. The worse case is discovering these phenomenon near the ground. Keep your turns and pitch controls gentle until you have enough airtime to get high and feel any imbalance in controls. Chances are, your powered ultralight won't exhibit strong characteristics of this sort, but be aware that some do. Generally, the low amount of horsepower and thrust with respect to wing area on an ultralight makes these turning factors barely noticeable.

If you are going to change the weight of your ultralight by adding equipment (floats, fairings, traveling gear, etc.), it may be useful to consider what changes to expect. First, the extra weight will increase your flying speed about 0.5 mph and decrease your climb rate about 5 feet per minute for every 10 lbs of added weight. This isn't bad, but you must consider the extra drag as well (except for fairings which generally reduce drag). All these factors must be considered when looking for fuel efficiency for cross-country or competition.

Of course, there is a lot more to learn about the theory of flight. Most pilots continue to pick up this information as they progress in their flying careers. The material provided in this book is what is necessary to understand the workings of your ultralight in order to fly safely. Coordinate those turns and avoid the five S's: slips, spins, stalls, skids and spirals.

The Soarmaster Powered Fledgling

CHAPTER V

AIRMANSHIP

Airmanship is the art of flying with unerring skill in a variety of conditions and situations. Like any art, flying requires patience and practice along with study and experience. In the preceding chapters we covered the material necessary to understand our aircraft's response to the changing air. Here, we will apply this understanding to advanced flying as well as explore the many situations that arise in everyday flight.

An ultralight aircraft shares many flight characteristics with conventional airplanes. Both types require a good bit of responsibility on the part of the pilot in dealing with air traffic operations. However, there are some differences. For example, ultralight pilots don't need to learn radio communications and in-depth navigation, while pilots of large aircraft aren't worried about small-scale weather effects.

The following material will cover flight from the viewpoint of an ultralight pilot, but experience gained in conventional aircraft will certainly prove useful. The knowledge and practice of safe flying comes through study and careful attention to detail over a period of many years. Start the learning process now and continue improving your skills throughout your flying career. May it be long and rewarding.

SET UP

Unless you store your ultralight in a hangar, every day of flying starts with setting up and pre-flighting. When you first learn to set your ultralight up, it may seem confusing and complicated, but follow the directions in the owner's manual step by step and soon the procedure will become routine. Some items to watch for are listed below.

If you have the type of aircraft that folds open, be sure the frame is not twisted so that excess stress is not placed on the attachment junctures. A long tube can easily apply enough force to bend bolts and fasteners. When tightening bolts, be sure to use lock nuts or safety pins to prevent their loosening due to vibration. One of the most common mishaps during set up is dropping safety pins, washers or nuts. This is not dangerous, but sure can ruin your day if you don't have any spares handy. To avoid such a fate, try putting the small parts in your mouth. It won't do much for your taste buds, but certainly will help prevent the use of strong language.

Again, when tightening bolts, be careful not to pinch the sail between tangs or tubes. This will spoil the airfoil shape of the wing. Other things to look for are thimbles twisted in the tangs and twisted cables in general. When you tighten a turnbuckle, be sure to hold the free end and turn the barrel (center part) so that both ends screw in equally and the cable does not twist. If a turnbuckle is hard to tighten, use a nail through the hole in the barrel, apply silicon to the threads or tighten one side of the turnbuckle at a time, being careful not to leave the cable twisted permanently.

The albatross, one of the most magnificent seabirds, is admired for its unsurpassed soaring ability. However, it is awkward and clumsy on land, a trait that has earned it the nickname gooney bird. Many ultralights share the albatross' Cinderella syndrome, especially when partially set up. When an ultralight is being assembled, pins and cables are not holding the structure solid so it is very apt to be damaged if a gust blows it around. For this reason, select a well sheltered set up site, or enlist the help of a friend or two to hold the wings. *DON'T* let anyone set your aircraft up for you—they don't have as much incentive to perform as careful a job as you do, since your life, and not theirs, is at stake.

PREFLIGHT AND ROUTINE INSPECTION

Before every day's flying begins, a thorough preflight must take place. A preflight is a careful inspection of each component of an aircraft. Obviously, a pilot of a conventional aircraft cannot crawl around the fuselage looking at every nut, bolt and bellcrank, but a pilot of an ultralight can cover every part of his ship. It is important that the ultralight pilot do this since daily set up and breakdown allows human errors as well as wear to occur. In addition, ultralights generally experience more vibration than conventional aircraft.

To do a faithful and consistant preflight, you must establish a routine. This means starting at a given point and completing a circuit in the same order and sequence every time you preflight. A good place to start is at the nose of the aircraft. Check all bolts and nuts. No wear should be evident, bolts should be straight, safety pins or lock nuts should be used. At least 1½ threads of the bolt should show past the lock nut in order for it to hold properly. Lock nuts should not be removed and reused, since the nylon gripper wears out.

Carefully inspect all tubes for bends, dents, corrosion, and loose bushings or elongated holes. Rub a rag along every cable to check for broken strands, especially near Nico fittings. Make sure thimbles are not twisted or bent. Ball Lock pins must be operated to assure that the balls move freely in place. Check the wing covering or sail for rips and holes. Next, sight along both wings for symmetry and proper balance.

Preflight the control lines and surfaces as well as the engine controls. Work all controls to check their operation. Preflight the engine system looking for loose parts, carburetor leakage or oil on the engine indicating a leak that would lead to engine seizure. Carefully check the prop for cracks or nicks as well as bolt tightness. Finally, preflight your parachute system. Is the velcro secure and the bridle hooked up?

If any part or component appears to be damaged, have a competent repairman fix it or replace it. Remember, your good health depends on the good health of your aircraft. Don't let *anything* go. Nothing can be more disconcerting than to hear a sudden ping! twang! crack! when you're 2000 ft. up.

Besides the preflight that occurs with each step, a periodic safety inspection must be performed. A safety inspection consists of the same rountine as the preflight, but on a more thorough basis. All junctures should be disassembled to allow close inspection of every component. If possible, remove each tube (one at a time to prevent confusion) and check its integrity.

Perform the complete safety inspection at least once every 10 hours of powered flight until you know what parts receive the most wear. Then you can give the trouble spots constant attention and increase the time between complete safety inspections. Needless to say, a safety inspection must be performed after every crash, no matter how minor. The engine should receive a safety inspection as well as a preflight along with the rest of the glider. The schedule for overhaul and maintenance is given in Chapter VI.

The Tomcat

CARE AND CLEANING

Obviously, the better you care for your flying machine, the less chance there will be of damage occurring to the various components. Most wear and tear occurs during set up, storage and transportation. Keep your ultralight sheltered from the elements in a shed or garage (preferably locked). At the very least, cover it with plastic to ward off moisture and an opaque sun-shade to keep harmful ultraviolet radiation from damaging the Dacron covering. Dacron left in the sun will lose strength in a matter of months and eventually deteriorate to a dangerous level. It is especially important to keep the engine dry. Stuff a rag into the intake and exhaust ports to block moisture and dust.

For long periods of storage, drain the fuel from the feeder line and the carburetor. Wipe the engine clean, paying special attention to the exhaust port. Place a little oil in the cylinder(s) to prevent rust. Again, cover all ports with rags. In the case of long-term storage, it is best to remove the propeller from the drive shaft. Humans have a strange fascination for rotating props. Some engines can be harmed if the propeller is spun in the wrong direction. For this reason, tie the prop to the engine, or hang warning signs on it to ward off curious bystanders between flights or during storage. Always position your propeller sideways when storing the ultralight so that the sap or moisture in the (wooden) prop doesn't run to one end and unbalance it.

Avoid bumps and rough handling during transportation. Use padding when strapping your glider to a car or trailer. If your ultralight folds into a long, thin bundle (as with flex wing), be sure to support it at both ends when carrying it on a car roof. Otherwise, bouncing during a drive will cause excessive bending and stress in the tubes. Needless to say, use strong ropes tied securely during transport. The force of the air on your aircraft is considerable when driving at maximum legal speed.

Despite any amount of meticulous care, an aircraft will eventually get dirty. Birds preen their wings, we must clean ours. Oil on Dacron wing covering (common on powered ultralights) can be removed with mineral spirits. Tar and other sticky substances can also be treated in this manner. Wash the mineral spirits, as well as dirt and grime in general out with a non-alkaline detergent and soft brush. The reason we specify non-alkaline, is that alkaline material in the presence of sunlight deteriorates Dacron. Rinse the soap out thoroughly (several times) and leave the aircraft open in a ventilated shady area to dry. Never store your wing folded for any length of time when it is wet.

A special silicon spray is available from most boating supplies for use on undoped Dacron. Get the type of fabric spray with a sun screen. Apply this to your wings to repel moisture, dirt and chemicals. Silicon is also ideal for wiping on aluminum tubes to prevent corrosion. Clean your engine regularly to assure proper cooling. Motorcycle shops can supply a cleaner ideal for small engines. As a final note, keep the leading edges of both your wings and propeller free of bugs and other

debris. Foreign matter at these critical points will decrease performance dramatically. Varnish and wax your propeller on a regular basis
to help keep it unfouled. Balance it and true its path as described in
Chapter VI. Again, the key to continuous safe operation and
performance is keeping a clean machine.

GROUND HANDLING

Ground handling refers to carrying, pushing, pulling, positioning,
maneuvering and taxiing an ultralight on the ground. When a wind is
blowing, ground handling requires the strength of Hercules or finesse.
Since this is not a weight lifting course, we will concentrate on finesse.

If your ultralight has wheels, you will need a helper to hold the
upwind wing when moving the ship across the wind. If you are moving
into the wind (upwind), pull the aircraft by its nose. If you are moving
downwind, pull it by the tail (keeping the nose pointing into the wind),
but be sure to hold the tail high enough so that the air pushes down on
the top of the wing, thus preventing a gust from blowing the aircraft
around like a newspaper tumbling down the street.

Groundhandling the Weedhopper

It's also nice to have a helper when taking off. The helper can steady
the wing or hold the nose of the ultralight while the pilot completes the
preflight check of the engine system. When every item is checked out,
the helper should assist the pilot in positioning the craft or looking for
traffic. When the pilot is ready, he should give the helper a visual
signal (vocal commands will be drowned out or garbled by the insis-
tant engine), allow him time to jump out of the way, then begin the
takeoff.

An important part of ground handling is tethering or picketing the

Picketing An Ultralight

aircraft when it is to be left unattended. Many a pilot has returned to find a broken craft after leaving it unguarded for a period of time. To avoid this, place your aircraft in a sheltered area if possible (behind trees, buildings, etc.) and tie it down. Keep the nose pointing into the wind and attach a hold down rope to the nose, tail and each wing. The ropes should be tied to a well-braced juncture on the aircraft then out to a stake or similar secure ground object. Large aircraft should be tied to cement or block anchors, but ultralights can usually get by with stakes. Spiral steel pet anchors make wonderful tie downs for your "pet" ultralight. It is a good idea to place chocks or wedges against the wheels to prevent rolling. A final precaution is to tie down all moveable control surfaces to prevent the wind from flopping them around. Secure the surfaces themselves to the wing, don't try to hold them still by fastening the control lines. Excess stretch can occur in the lines if you make this mistake. One trick sailplane pilots use is to tie a length of wood (a 2x4 works fine) on top of the wing at the high camber point. This strip acts like a spoiler to destroy lift and help prevent the wings from rising in gusts. The thing is, it's hard for an ultralight to suffer much abuse in the air. Ground handling is the place to work carefully to extend the lifetime of your ship.

ULTRALIGHT TRIMMING

The word "trim" refers to a proper balance of weight and aerodynamic forces on an aircraft in flight. For example, an ultralight that is in trim will fly at a steady cruise speed when the pilot lets go of the controls (hands off) and the engine is set about ¾ throttle. Trim speed is the flying speed attained in this hands off condition.

There are three ways to effect a change of trim speed in a given aircraft. The first method consists of changing the wing configuration. The designer controls the twist and dihedral in the main wing by setting the length of the flying (lower) wires. A pilot must be sure to never alter these lengths at the risk of producing dangerous instability. In many ultralights put together from a kit, the incidence or angle of the horizontal tail can be altered by adding or removing washers at the attachment bolts. Raising the front of the tail produces nose down trim while lowering the front of the tail produces nose up trim. Too much nose down trim (front of tail lifted too high) can cause dangerous instability. Be sure to consult the manufacturer (or owner's manual) to find the limits for this adjustment.

Flex wing ultralights can be trimmed by shifting the sail. These craft can be trimmed for turns as well as speed in the above manner. There are many subtle effects involved with trimming a flex wing, so contact a dealer of such craft to get a proper trim job.

The second method of trimming an ultralight for speed is weight shift. As a pilot of a weight shift controlled ultralight is well aware, moving weight forward speeds the aircraft while moving weight back slows it. Since ultralights aren't designed to carry much baggage, there is not much consideration given to the location of added weight beyond the engine and fuel. However, it should be noted that moving weight too far backward results in instability. As the center of gravity of an aircraft is moved back, a point is reached beyond which the aircraft becomes impossible to control. For this reason, the addition of cameras, excess fuel or traveling gear to the rear of the ultralight must be carefully counterbalanced with equal weight at the front.

Larger ultralights are not controlled by weight shift. Therefore, the designer must place the pilot's seat exactly right to achieve the proper trim speed. For this reason, do not make modifications in the seating arrangement or configuration of your ultralight without the manufacturer's approval.

The third method of trimming is to alter the position or angle of the engine's thrust line. This too can have dangerous consequences. Much thought and design work goes into the stability control of an ultralight. If you have a trim problem consult the manufacturer or you may make a trim correction at the expense of stability.

WEATHER CONDITIONS

A sensible pilot of any aircraft makes a thorough check of the current and expected weather conditions before deciding to fly. The material in Chapter III will help your judgement. In addition, a call to the local weather station and Flight Service will fill you in on the situation at any altitude and distance from your ground position.

Flight Service is available at many airports. This service consists of weather information for airmen, including ultralight pilots. When calling Flight Service, ask for the wind direction, velocity and temperature at various altitudes (for example, ground zero, three thousand and six thousand feet). Also, it's a good idea to inquire about thunderstorms or any other unusual activity in the vicinity.

Be on the lookout for winds in the general direction of your launch (obviously, it's an asset to have operating strips covering all directions) with speeds under 10 mph (16 kph). Also be aware of how fast the winds increase as altitude is gained. One of the dangers somewhat unique to powered ultralights is the ability to fly into shear turbulence strong enough to jeopardize control. Large aircraft are not affected by small-scale shear turbulence, and hang gliders usually don't have the means to reach shear layers. A strong increase in wind within a short change of altitude is indicative of possible shear. Likewise, shear turbulence is present when the wind changes directions radically within a small vertical distance.

Shear layers, in the absence of clouds, cannot be seen. Airplane pilots often report the presence of shear layers, but remember that they fly much larger craft and may not notice some turbulence significant to ultralights. The safest policy is to limit your flying to days when the upper winds are less than 15 mph (24 kph).

Do not fly when thunderstorms are reported in the area. Thunderstorms and squalls can develop rapidly in hot, humid weather. Flying an ultralight in a thunderstorm is like paddling a canoe over the Niagra Falls. If you come out unscathed from such an encounter, you simply have an over-achieving guardian angel.

The air is always changing. Keep a constant vigil on the subtle signs that serve to inform you of these changes as the day progresses. Watch for soaring birds, dust devils, drifting smoke and seeds, waving flags and trees, clouds and smog to continuously monitor the air structure and wind velocity. Remember, an ultralight has no business flying in strong thermal turbulence. Respect the power and fickleness of Mother Nature and she will reward you with plenty of benign, mellow air.

ULTRALIGHT INSTRUMENTS

We have already discussed instruments in Chapter I. Here we will look into the operation and use of altimeters, variometers and airspeed indicators.

By now, we are aware that air pressure reduces as altitude is gained. We can take advantage of this natural phenomenon to get a measurement of altitude. An altimeter operates in exactly this manner. When the air pressure changes, a sealed container (aneroid) expands or contracts to equalize the pressure within (see figure 33). A mechanical linkage (levers, gears or a chain as shown in the figure) moves a dial to give an accurate indication of how much pressure and thus altitude change has occurred.

Since the air pressure varies at any given location, some means for setting the dial to the desired starting point must be incorporated in the design. This usually consists of simply turning the face of the dial until the needle points to the desired value. More expensive altimeters have an adjustment to turn the needle itself to the correct setting.

You should always set your altimeter to the altitude above sea level of your take off point when flying powered ultralights. The reason for this is that you must obey certain traffic regulations that require flying specific altitudes. Other airplanes in the vicinity will be following these rules and flying according to their altimeter settings above sea level. When all aircraft set their altimeters to read height above sea level, everyone is assured of having syncronized instruments. Find the height of your takeoff field from a topographic map (if you fly from an airport, ask the manager), then adjust your altimeter to this height. In this manner, you will compensate for changes in barometric pressure.

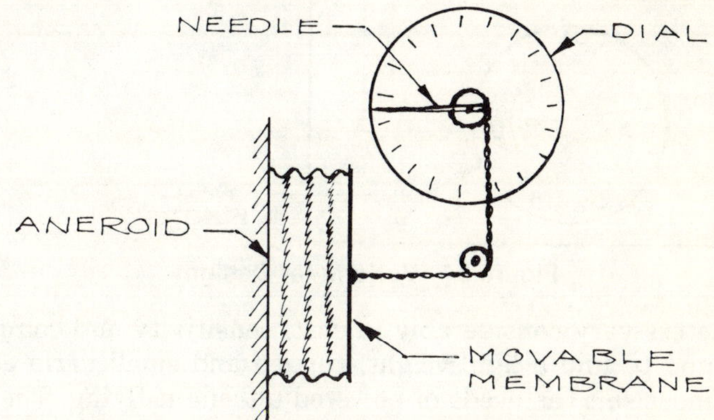

Figure 33 - Altimeter Design

The next instrument in our line-up is a variometer or rate of climb indicator. All variometers work on essentially the same principle: measuring the rate of change of the pressure as vertical movement takes place. Since air pressure changes on a fairly regular basis with height, measuring how fast this change occurs will provide an accurate indication of how fast we are moving up or down.

A typical variometer for ultralight applications consists of a flask with a tiny hole at one end. As the flask is lifted, the outside pressure becomes lower than the pressure in the flask. Consequently, air flows out of the hole at a rate according to how fast the outside pressure is being reduced. If the flask is lowered, the air flows into the hole, again at a rate proportional to the rate of descent.

A sensor consisting of thermistors (heat sensitive resistors) is placed in front of the hole to measure how fast and in which direction the flow moves. The entire train of events that occurs when the instrument is raised is as follows: the lowered outside pressure causes an outward flow of air from the flask which is detected by the sensing circuit which in turn puts out a signal used to excite a dial indicating the rate of climb. This process is shown schematically in figure 34.

Another common variometer mechanism employs a set-up similar to the altimeter in figure 33, except that the aneroid has a small hole (capillary) which allows a small amount of airflow. If the outside pressure is changing continuously (as when the instrument is rising), the pressure inside the aneroid will never quite equal the outside pressure. Thus, a value will be indicated on the dial. However, when the vertical movement stops, the pressure inside the aneroid will quickly equal the outside pressure, so that dial returns to zero.

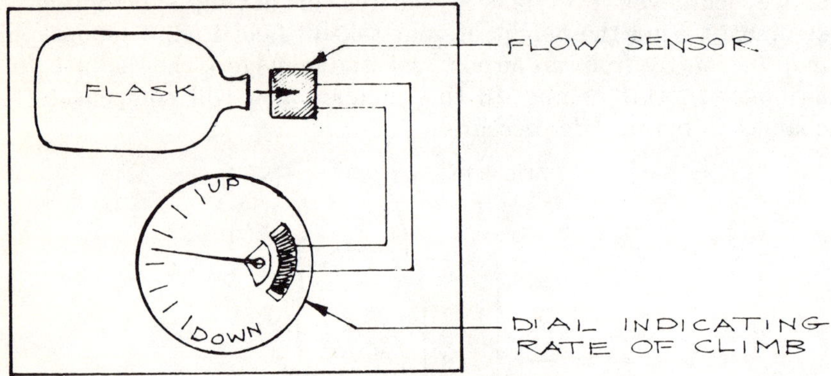

Figure 34 - Variometer Design

Variometers vary considerably in cost, sensitivity and complexity. Shop around to find a lightweight, rugged and small vario as these qualities most suit the needs of powered ultralight flying. The size of your bankroll will probably ultimately determine which instrument you buy, since there are so many different types available. Note that a vario with an audio tone will be useless when you are under power, but will free your eyes from the dial when soaring with the engine shut down.

The last instrument to consider is an airspeed indicator. Since the sense of sound is blocked out by engine noise, powered ultralight pilots should use an airspeed indicator to help keep the proper speed.

There are four basic types of airspeed indicators. The first consists of an impeller or propeller that spins in the airflow. A dial reads out the rate of spin and thus the airspeed. The second type employs a small vane that is pushed back by the drag of the air, giving a higher reading as faster airflow pushes harder on the vane. The third type measures the reduction of pressure caused by the air flowing through a restricted passage called a venturi. The fourth airspeed indicator mechanism consists of a pith or foam ball that rises up a tube as the air blows into an opening in the bottom of the shaft. The shaft is tapered so that the ball only rises so high according to how fast the air is moving by the instrument.

Airspeed indicators are as varied in price and style as variometers. There is a wide range of accuracy and sensitivity inherent in the different designs. One thing to note is that stall speed changes as wing loading changes. Adding more weight to your craft does not increase the stall speed appreciably, but the increased loading in turns and pull-outs does. For example, in a 60° banked coordinated turn, you will feel 2 G's (twice as heavy). The aircraft feels this also, so if it originally stalled at 20 mph, the new stall speed would be over 28 mph.

Now, it would be impossible to learn the stall speed at every angle of bank, but there is one handy solution. If you use an airspeed indicator that employs the floating pith ball, your stall speed will always read the same, since the ball too is pulled down by the G forces. In the example above, with a 60° bank, the pith ball indicator will read 20 mph when the craft is flying 29 mph so that stall speed is automatically given no matter what the bank angle. Of course, the indicator does not give the true airspeed in curvilinear flight, but so what?

Altimeter And Airspeed Indicator

It's a good idea to mark the important speeds on your airspeed indicator (stall speed, minimum sink speed, best climb speed, etc.). However, your flying should not be so mechanical that you must constantly watch your instrument. Your body in the airstream has a built in system of sensors that allow you to judge airspeed fairly accurately, with a bit of practice. Note that as your altitude increases you fly faster due to the thinner air (about 2% increase per 1000 feet). However, your airspeed indicators (and body) will sense no difference since the same amount of drag or pressure forces will result due to the thinner air but increased speed.

To avoid confusion, mount all your instruments together at a point on the aircraft that is in your field of vision when looking straight ahead. Some convenient mounting brackets and cases are available for ultralights that fold up out of the way and protect the instruments during ground handling and transportation. Take care of these modern devices and they will serve as an extra set of eyes and ears throughout your flying career.

COCKPIT CHECK

Although most ultralights don't have a traditional style cockpit, the pilot still should perform a routine check of the items that surround him in flight. The cockpit check is not included with the preflight check because it exists as a separate procedure just before takeoff.

The list of items on a cockpit check will vary with the equipment used. Here are some of the important matters. Check the harness or seat belt adjustment and make sure no free ends are loose enough to be sucked into the propeller (a guard in front of the prop is a necessity in some applications). Move the controls to see that they operate freely with no slack. Turn your vario on, zero it and set the altimeter to the takeoff field altitude.

Now, yell "clear prop", check to make sure everyone is clear, then start the engine, rev it up and down to check the throttle and set the proper mixture. Try the kill switch at least twice to make sure it is working flawlessly. Finally, clear all obstacles, spectators and heavy thoughts, check the wind and take to the sky. Be aware of your prop danger zones (see Chapter VI) and avoid putting spectators in jeopardy by having them stand well clear behind and beside the ultralight.

A Typical Ultralight Cockpit — Spare

TAKEOFF PROCEDURES

The takeoff is one of the most critical parts of any flight. The reason for this is that the aircraft is flying at a fairly high angle of attack and ground clearance is minimal. An engine failure or gust induced stall could have severe consequences.

The first matter to consider is the field of operation. Is it long enough to allow a straight ahead landing if engine failure occurs? You should be able to fly straight until you have enough altitude to turn back and land safely in the case of an engine out. For this reason, the narrower a field is, the longer it should be for safe operation.

The size of a field will vary according to the aircraft used. Those with less climb performance will, of course, need more room. Obstructions that can produce turbulence in a wind effectively reduce the size of a field since you must give them wide berth in order to avoid the rock and roll air.

The quality of the field surface must be given some consideration as well. Ruts, tall grass or soft areas can greatly hamper your take off roll. Different types of landing gear will handle these adverse conditions in varying degrees of success (larger wheels for weeds and ruts, wider wheels for soft ground).

Preparing To Take Off

Also, taildragger designs tend to be better for adverse terrain conditions. The rough or soft field takeoff procedures are as follows: Set the pitch control for the rotation angle of attack (slightly nose up from normal), apply full power and lift off as soon as possible. When the wheels break free of the ground, lower the nose immediately to pick up flying speed in ground effect. Once climb-out speed is achieved, add nose up control and power merrily up and out.

Short field operation is the opposite in the respect that you should keep the angle of attack low to stay on the ground and gain as much speed as possible while producing minimum drag, then pop into the air and climb rapidly. However, we only include this information for the sake of completeness and do not condone *any* short field operations at all. There is no reason to risk your life and depend on the dubious integrity of your engine, skill and luck to pull off a narrow escape from the confines of a too small field. There have been a number of pilots that have ended up in power lines or trees through such a misjudgement.

Normal takeoff procedures consist of aiming into the wind, applying full throttle until taxi speed builds up to about 5 mph above stall. At this point a nose up control is applied and the ultralight rotates into the air. Once airborne, the pilot generally noses down a little to maintain proper airspeed.

There are two climbing speeds of which every pilot should be aware. The first is the speed for best climb. This speed allows you to get the highest in as short a time as possible. The speed for best climb occurs at the aircraft's "best glide speed" or the speed where the lift to drag ratio (L/D) is highest. The second speed is the speed for best angle of climb. At this speed, the aircraft climbs the steepest path possible although it doesn't climb as fast as in the former case. The speed for best angle of climb occurs at the aircraft's "minimum sink speed." The min. sink speed is always below the "best glide speed."

Figure 21 in Chapter IV shows the relationship of the above two speeds. You can find these speeds through experiment (fly the aircraft with the engine off and note where minimum sink and best glide speeds occur) or from the owner's manual. Be aware that the speed for best angle of climb may occur near stall so it should be avoided near the ground. Also, this slower speed may overwork the engine and reduce the cooling due to lower air flow. Consequently, you should always climb with the best rate of climb airspeed.

Occasionally, you may go out to fly and find the wind unpleasantly crossing your runway. Ultralights handle crosswind takeoffs (and landings) with various degrees of success. In general, it is best to cross the runway and head into the wind if possible. Allow plenty of clearance for ground roll and climbing over obstacles.

Once you have much experience flying your craft, you may try a crosswind takeoff by using control inputs. This is very difficult without three-axis controls. Some experts on two-axis ships allow the upwind wing to lift while balancing the roll force with the yaw input of the rudder and running on only the downwind wheel of the main gear. This takes very precise control and is not viable in gusts. It should be left to the experts.

The conventional way of handling crosswinds in a three axis ultralight is to hold down aileron on the upwind wing and compensate for the yawing effect of the wind on the tail with opposite rudder. (The wind will tend to yaw the aircraft to point into the wind). Once airborne, the wings are leveled and the rudder moved in the opposite direction to yaw the craft into the wind to set up a crab angle in order to go straight down the runway. This is shown in figure 35. Again, this procedure requires a certain degree of skill and should be learned gradually in light winds.

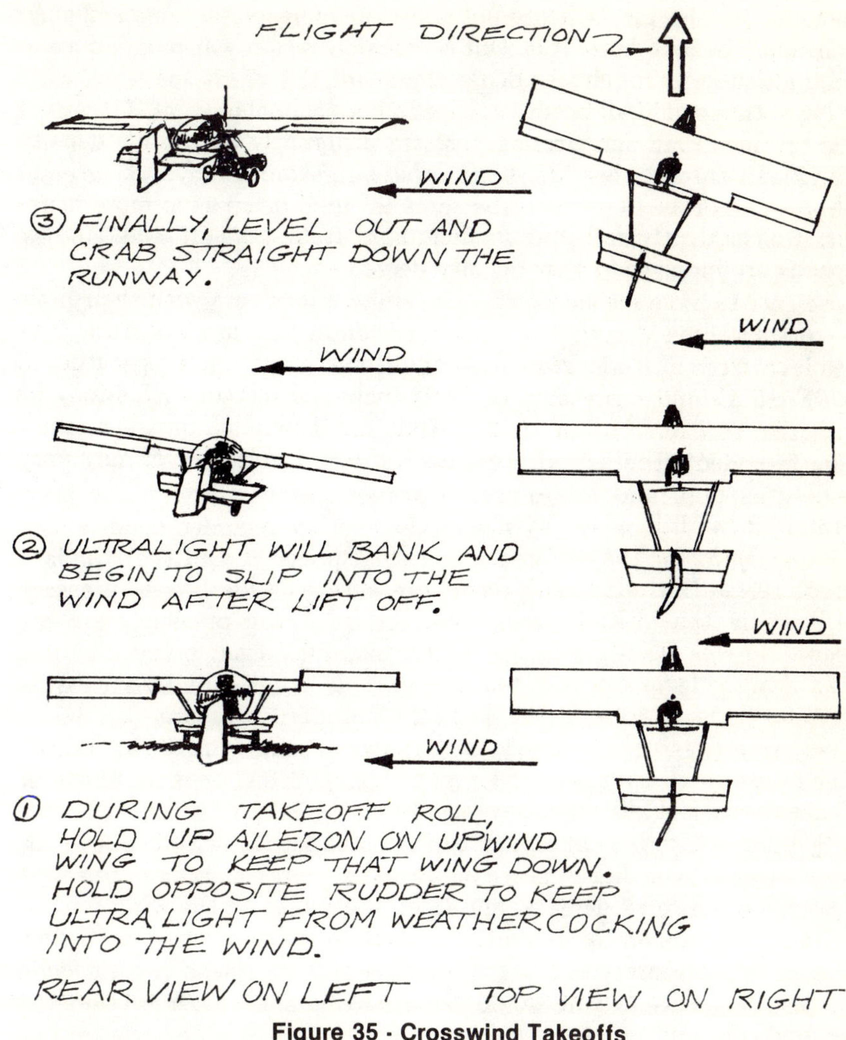

Figure 35 · Crosswind Takeoffs

DENSITY ALTITUDE

The air through which we fly is compressible and possesses a certain amount of weight. The pressure felt at any point is dependent on the mass of the air above that point. Consequently, the higher we go, the less mass of air there is above us, so the lower the pressure. (An altimeter takes advantage of this change in pressure to measure altitude).

It is well known that the air density varies with pressure, temperature and humidity. As the pressure increases, the air is compressed and becomes more dense. Likewise, as the air cools it contracts (the molecules move closer together) and density increases (remember, the air is not in a closed container, so pressure does not increase as the air is heated). Also, the more water vapor the air contains, the less dense it is. Our conclusion is that warm, moist air at high altitudes is much less dense than cool, dry air at sea level.

Now, this would all be an exercise in high school physics if it wasn't for the fact that our aircraft perform differently as the air density varies. In thinner, less dense air, the wings must move at greater airspeed in order to develop the same lift (and drag) as in more dense air. Consequently, all speeds including stall, take-off and landing speeds are increased as air density decreases.

Scientists have measured the atmosphere for years with their little meters and have determined "standard conditions" at all altitudes. At sea level (zero altitude) standard conditions refers to a temperature of 59 °F (15 °C) and a pressure of 29.92 inches of mercury (this may be given as 14.7 lb/inch ^{2} or 1013.2 Millibars, depending on the application intended). The actual pressure we record at sea level may vary widely as high and low pressure systems move through the area. Standard conditions simply means the average recorded conditions.

To account for the difference in actual pressure and the standard pressure, we introduce the term "pressure altitude." Your pressure altitude is the altitude you would be at if the pressure you are recording was standard pressure. For example, assume you are 1000 ft. above sea level and your barometer reads 27.83. Standard pressure at 1000 ft. is 28.86 while 27.83 is the standard pressure at 2000 ft. Thus, your pressure altitude is 2000 ft. even though you are at 1000 ft. The pressure altitude will often be a thousand feet or more above or below the actual altitude above sea level.

Pressure altitude is always used in lieu of actual altitude above sea level when discussing aircraft performance, since it is pressure that determines the air's density, and thus, the forces on the wing.

Now, if we add one other variable factor to pressure altitude – namely, the temperature – we can find density altitude. Density altitude is simply the altitude you would be at taking into consideration the temperature and pressure altitude. For example, assume you are at 1000 ft. and your pressure altitude is 2000 ft., while the temperature is 77 °. The density altitude is then 3800 ft. This is startling . Even though you are only 1000 ft. above sea level, the air is as thin as the 3800 ft. average (standard condition). Of course, there can be an even greater difference between your actual altitude and the density altitude.

Since density altitude is a measure of the actual air density, we use this to calculate the effect of the air on our performance (note that humidity changes are ignored for the sake of simplicity). We are most interested in the way air density effects our takeoff and landing run or roll as well as climb rate. The easiest way to determine this is to use a Koch chart as shown in figure 36. First, find your pressure altitude by calling a nearby airport, or reading an altimeter set to 29.92 inches of mercury. Now obtain the temperature from a thermometer and locate this temperature on the scale at the left of the chart. Draw a straight line from the temperature scale to the current pressure altitude on the right hand scale. Where this line cuts the scales in the center of the chart indicates the percentage increase in your normal takeoff distance and percentage in your rate of climb.

As an illustration, again assume the pressure altitude is 2000 ft. and the temperature is 77 °F. A line drawn on the chart as shown indicates an increase in takeoff roll of almost 50% and 35% decrease in climb rate over its standard air sea level values. From this we can see the significance of weather in powered ultralight performance.

Here's an easy rule of thumb to figure out how speed changes as density changes. Just add 2 percent for every 1000 ft. of pressure altitude and 1 percent for every 10 °F difference from standard conditions to your normal running speed. For example, assume you lift off at 18 mph at sea level with a temperature of 59 °F. However, you read a pressure altitude of 2000 ft. and a temperature of 80 °F. The total change would then be 2 perecent (from the pressure) and 2 percent (from the temperature difference of 21 degrees), or 18.6 mph.

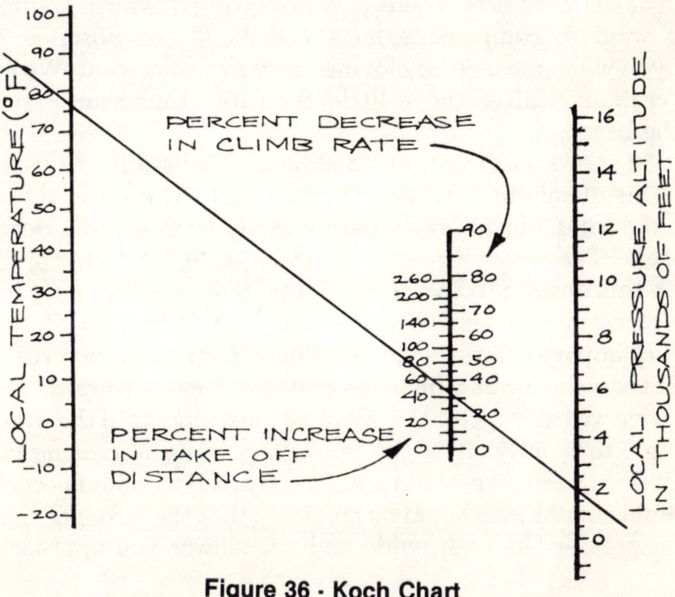

Figure 36 - Koch Chart

Most pilots of ultralights don't use a calculator and chart to figure out their density altitude before each flight. However, a little practice of this nature is recommended to provide a feel for the daily changes in performance that can be expected. Remember, there may be times at high altitude sites in hot, humid weather that you may not be able to take off at all. Be aware of the extra distance needed and the reduction in climb rate. Leave plenty of room to clear distant obstacles. Also remember your engine and body are less efficient workers in thinner air. Of course, a little bit of headwind will do wonders in cutting down runout distance and velocity.

FLYING IN WIND

As we have said many times, wind is a complicating factor in all flying. Here we investigate some of the complications in more detail.

The first matter is the effect of wind on our ground track. As we have already seen, flying into the wind slows our groundspeed down while flying with the wind speeds it up. What about crosswind? If you can imagine a boat crossing a swiftly flowing river, you will see that it drifts downstream as it crosses so that it reaches the opposite bank well downstream from the starting point. If it wants to reach a point exactly across from the starting point, it must aim a little upstream—the amount depends on the boat's velocity with respect to the stream—so that it seems to be moving sideways somewhat. The boat moves directly across the stream but is aiming a bit upstream to compensate for the downstream drift.

An aircraft follows the same procedure when moving across the direction of the wind flow. To keep from drifting downwind, aim a little into the wind to compensate for the drift. To an observer on the ground, you will appear to be moving sideways somewhat. We call this action "crabbing" after those little creatures that scurry sideways across the beach.

Figure 37 shows a top view of a crabbing ultralight flying from point A to B. This ultralight is labeled C. Note that the craft is aimed a bit towards the wind, but follows a path directly from A to B. How do we explain this? The arrow F represents the ultralight's flying speed. We can break this down into two components: S directed to the side in the opposite direction to the wind and P along the flight path. Note that S is equal but opposite to the wind and thus offsets the wind drift action. P then is the velocity at which the craft progresses towards B.

If the wind velocity increases, we must turn more into the wind, thus increasing S to exactly offset the wind effect while decreasing P. If the wind dropped to zero, we would aim directly at B; S would become zero and P would equal F. It should be apparent that the stronger the crosswind, the greater the crab angle and the slower you approach your goal.

How do we set up a crab angle? Simply look at your goal and turn into the wind until you are moving straight at your goal. We said moving at your goal, not aiming. If you try aiming at your goal you will end up flying the path of ultralight D in the figure. You will get there eventually, but this is obviously a longer route. If you are moving sideways directly toward your goal, you are crabbing properly.

What if you can't see your goal as on an extended cross country? In this case, you will probably be following a compass heading. Read the section on Navigation and you will see how to get the correct compass heading in a wind. With this correct compass heading you will be automatically crabbing properly towards your goal.

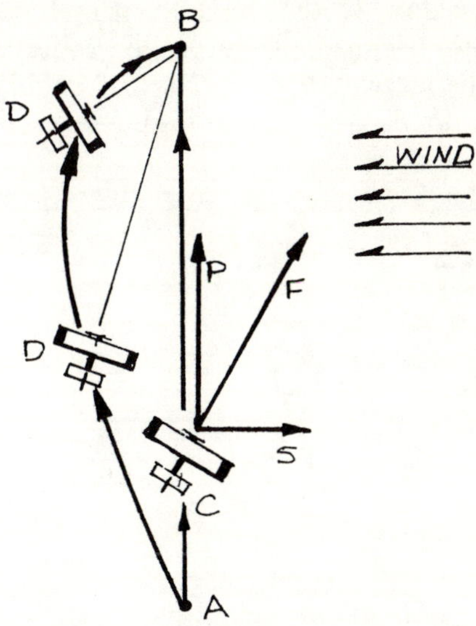

Figure 37 · Crabbing in Wind

Another complication wind presents is drift when turning. For example, when flying downwind and intending to turn over a point to line up on a cross wind leg, you may find you have drifted well past where you intended to be. Similar examples can be made for turns in other directions with respect to the wind.

The problem of perception is of great significance to aircraft such as ours that fly so near the ground. When turning to the downwind direction, our ground-speed increases dramatically and the perception is one of traveling too fast. The natural tendency is to slow down which, of course, can lead to a dangerous downwind stall. Whether flying downwind, upwind or crosswind, always monitor airspeed. The aircraft flies on airspeed only, not groundspeed.

Away from the effects of the terrain, an upwind and downwind turn are controlled exactly alike. There is no difference in an upwind and downwind turn except in the groundspeed and perhaps the perception of the pilot. The aircraft feels the same forces and controls the same.

However, in a wind gradient there is a difference. The aircraft will tend to underbank (bank less than normal for the amount of control applied) when turning from crosswind to upwind and overbank when turning to the downwind direction. Don't let anyone tell you different, for there's much confusion on this point and some unclear thinking.

To simplify our understanding, look at figure 38. On the left is a wind velocity profile showing how the wind increases above the ground. An aircraft flying across this wind would drift to the side (if it wasn't crabbing) an amount equal to the wind velocity at the level at which it was flying. Therefore, we redraw the gradient to appear as the aircraft sees it: zero wind at its flight level, increasing wind above and an *opposite* wind below. Note, we have not included the ground in the second wind profile because although the ground causes the gradient due to friction, the aircraft flies the air and could care less where the ground is (unless it's directly in the flight path!)

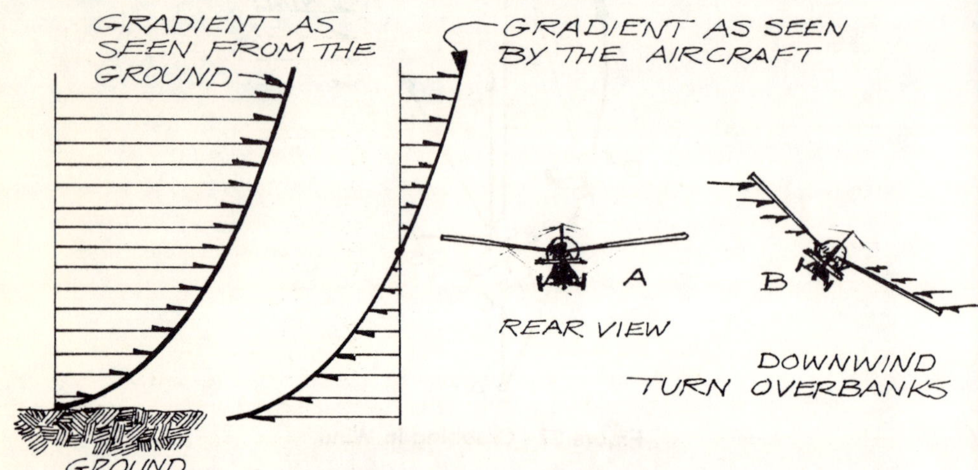

Figure 38 · Turns in a Wind Gradient

Removing the improper ground reference helps clear up a lot of the confusion, for now we can see that an aircraft flying away from us at A (in a crosswind) will experience very different relative wind on its wings as it banks right to turn downwind. The upper wing experiences an increase in velocity and angle of attack (it "sees" a gust from below and to the side) while the lower wing experiences an increase in velocity and a decrease in angle of attack (it "sees" a gust from above and to the side). The result is an overbanking an amount depending on the severity of the gradient. In an upwind turn the opposite changes are felt.

The problem with such overbanking or underbanking is that it may surprise the pilot and put him or her in the wrong position unexpectedly. Be careful when turning downwind so that the lower wing doesn't drop more than expected or you don't turn further than planned. Also, be aware of the perception difference and think "airspeed" only.

One other factor we should consider in wind is the presence of gusts and turbulence. Besides gripping on tight in the bumpy air, what are your proper reactions? Very often the nose of your ultralight will be lifted radically. Airspeed may increase momentarily and then decrease. In any case, your first reaction should be nose-down pitch control. This is to prevent a stall if the gust suddenly dies.

If the nose drops suddenly, your normal reaction might be to raise it up, but usually you will have lost airspeed due to a rearward gust so the correct procedure is again to lower the aircraft's nose. Once you have resumed proper airspeed, raise the nose to pull out of the dive. What is the proper airspeed? The aircraft's best maneuvering speed (a little above best glide or best rate of climb angle of attack) is the speed to fly in turbulence. Do not fly too fast or you can overstress the aircraft in strong gusts. If you fly too slow, you won't have the control response necessary to maintain level flight. Throttle back to reduce speed in a dive. The engine tends to smooth out the bumps so carry about ½ power. If one wing gets lifted, give it roll control to level out.

Now here's a summary for flying in turbulence: Bring the nose down when it gets lifted. Maintain the airspeed then level out if the nose drops. Keep the wings level. Throttle back to about ½ power. Maintain best maneuvering airspeed. Use quick, precise controls and avoid over-controlling. If at any point you feel safety is compromised, land immediately and imprint on your mind the conditions that led to such turbulence.

Remember, flying turbulence is an acquired skill (some say taste) so take it easy. There is considerable variation in the turbulence capabilities of different ultralights—don't get caught by the lemming principle and fly in rowdy conditions just because others are. Again, the stronger the wind, the more likely you are to encounter strong turbulence.

CROSS-COUNTRY

Let's take a flight. We get up on a clear, crisp Saturday morning and decide that this is the weekend to explore the countryside by air. A call to Flight Service confirms the decision with a fair weather prediction. All there is left to do is grab a quick breakfast, locate a small sleeping bag, stuff some money in our pocket, fill the fuel tanks and zip over to our launch site.

After a careful set-up and preflight, we take to the air, circle the field twice to gain altitude, then set a course along a nearby highway. Soon we are cruising at two thousand feet watching the fields, trees and houses slip by far below. We spot a herd of cows heading for the pasture, a housewife hanging out the wash and a few cars crawling along the road, their drivers unaware of our lofty presence. The morning sun glints from a winding river as a fisherman rows his boat to shore. The scenery unfolds for a couple of hours until we see a gas station and decide to land for refueling.

By now the sun has warmed the land and a slight breeze is rustling the trees. Smoke from a chimney confirms the wind direction and we set up our approach in a convenient field. As soon as we touch down a band of children, dogs, farmers, housewives, aunts, uncles and cousins surround us and pelt us with questions. After a leisurely chat, a good rest and lunch with the local farmer, we again take to the air with full tanks.

The day passes on, full of similar scenery and encounters. We may see a farm auction and fly down to take in the action, or land near a lake to splash around, or even swoop low over a field to wave at a few girls. The possibilities are unlimited. We fly as long as we want, then spend the night in our sleeping bag under our wing. By the time we return Sunday evening we are not the same for we've had an adventure that few will ever experience. We walk on air for the rest of the week.

This little episode may sound like more of a dream than a reality, but flights of this nature are easy to accomplish with most powered ultralights. In fact, five pilots — Pat Hirst, Jack McCornack, Kevin Bell, Keith Nicely and Jack Peterson — flew coast-to-coast from California to North Carolina on powered ultralights in July, 1979. They followed two different routes — one north through Wisconsin to the EAA Oshkosh fly-in, and one south through Arizona, Texas, Mississippi, etc. They flew motorized Fledglings and one EasyRiser, completing the thousands of miles in hundreds of short hops over the period of about four weeks.

Cross-country flights of such magnitude are special expeditions, of course, but the average pilot can take a weekend jaunt with only a little preparaion. The most important concern is the weather. Powered ultralight aircraft are susceptible to strong winds and are obviously no match for thunderstorms, nor can they fly safely when visibility is poor. To avoid such conditions, learn to predict the weather from newspaper weather charts (only a few of these maps provide adequate data — the New York Times is best) and interpret radio weather reports.

One of the best sources of weather information for pilots is Flight Service, as mentioned. All larger airports provide this service free of charge. You simply phone the Flight Service number and you will receive the weather information. Ask for the wind velocity and direction at the various altitudes you intend to fly. Also check for turbulence and stability to get an idea of the nature of the air. Be sure to get an extended forecast so you don't get caught a hundred miles from home in a rainshower. It should be noted that pilots of conventional aircraft are usually requested to give their airplane registration number when calling Flight Service. Pilots of ultralight craft should use their number or state their name and the fact that they are flying ultralights.

During an extended flight, it is important to monitor the weather en route through visual clues such as clouds and smoke. The most insidious weather phenomena is the thunderstorm. During the summer months, these huge beasts can develop quite rapidly with enough power to shake un ultralight like a rat in the jaws of a dog. Learn to recognize the various stages of thunderstorm growth and give them a wide berth. As seen in Chapter III, the dangerous effects of a thunderstorm can extend for miles ahead of the actual cloud boundaries in the form of a gust front.

The Pterodactyl With Rough Field Gear

The way to learn to fly cross-country is the gradual approach as in all our training. Start by heading out a ways from your home strip and then return. Maintain enough altitude so you can easily glide back home. Next, select a field nearby and set up your ultralight (have an instructor fly your ship over if you can't transport it). Now practice a few take offs and landings at the new field then fly back to your home port. After a few times back and forth you will be familiar with altitude requirements and judging new terrain from the air. You can now progress to longer and longer jaunts until you are ready for some serious X-Cs! Be sure to use a standard pattern to gain altitude and approach both fields.

A real concern when flying cross-country (or any time) is the possibility of engine failure. Two-cycle engines are fickle, so ultralight pilots must have plenty of dead stick (engine off) landing practice before attempting cross-country flight. Because of this engine failure possibility, **never** fly low over trees or other unlandable areas. If you have to cross a large tract of wilderness or other hostile (to ultralights) territory, simply motor up until you are high enough to glide to a landing area on one side of the unlandable tract. Ignore this simple rule and one day you'll find yourself eating pine (or enclosed in pine as the case may be).

When crossing a ridge or a high power line, do so at an angle as shown in figure 39. This will allow you the option of turning left or right to miss the obstruction in the case of an engine failure or a surprise downdraft. Of course, you should never get so low above such ground objects due to the risk of downwind turbulence or a high voltage surprise.

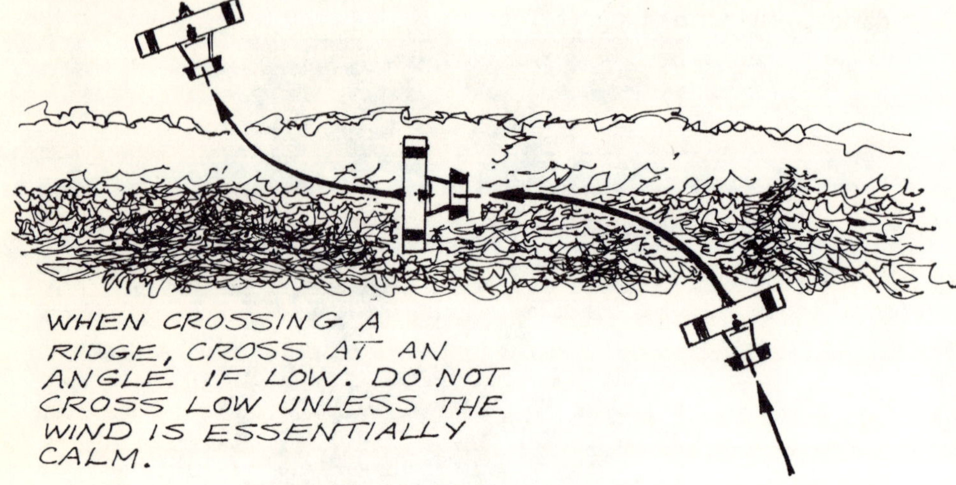

Figure 39 · Crossing A Ridge

As you fly along, always have a landing field in mind. You can practice this by looking for fields and imagining a landing set up as you drive along in your car. Also, keep a constant check on the wind to control your drift and help in emergency landings.

In most cases, you can scope out the area you intend to fly over from the ground. Drive over your intended route and check all the potential landing areas for hidden dangers. Keep an eye out for sources of fuel and food. The more familiar you are with an area, the safer your initial cross-country excursions will be. Pick out prominent topographical or terrain features to guide you along the way.

At times you may have to go around certain areas. Towns are illegal to fly over and large bodies of water are risky unless you are equipped with floats. A ditched ultralight will sink in seconds. In the case you have to alter your course, choose two points beyond the area that you must skirt that line up with your intended path. Once around the area, position yourself to realign the points and continue on your merry way. This is an old boy scout trick that works just as well in the air as in the woods.

Other areas to avoid are those prohibited by the FAA (see the next section) and wild life preserves, National parks, game farms as well as other areas of high concentration of people or animals. Remember, the less obtrusive we are, the fewer the demands for regulation.

Matters to prepare for when taking an extended cross-country flight are meals and accommodations. Of course, you can't carry too much baggage on an ultralight aircraft, so a small sleeping bag is about the best you can do. Meals will have to be found along the way, although in many situations—over the desert, for instance—it is advisable to carry a bit of drinking water.

One of the most important considerations is proper clothing. Weather changes, high altitude flying and daily temperature variations must be prepared for through the use of multiple layers of clothes that can be easily added or rolled in your sleeping bag. Other items of importance are a compass and maps for the purpose of navigation , and the avoidance of air traffic. We will discuss these in later sections.

The range of an ultralight is a major factor in determining its suitability as a cross-country ship. Generally speaking, the larger, fixed wing type of ultralights will fly further on a given amount of fuel due to their greater aerodynamic efficiency.

Different designs achieve widely different fuel economies, however, one example will illustrate what to expect. One ultralight equipped with a 30 horsepower engine, and a 3 gallon tank flies for approximately 54 miles and a fuel economy of 18 miles per gallon. Other designs can do much better. Of course, flying style, wing loading, weather conditions and powerplant efficiency can alter these figures drastically.

One solution to the relatively short range of most ultralights is to have a ground crew follow the flight in an automobile with ready fuel as each tank runs dry. Of course, this may somewhat dampen the nature of the adventure since the feeling of freedom is compromised. However, there's nothing like having a friend waiting in the landing field after a long day of flying, ready to point out the wind direction and listen to tales of spectacular views and vistas. Whenever you choose to perform your aerial trek, be sure to be well prepared, and fly safely.

NAVIGATION

Compared to conventional aircraft, navigating a powered ultralight is ridiculously simple. Instead of dead reckoning computors and radio direction finders, all we need is a compass and a map, if even that. The reason for this is that we fly only when visibility is good, at such low speeds and altitudes that it is easy to follow markings on the terrain, such as rivers, mountain chains or railroad tracks. Furthermore, being off course is no major catastrophe since it is so easy to find a convenient field, land and ask directions.

For merely getting from one point to another, the best maps to use are road maps or topographic maps. The latter are very detailed and can be purchased from the government or outdoor recreation supply stores. These maps can be folded and held on the leg with rubber bands or carried in a pocket for consultation upon landing.

The most important maps are sectionals. These are charts of the airways in the U.S.A. and Canada. Pilots of all aircraft must know how to interpret a sectional to avoid air traffic in general, and airport congestion in particular. You can purchase sectionals at any commerical airport. There are 37 sectionals that cover the United States. Be sure to obtain those that pertain to the area you intend to fly over.

The interpretation of a sectional is fairly easily understood by reading the legend. The important matters for ultralight pilots to understand are:

1. Controlled airspace is outlined in blue and magenta (violet). If outlined in blue, an area is controlled from 1200 ft. above the surface, on up. Note that most of the land area in the U.S. is outlined in blue and is thus controlled airspace above 1200 ft. Areas outlined in magenta are controlled airspace from 700 ft. on up. These areas are located around commercial airports and may be quite large in busy areas. When flying in controlled airspace you must have at least 3 miles visibility. When flying outside of controlled airspace, one mile visibility is required.

2. Victor airways are aerial routes that airplanes follow most commonly when traveling from airport to airport. Expect heavy traffic along Victor airways and avoid them if at all possible. They are indicated on a sectional as a pale blue line and identified with a V followed by a numeral. They usually start above 1200 ft. and extend several miles either side of the center line.

Military Training Routes (MTRs) appear as grey lines on sectional charts. These are the routes followed by fast flying jets. They are divided into VR (visual flight rules) and IR (instrument flight) and are identified by the letters VR or IR followed by a number. A four digit number means the route is confined to 1,500 ft. or below. Above 1,500 ft., they are shown by a three digit number. The line on the chart does not indicate the width of the MTR. It may be several miles or tens of miles wide. Check with the nearest Flight Service Station to find out when a MTR is active, and avoid it carefully during these times.

3. Restricted areas, Prohibited Areas, and Military Operations Areas must be avoided at all times without special permission. These areas are identified by blue or magenta hatching on the sectional.

4. Airports are clearly identified with various circular symbols. Those marked in blue are equipped with a control tower. *Avoid these airports at all times* if you are flying a powered ultralight. An incident of interference between an airplane and an ultralight will quickly result in the curtailment of all ultralight pilots' freedom. If you normally operate your ultralight at an airport, be sure to get the limits of your operation in detail from the airport manager.

Along with maps, a compass can be used to follow a given heading. Your heading in flight is the direction you are traveling denoted by the angle between true north and your path, measured in a clockwise direction. For example, figure 40 illustrates headings of 45°, 180° (south) and 305°.

Now, if you want to fly from point A to point B on your map, simply draw a line between the two points, measure the angle this line makes with true north, then fly in the direction that gives a compass reading or heading equivalent to this angle. This is easy enough, but there are two sources of error that must be accounted for.

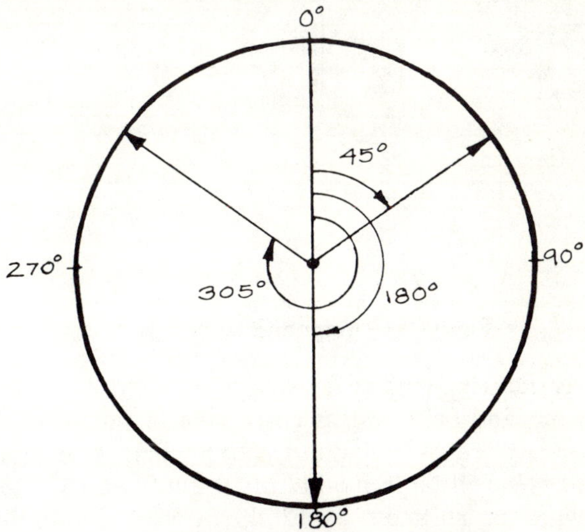

Figure 40 · Compass Headings

The first is compass variation and deviation. Unfortunately, the magnetic north doesn't quite coincide with true north. The difference varies with the location and even drifts over a period of years. A ten degree variation is possible (see figure 41). Deviation refers to the deflection of the compass needle by the metal mass of the aircraft.

To avoid the adverse effects of magnetic variation, plot your course on a sectional and use the compass rose around the commercial airports to measure your heading angle. These compass roses are tilted so that the zero degree readings are pointing at magnetic north, not true north. Your heading will then be automatically compensated for compass variation. An alternate method is to find the magnetic variation for the area you are traversing from the sectional and add it to your heading if it is a west variation, subtracting it if it is east. Remember, an error of one degree results in about a mile error in position after six miles of flight. Obviously, it pays to be as accurate as possible.

The second source of ground track errors when flying by "dead reckoning" is the drift caused by the wind. You can control this problem by calling Flight Service and asking for the wind direction and speed at the altitude you expect to fly. (Note the wind direction is given as an angle in the same manner as heading. The angle always in-

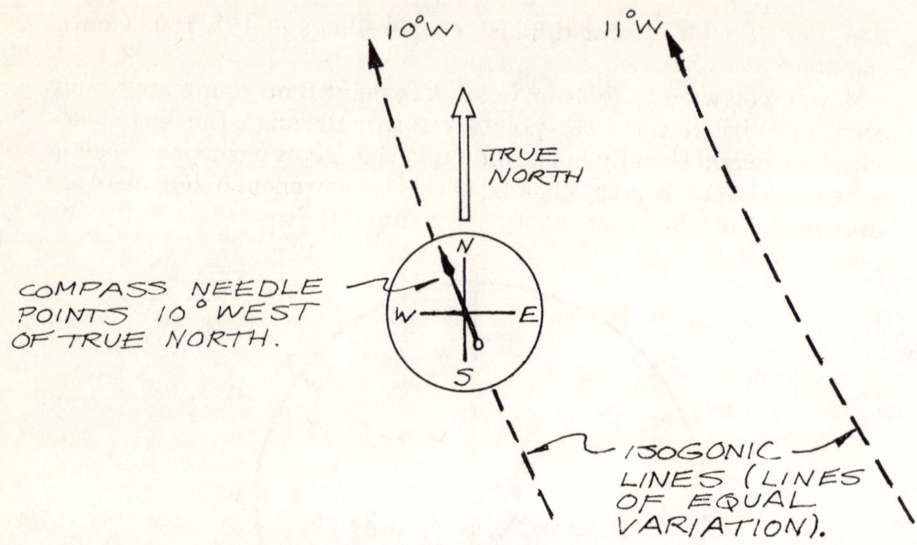

Figure 41 - Magnetic Variation

dicates the direction the wind is *from*. A 270° wind is a west wind.)

An example of wind drift course correction is shown in figure 42. Suppose you wish to travel from point A to point B. Your flying speed is 30 knots and you will be in a wind of 10 knots at 15° (note: Wind speed is always given as knots by Flight Service—knots divided by 1.15 gives miles per hour). Now, draw an arrow along your intended course to represnt your velocity (line AC). Now draw an arrow to represent the wind (line AD). The length of the wind arrow should be proportional to your velocity arrow according to the proportion of the windspeed to your airspeed. Now draw a third line, DC. The heading of this line will be the necessary heading to follow from point A in order to end up at B given the indicated wind velocity. Be sure to correct this heading for magnetic effects.

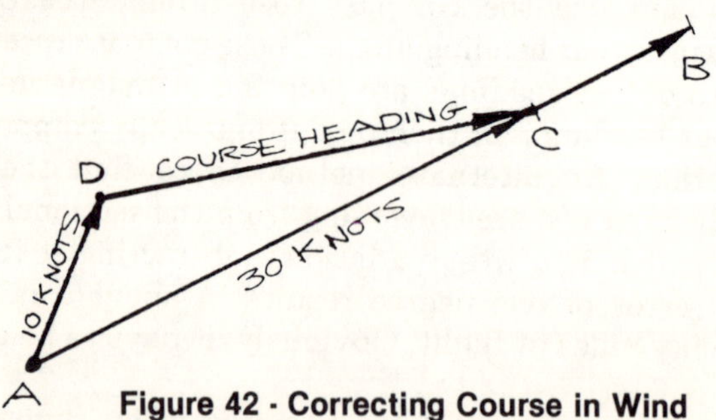

Figure 42 - Correcting Course in Wind

Once you practice this simple form of navigation it will become a challenge to see how accurate you can be over an extended flight. Some fun type competitions use this sort of "road rally in the air" as a cross-country event. Navigation of this sort is called pilotage.

AIR TRAFFIC RULES

The Federal Aviation Administration (FAA) imposes a number of rules on aircraft operations in the interest of preserving order and safety. It is imperative that ultralight pilots obey these rules assiduously to avoid endangering human life and flying freedom. We will review the general rules for all aircraft here, while the specific rules applying to ultralights are given by Part 103 in Appendix I. Failure to obey these rules may result in a FAA levied fine.

The first set of rules dictate the mandatory flying altitudes, depending on heading. In controlled and uncontrolled airspace above 3,000 ft. above the surface, you must fly *odd* thousands above sea level (MSL) plus 500 ft. (example: 3500 ft., 5500 ft., etc.) when heading from 0° to 179 ° magnetic course. You must fly at even thousands, MSL, plus 500 ft. (4500, 6500, etc.) when heading from 180° to 359°. Below 3,000 ft. (3,500 ft. in Canada), these rules do not apply, but it is strongly suggested (by the FAA) that they are followed whenever possible.

These flight levels change above 18,000 ft. and during instrument flight (IFR), but powered ultralights shouldn't encounter these conditions. The complete chart of these rules is in the Airman's Information Manual, available at airports or from the FAA.

The next set of rules dictate the necessary distance from clouds when flying visual flight rules (VFR). These are summarized below:

I. When flying 1200 ft. or less above the surface, you must stay clear of clouds in uncontrolled airspace while controlled airspace requires a clearance of 500 ft. below, 1000 ft. above and 2000 ft. horizontal from clouds.

II. When flying between 1200 ft. above the surface and 10,000 ft. MSL, both controlled and uncontrolled airspace require a cloud clearance of 500 ft. below, 1000 ft. above and 2000 ft. horizontal.

III. Above 10,000 ft. MSL (and more than 1200 ft. above the surface), cloud clearance must be 1000 ft. below, 1000 ft. above and one mile horizontal. These rules are intended to prevent accidents when pilots flying on instruments suddenly pop out of the clouds.

In addition to the above rules, aircraft are given a priority of right-of-way depending on their ability to maneuver and control altitude. This order in terms of highest priority is:

1. Fixed or free ballons
2. Sailplanes
3. Airships (Blimps)
4. Fixed or rotary wing
   aircraft (airplanes and helicopters)
5. Hang gliders
6. Powered ultralights

As can be seen from the chart, powered ultralights must give way to all other aircraft, even hang gliders. Since this chart is supposedly based on ability to avoid other air traffic, it doesn't make sense to expect ultralights to be able to evade an airplane or helicopter, but that's what we have to live with. Obviously, you must maintain vigilance and take evasive action long before another aircraft gets near.

An aircraft towing another has priority over all other powered aircraft. An aircraft in distress has top priority. When landing, the lower aircraft has the right-of-way as shown in figure 43. Two aircraft approaching head on must alter their course to the right (as with automobiles). An aircraft overtaking another must pull around to pass on the right (the opposite of automobile practice). When two aircraft are on a converging course, the pilot on the right has the right-of-way. However, both pilots must take avoidance action if necessary. See Chapter VII for variations when soaring.

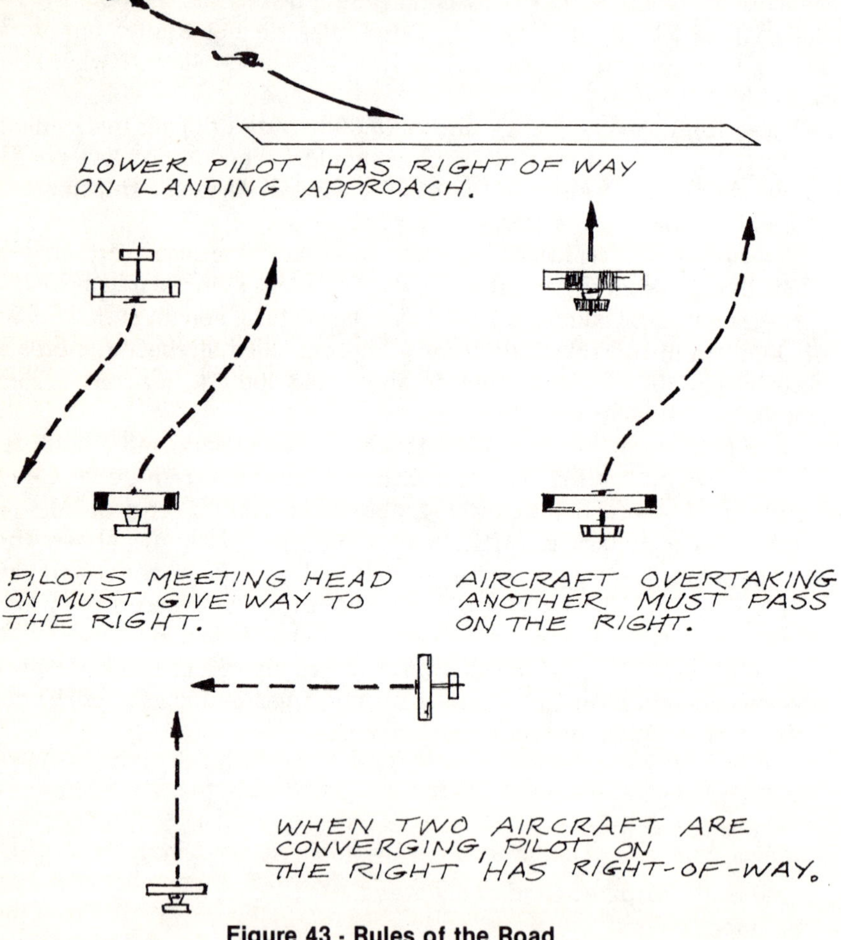

Figure 43 · Rules of the Road

Figure 44 illustrates the method for determining whether or not you are on a collision course with another aircraft. If you are going to collide, the viewing angle from your position to the other aircraft will remain the same as you get closer as in 44 (a). If the other aircraft is going to pass in front of you, the angle will get smaller as in 44 (b). If you will pass in front of the other aircraft, the angle will get larger. To use this method, keep your eye on the aircraft in question and note any change in the angle at which you are viewing. If no change occurs, take evasive action.

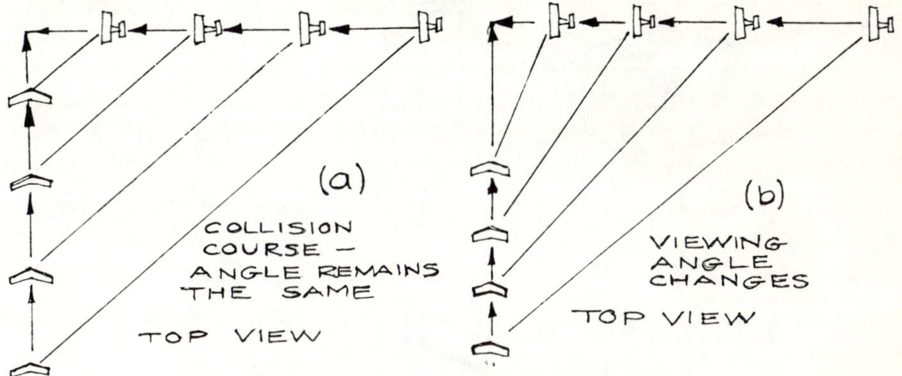

Figure 44 · Judging a Collision Course

Obviously, it does no good to have the right-of-way and risk a midair while waiting for the other pilot to avoid you. He may be daydreaming. In addition, an ultralight may be hard to see or may even attract certain careless pilots closer to see the "strange" craft. The problem with close passes from larger aircraft are wing tip vortices. These strong swirls that originate from the tips of all aircraft can cause serious control problems or structural damage to ultralights.

The higher the angle of attack at which an airplane flies, the worse the vortices are. For this reason, special care must be maintained when landing around other aircraft. Helicopters are extremely dangerous, especially when hovering. Incredibly enough, many helicopter pilots are unaware of the dangers they create for ultralight pilots. They love to buzz over to take a look, so get to the ground as quickly as possible if you see a helicopter approaching.

Wing tip vortices tend to sink as they leave an aircraft. If they encounter the ground they drift apart rapidly. Once an aircraft lands, the vortices terminate since the weight is off the wings. If you land beyond another aircraft's touch-down point you will avoid his vortices unless a wind is present to cause them to drift. When taking off behind another aircraft, your lift-off point should be well before the other aircraft's lift-off point. These guidelines are shown in figure 45. Remember that vorticies can linger for several minutes, so give them wide berth. From the foregoing, it should be obvious that an ultralight pilot's greatest concern is avoiding other air traffic entirely. The best way to do this is to follow the FAA rules and guidelines.

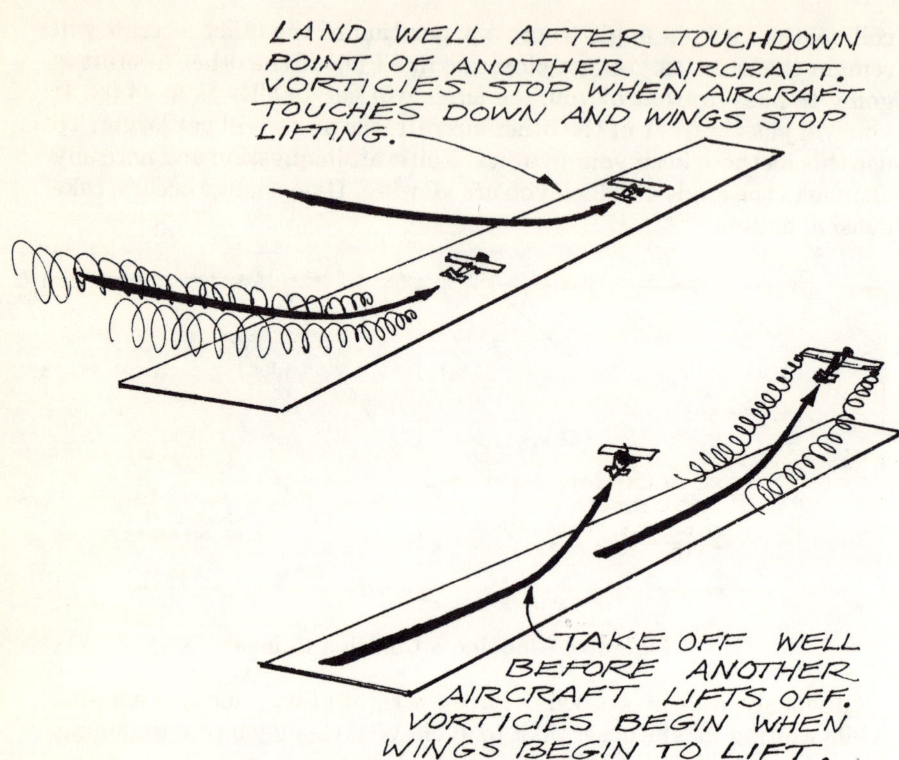

Figure 45 · Avoiding Vorticies

AIRPORT OPERATIONS

Because of the wake turbulence complications described in the last section as well as the difference in airspeeds, airplanes and ultralights do not really mix very well. However, many airports allow ultralight activity for the mutual benefit of ultralight pilots and the airport's business. To do this safely, certain guidelines must be observed.

Generally, ultralight operating areas are set up inside or to the opposite side of the standard airplane pattern. This is shown in figure 46. The different systems depend on wind direction. Note how in both cases the takeoff and landing directions for all operations are the same and may be reversed according to wind conditions.

Runways are designated by the direction to which they point. Thus, runway 27 means the runway points to 270° (the last digit is dropped) or west. If we are landing the other way, we designate the runway 180° opposite. In our example, this would be runway 9 (for 90° or east heading). This is the significance of the numbers painted on the ends of the runway. A U after the number means ultralight runway.

In the figure we have identified our runways 27 and 27U or 9 and 9U as an example. It is important for ultralight pilots to understand this simple notation system so that they know what to do when given certain operational directions.

Each airport may set their own rules, but in general, airplane and ultralight patterns are separated further in the following manner: Conventional airplanes must fly their pattern at 800 feet (or better) above the ground while ultralights must fly their pattern 300 feet above the ground. A further separation method may be to restrict ultralights from the altitude between 400 and 1300 feet above the ground within two miles of the airport. Remember, each airport may choose to impose its own restrictions and patterns, so check with the proper authority before flying.

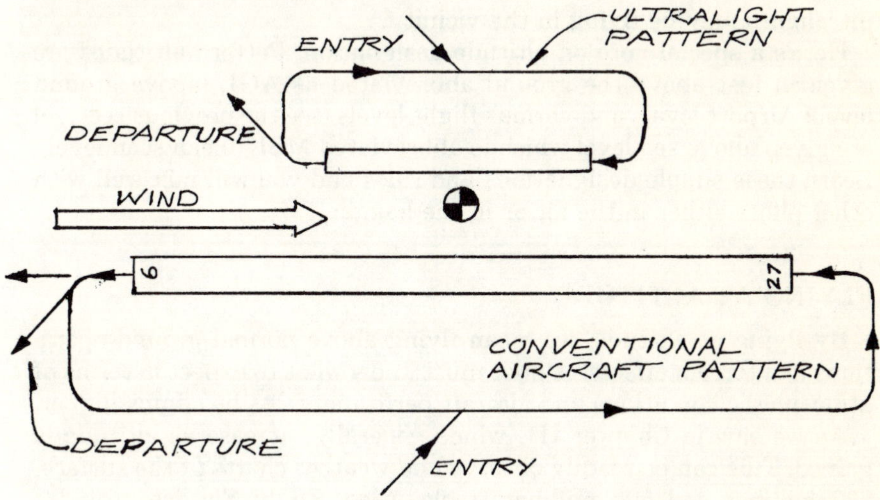

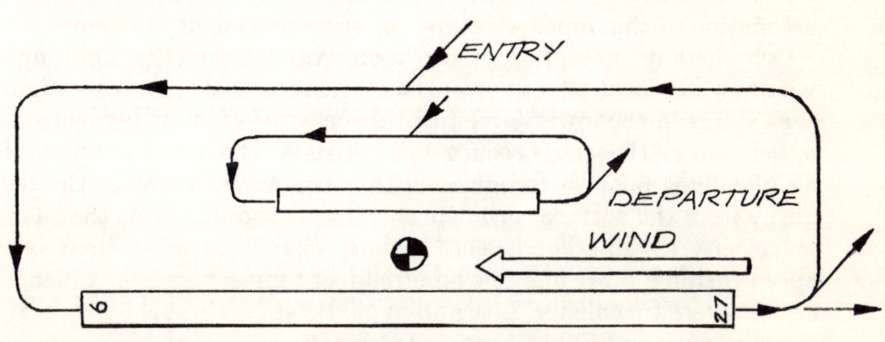

Figure 46 - Airport Operations

Look at the figure again and observe the flight patterns. Note that in both cases the airplane pattern is left handed (all turns to the left), while the ultralight pattern switches from left to right. This is necessary to avoid switching the ultralight runway from one side of the main runway to the other.

Now look at the entry and departure points. This is standard procedure. Entry is at a 45° angle midway on the downwind leg. Departure is from the crosswind leg. However, an ultralight may have to fly around the pattern to gain altitude in order to leave the airport area. Work out the proper procedure for departure, with your airport director.

The symbol for ultralight operations is shown on the figure as a circle divided into quarters with contrasting colors. This symbol is designed to let airplane unfamiliar with the airport know that ultralights may be flying in the vicinity.

Here's a special note on altitude designation: Pattern altitudes are given in feet above the ground abbreviated as AGL (above ground level). Airport levels and various flight levels (see the previous section) are given above sea level which is abbreviated MSL (mean sean level). Learn these simple designations and rules and you will mix well with other pilots either in the air or in the hangar.

FLYING AT ALTITUDE

By flying at altitude, we mean flying above normal ground operations and terrain effects. A pilot must know what to expect in terms of atmospheric conditions and aircraft performance as he climbs higher.

As we saw in Chapter III, winds generally increase as altitude is gained. This can be readily observed on weather charts of the surface, 800 millibar and 500 millibar levels. Also, Flight Service provides information concerning the winds at different levels, which serves to verify the existance of higher winds aloft. Often, you can get a good estimation of the upper winds by observing the drift of clouds.

Occasionally, a high pressure aloft will create very light upper winds, while local effects or surface pressure systems create significant winds in the lower levels. In this case the effect is opposite that noted above—the winds reduce with altitude. The important thing for an ultralight pilot to recognize is that the actual speed of the wind (away from the surface turbulence) is not as significant as the change in velocity at different levels. A sharp change in wind direction or speed within a layer of a few hundred feet represents shear which can cause severe turbulence. Learn to avoid these conditions by analyzing weather data and Flight Service Information.

When flying at altitude, it is possible to be around the level of clouds. Review the cloud clearance rules listed previously and obey them carefully (they are for your protection as well as that of other aircraft).

It is possible to be flying in lift and be suddenly, engulfed in cloud. The simple way to avoid this is to pull out of the lift long before you get near the cloud (remember that 500 foot clearance). However, if the unexpected happens you should know what to do. Often in a cloud, conditions will be very smooth, but normally it is quite turbulent since condensing water vapor releases a large quantity of heat that keeps the cloud billowing.

The big problem in clouds is you cannot see—a condition known as "white out." Without a compass you cannot tell where you are going and the action of turbulence can turn you without any means of determining in which direction. To further compound the problem, you may be in a turn and not even know it. Once a turn is established, the body senses no forces except an increase in weight. In less than 20 degrees of bank, a pilot can't even detect this weight increase.

What do you do? The best policy is to try to keep the controls centered and fly straight to exit the cloud. If you try turning around to come out they way you entered you may turn to an entirely different heading than expected unless you have practiced turns with your eyes closed to learn what controls held for how long provides a 180° turn.

A common occurance when flying blind is for the aircraft to enter a spiral dive. If you watch the airspeed indicator you may think you are simply diving straight ahead so you apply nose up control. This will tend to tighten the spiral which confuses you and may lead to more nose up control. The correct procedure is to try rolling the wings slightly one way and watch the airspeed. If it lessens, continue to roll. If it increases, roll the other way. Once the airspeed no longer decreases with roll control, level out gradually with a nose up control.

The Solar Riser

Be aware that severe disorientation can occur as you exit the cloud for the ground may seem to be moving the opposite way you expect it to. This can lead to instant nausea and confusion.

A very common sad tale is the case where a pilot climbs up through a hole in a layer of clouds for a look around only to find the holes close up

107

once he is above the clouds. This is very dangerous, very foolish and not conducive to easy solutions. Ultralight pilots have been caught in this manner. One such pilot flew around looking for a way down until his fuel ran out and he dropped into the clouds. He came out the bottom of the layer in a severe spiral dive over a wooded area. Fortunately, he was able to find a small landing field and lives to tell the tale. Probably the best thing to do in such a situation is descend through the clouds while you still have ample fuel before the cloud layers thicken and possibly extend to the ground.

From the preceding, it should be apparent that flying in clouds is extremely risky and should be avoided at all times. The risk increases the closer the cloud is to the terrain. A compass increases your chances of exiting a cloud safely, but will not guarantee your safety.

As we climb higher, we experience a noticeable drop in temperature. The average drop is 3.5° per thousand feet (2°C per 300m), but it can be over 5°F/1000 ft. Now add to this the wind chill factor and you'll find it getting pretty cold as you reach skyward. The point is, you must dress for the expected cold. Don't let balmy weather on the ground fool you into thinking the upper air is also warm. All exposed flesh should be covered in very high flights. Be especially careful to protect your extremities with warm socks and gloves. There's nothing worse than having to cut a flight short due to aching toes and frozen fingers.

Another problem encountered as altitude increases is the lowered air density. This decrease in density hampers the performance of our bodies, wings and engines. The rarefier air means less oxygen for the functioning of our brain and muscles. At about 10,000 ft. MSL (3,000m), we begin to experience the debilitating effects of too little oxygen in the blood (hypoxia). This will be discussed in Chapter VIII. Remember that the FAA requires supplemental oxygen at altitudes above 12,500 ft. MSL.

The powerplant of an ultralight also consumes oxygen. As the air gets thinner, the fuel mixture gets richer (greater percentage of fuel to air) so the carburetor should be leaned in flight as altitude is gained for maximum efficiency. When descending the mixture must be richened to avoid overheating from too little fuel/oil lubrication. The best way to determine the appropriate setting is to monitor your temperature gauges and tachometer to maintain the same approximate operating range.

At some point, peak engine efficiency will fall off as you reach maximum throttle setting and very lean mixture. There just won't be enough oxygen in the rarefied air to feed the engine. In addition, the thinner air results in less efficiency of the propeller and greater flying speeds. Consequently, a ceiling is reached above which you cannot climb. This upper limit is determined by your wing loading as well as the design of your particular craft and power plant.

Ultralight aircraft have motored up to over 15,000 ft. MSL and have climbed above the ceiling of some conventional aircraft. The ultralights capable of doing this are those with lots of power and efficient wings. Remember, your climb rate slows as you get higher, so it may take over an hour just to climb to 10,000 ft. Of course, the effort is worth it. There's nothing like the breathtaking view offered to the high altitude pilot.

Three Axis Controls On The Flightstar

STALL CONTROL

As you know, a stall occurs when the air separates from the surface of a wing, drag increases dramatically and lift drops.

The abruptness of a stall depends on the design of a wing and the rate at which the angle of attack changes. An abrupt stall results in the nose of the aircraft dropping rapidly.

In most cases, you should return the control to neutral and add power. Do not apply a strong nose down control as the aircraft may dive much more abruptly and further before pulling out. A quick nose down control is only applicable if you catch a rapidly rising attitude before the stall occurs. The reason we add power is that the increase in thrust will lower the angle of attack. Here we should make a qualification, for some older designs without the pitch dampening effect of a tail and with high thrust lines may pitch down radically when power is added as a stall break occurs. The best guideline to follow is the manufacturer's recommendations.

A stable aircraft will pull out of stalls automatically as long as the pilot doesn't bully it around with rough controls. In turbulence, the possibility of inadvertent stalls always exists. Reduce power so you can add power in turbulence induced stalls as mentioned previously.

When an aircraft approaches a stall slowly, there are certain signs that the pilot can learn to recognize to avoid the stall. First, the controls feel sluggish due to the reduced airflow. Also one wing may retard or "stick," yawing the glider. Furthermore, a slight buffeting may occur in the wing (caused by the turbulent flow on the upper surface). Finally, the feel of the wind will be reduced considerably if the pilot is not sitting in the propeller slipstream. Detecting all these signs takes a little practice, but they can be used as readily as a stall warning on a conventional aircraft.

Once you are experienced at flying at least 1000 ft. above the terrain, practice a mild stall on your craft with the engine off or idling. You will soon have a feel for how it reacts below normal flight regimes. Raise the nose slowly to stall the wings, then let the ultralight recover itself. When it is again rising to approach another stall, level the nose to return to the proper speed. Never allow your ulralight to stall at a high nose-up position. This is a result of pulling up quickly when carrying considerable speed and is known as a whipstall. The result of a whipstall is often a tailslide then a partial tumble to a steep or past vertical dive. The severity of the whipstall results depend on how abrupt the maneuver is made and this factor is hard to control, especially in varying air.

It will become clear from this practice how much altitude is lost in a stall or how much the aircraft "mushes." This should be a good warning not to fly too slowly when taking off, landing or cruising near the ground. Do not attempt full power stalls for they occur at too high a nose-up position.

USING CONTROLS

When an aircraft such as a glider flies without an engine, there is a simple relationship between angle of attack, airspeed and altitude lost or gained. For instance, dropping the glider's nose results in a greater airspeed and a greater sink rate. On the other hand, the addition of an engine changes matters somewhat.

Due to the thrust of the engine, an aircraft flies with a greater horizontal component of velocity under power. Thus, to set the wings at the same angle of attack as in an unpowered situation, the nose must be raised to a higher attitude. If, for example, you are flying at best angle of climb (near a stall), and you suddenly cut your power, you would be stalled. The same nose up or down position with respect to the horizon (attitude) does not apply to both powered and unpowered flight. In general, when you reduce power, you should lower your nose to avoid a stall. As you increase power, you can raise the nose to avoid speeding up.

Practice controlling your throttle settings in conjunction with pitch control. This will provide you with a good feel for all aspects of your craft's personality. Learn to perform speed changes by varying your angle of attack, while making altitude adjustments by changing your power setting. This is classical aircraft flying technique and is very useful when setting up landings.

As we have seen, ultralights vary greatly in their methods of control. Here we will make a few notes concerning some properties of common systems. Often a rudder, elevator and spoilers will be used as a system of three-axis control. Usually the rudder is very effective for roll control (in conjunction with the wing's dihedral) and the spoilers aren't needed at all. For this reason, many of these designs will have the rudder hooked up to the stick in order to avoid making all turn controls with the feet as is the case if the rudder is hooked up to pedals as in a conventional aircraft.

A Three-Axis Control Stick And Rudder Pedals

Spoilers can be used to initiate a turn quickly for they create drag and destroy lift. A spoiler system is especially effective for descending rapidly (a good example of this is when escaping a thermal cloud) or steeply (for glide path control). When both spoilers (one on each wing) are applied, the nose must be dropped to maintain airspeed. Even at a steep nose down position, however, the spoilers keep the speed from rising too greatly. A smooth entry and exit from spoiler mode should be practiced. Also, note that with both spoilers full on, turn control with the spoilers will be reverse from normal. For example, with spoilers off, depressing the left control will produce a left turn. With both spoilers on, letting up on the left control will induce a right turn.

Standard three-axis control is the most complicated. A turn is initiated with a side movement of the stick which deflects the ailerons (see figure 47). The upward moving aileron reduces lift on the wing while the downward moving aileron increases lift (the cause of this change of lift is a change in the wing section's net angle of attack). This imbalance produces a roll force.

Unfortunately, an imbalance in drag is also produced in the wrong sense. That is, the downward deflecting aileron produces more drag than the upward one (increasing angle of attack increases drag as well as lift). The result is the wing wants to roll one way and yaw the other-way. We call this wrong way yaw tendency adverse yaw.

To overcome adverse yaw, we add a rudder input by depressing the pedal on the side to which we are turning. The rudder then angles to that same side, swinging the tail around to produce the proper yaw. The rudder control should be initiated just after the roll control is applied.

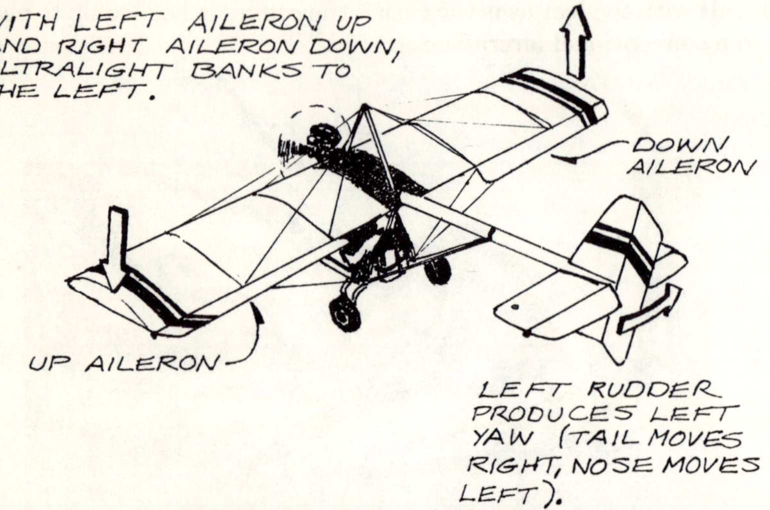

Figure 47 - Three-Axis Control

Finally, once the aircraft starts to bank, up elevator is applied to off-set the craft's tendency to nose down in the turn. The amount of rudder and elevator control depends on the steepness of bank (greater bank, greater control movement) which, of course, depends on the amount and duration the roll control is applied. Once the desired bank angle is established, the roll control (ailerons) is centered while the pitch control (elevator) continues throughout the duration of the turn. The yaw control (rudder) may have to be held a little to offset varied prop-wash in a turn.

Obviously, a bit of practice is required to coordinate these controls properly. Pilots learning to fly for the first time usually do better on ultralights with simpler control systems. The major advantage of three-axis control systems is their great superiority in crosswind operations and ability to handle turbulence.

LANDING PROCEDURES

Every flight must end with a landing. You can't have a good flight without a good landing, so practice to perfect your landing skills in all situations.

One of the most important rules when flying powered ultralights is to keep a landing field in sight at all times. Small two-cycle engines tend to be fickle, so don't risk a tree or water landing and don't rely on someone's backyard as an emergency landing field. On cross-country flights, the above rule is especially important. Keep looking ahead for landing fields and look back at those you have passed until they are out of reach. If trouble threatens, start choosing your landing field long before a loss of altitude forces the choice upon you.

How do we choose a good landing field from the air? Observation is the key. When flying over unfamiliar terrain, there are a few techniques we can use to judge a landing field before we get too low to reach another. The qualities we are looking for are size, lack of obstructions, smoothness of surface, levelness and ease of approach into the wind.

The size of a landing area is fairly easy to judge from the air. However, the presence of trees, power lines or other obstructions increases the required size of a field dramatically since we must clear ground objects by a comfortable margin, yet still get down in the field. Trees, of course, are visible, but look carefully for that lone pine in the middle of the field—it will surprise you every time. Remember that trees tend to look smaller from the air than they do from the ground. Remember that it usually takes a larger field to climb out than land, so don't box yourself in by landing in too small of a clearing.

Power lines are particularly insidious. The only way you can detect them is by looking for poles. There are always power lines running to buildings, and most often along roads. Occasionally, a power line will run across a field with the poles hidden in the trees at the edge of the field. To avoid this situation, look for power line cuts in the forest and land as far away from buildings as possible.

The slope and roughness of surface is the hardest quality to detect. Here are a few general rules. If a field is planted in crops chances are its not too sloped (but don't rely on this fact alone). A farmer generally uses his roughest, rockiest, steepest fields for pasture. Look for streams (not man-made ditches) besides fields. This generally means the field slopes toward the stream. Also, a farmer will plow across the fall (downslope) line of a field, so you can at least get an idea of the direction a field slopes. If fields are plowed or planted in nice straight rows, chances are it is flat and level (and you're in Iowa). At any rate, land in the direction of the farmer's cultivation tracks and you will generally be choosing the most level path.

If you have to land on a slope and wind isn't a major factor, choose the uphill direction. If you land downhill it will be extremely hard to judge your touchdown point as you will glide much further over the ground. Also, your rollout will be much longer downhill. To perform an uphill landing, carry on a little extra speed then flare (raise the nose) gradually to trade off the speed for a slight climb to follow the rising terrain. End with a quick final nose up control just as you touch down to slow your groundspeed.

When landing in rough fields, bleed off speed gradually then flare hard just before touchdown. The object is to minimize your ground-speed. Apply the brakes as soon as the wheels touch. Jarring along rough ground can be very hard on your ultralight's structure. Practice this rough field technique on smooth ground first.

Landing in corn and other high crops is taboo. Corn cobs have a horrible sound when they pound a wing into odd shapes; wheat, beans and other staples are hard to run or roll in; farmers sometimes aim shotguns at idiots destroying part of their summer's labor. Try to land in pastures that are cowless or at least bulless. The next best choice is a hayfield. Its hard to do much damage to hay.

Of course, one of the most important factors in landing is the wind. In order to land into the wind, you must first determine the wind direction. Look for smoke and flags as being the most accurate indicators. You cannot use the clouds when flying, but you can watch their shadows to see which way they are moving. However, its fairly common for ground winds to be blowing an entirely different direction from winds aloft. Lines on water are good wind indicators. There is usually a calm spot on the water near the shore that the wind is blowing *from* (see figure 48). The best indicator is vegetation. Grass will ripple with waves flowing in the direction of the wind. Trees will show whitened leaves on the windward side and branches will sway in the wind direction. Finally, if none of these indicators are present, you are landing in an unobstructed plain in which case the best method is to turn several smooth, continuous 360s and note your drift. Trying to determine drift in light winds by flying in straight lines is difficult, while 360 turns displace with the wind and are good indicators (see figure 73).

Figure 48 - Wind Lines on Pond

There is one classic landing approach that all pilots must practice to the point of proficiency. This consists of a downwind pass, a base leg and a final approach as shown in figure 49. This is the approved pattern for airports and is very useful for landing ultralights in strange fields. The downwind leg allows you to judge the windspeed and vary your altitude by varying where you make turn A. This first turn can be gradual or steep to again vary altitude. The base (crosswind) leg also can be used to control altitude by changing its length or angling slightly toward or away from the field. Finally, the second turn into the wind for final approach. Practice this maneuver continuously from both directions (right and left hand turns).

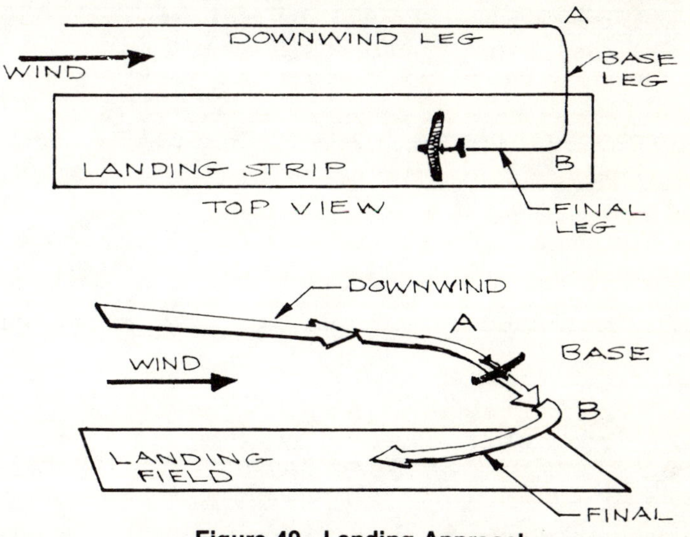

Figure 49 · Landing Approach

Judgement is always a major factor when landing. Acquiring this judgement requires time and practice, but here are a couple pointers to help you along your way. First, when flying to a landing field, do not fly directly at it for it is very difficult to determine distance when we are moving directly towards an object. A little sideways movement provides good depth perception. Note that the standard landing approach includes this flying sideways along the field.

Next, when judging a landing spot (or power line, tree, etc.) here's an easy clue to determine whether or not you will hit it. If the spot moves down in your field of vision you will land beyond it. If it moves up in your field of vision you will land short of it. If it remains stationary (except for getting closer) you will hit it. This is called the stationary spot method and is shown in figure 50. Obviously this technique is very valuable when trying to reach a field in the case of an engine out.

When landing on a sunny day, convection can greatly alter your glide path as shown in figure 51. For this reason, we avoid long, straight final approaches in an ultralight by setting up the traditional downwind, base, final approach. This is especially important in the case of an engine failure.

The engine can be a safety factor when landing. You can cruise low to make a pass to survey your field as well as play with the throttle to

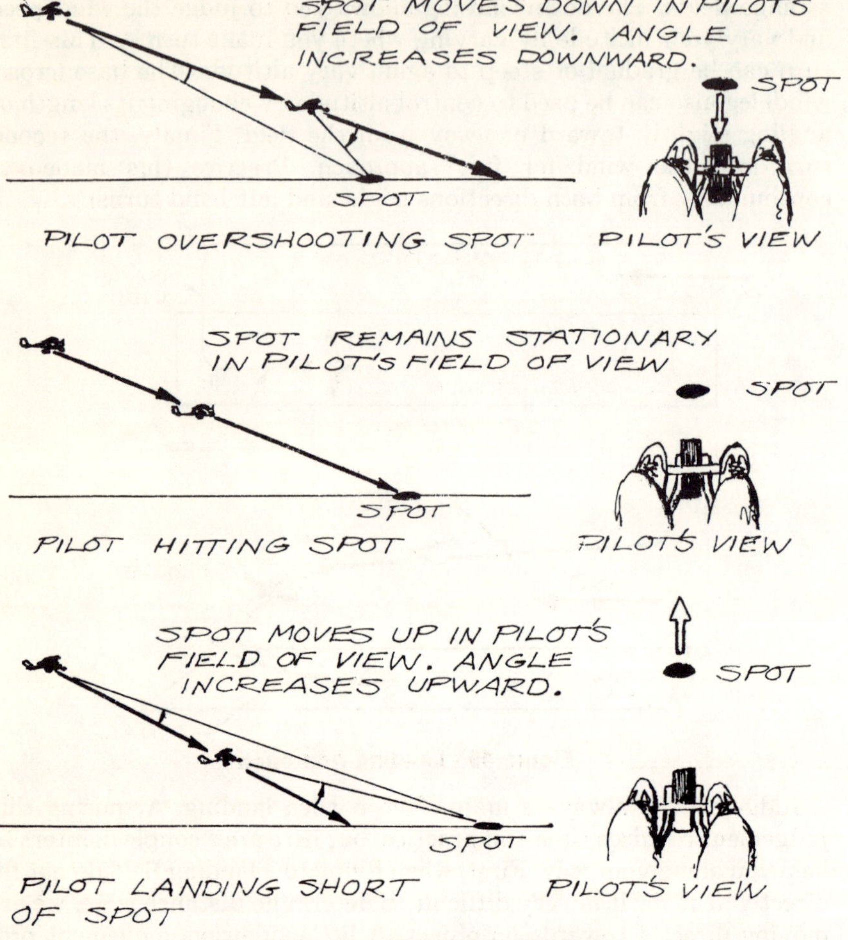

Figure 50 · Stationary Spot Method

control your altitude exactly on final approach. However, don't rely on this latter technique too heavily as you must always be within reach of the landing field when setting up landings even if your engine dies. Remember, an engine that is idled back after a long period of hard climbing is apt to shut down on its own.

At times we are forced to land in adverse conditions. In gusty air, keep your airspeed up to avoid an inadvertent stall near the ground. Don't flare too abrupty in these conditions or you may find a sudden wind speed change occurring at the same time you raise the nose, resulting in fifteen extra feet of altitude and no airspeed. Crosswind landings are best handled by crabbing into the wind to put your ground track straight down the runway, then straightening out just before touchdown. In any case, crosswind landings can almost always be avoided since ultralights land in such short distances.

One of the dangers of landing or taxiing in a crosswind is the possibility of a ground loop. A ground loop is an uncontrolled turn caused by a crosswind or a terrain irregularity. The problem occurs when the wind weathercocks the tail or one wheel is retarded in a rut or soft ground. Once the turn starts, centrifugal force acts to increase the turning force, especially on a tail dragger design. A ground loop can end with the aircraft tipping to the outside of the turn if the entry speed is high.

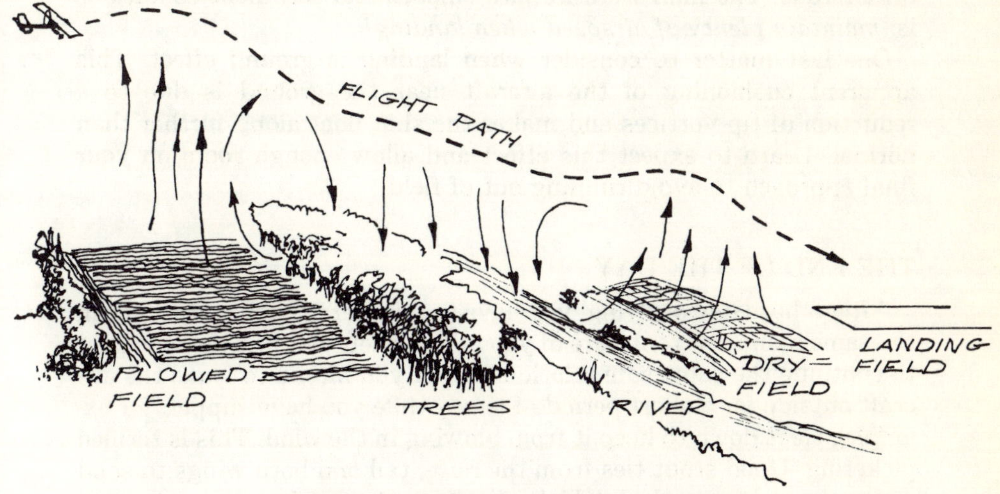

Figure 51 - Variation of Approach Path

To prevent a ground loop, use down aileron on the upwind wing or turn slightly downwind as you taxi or roll out in a crosswind. Once a groundloop starts, try correcting it with the rudder or brakes. If you use brakes, take great care for they maybe sensitive and cause their own problems.

Tail-dragger ultralights are more susceptible to ground loops since the center of gravity is behind the main wheels. Thus, centrifugal force

Landing A Trike

tends to make a turn sharper. An aircraft equipped with tricycle gear has the center of gravity in front of the main gear so centrifugal force tends to straighten out the turn.

When the wind is smooth, there can still be a stall problem on landing approach. This is due to the wind gradient as explained in Chapter III. In Chapter IV, the result of too slow an approach is depicted (figure 23). A stall this close to the ground could be disasterous. The final word in both smooth and turbulent conditions is: *maintain plenty of airspeed when landing!*

One last matter to consider when landing is ground effect. This apparent cushioning of the aircraft near the ground is due to a reduction of tip vortices and makes the ship float along further than normal. Learn to expect this effect and allow enough room on your final approach to avoid running out of field.

THE END OF THE DAY

After a hard day of flying, you have to take care of your ultralight in the same manner it took care of you at two thousand feet if you expect to continue the same safe relationship. If you intend to leave the aircraft outside for a short period of time (while you have supper, for example), tie it down to keep it from blowing in the wind. This is termed picketing. Good stout ties from the nose, tail and both wings to solid stakes in the ground should be suffcient for all but the strongest winds. Fold the wings if possible when winds are blustery. Be sure to enlist plenty of help. A side note: when taking apart small parts such as pins, nuts and bolts, hold them in your mouth to avoid dropping them. If you do not, it is guaranteed that you will lose something, sometime. Nothing is more frustrating than to be grounded by a missing 50¢ pin.

When storing your ultralight for an evening or a long period, take care to clean all parts while checking for wear and damage. Reread the sections in this Chapter on Care and Cleaning and Ground Handling to learn the proper treatment for your ultralight. Remember, the adage "an ounce of prevention is worth a pound of cure" is especially pertinent to such lightweight craft.

At the end of each flight you will probably encounter many curious onlookers (Wuffos). Be kind to them and answer their questions courteously, even after you've heard them a thousand times. Remember, you are an ambassador for your sport, and public opinion has some effect on your flying freedom. On the other hand, respect those close to you, and don't expect them to listen to your flying stories a thousand times, even if you were on top of the world for a few beautiful hours!

CHAPTER VI

THE FLYING MACHINE

Early airplanes were constructed with bicycle and automobile technology. A lot of trial and error along with crude experimentation was required to develop the concepts and construction details that are so familiar on today's aircraft.

Ultralight aircraft are a cross between the flying machines of the past and modern airplanes. On one hand, our light ships are put together with cloth and glue, while on the other hand, only the best stainless cable, aluminum alloy tubes and AN bolts are used along with up to date airfoils and propellers. Powered ultralights borrow technology from a number of sources: conventional aviation, hang gliding and snowmobile manufacturing to list a few. The result is a neat little airplane that flies with a minimum of fuss and budget.

There is, however, a bit of maintenance and care required to keep our wings in shape. In this chapter we will look at three components of powered ultralights—the aircraft structure, the engine and propeller—to see how we can get the maximum performance and useful life from each. The better we care for our entire system, the longer we will enjoy trouble-free flight.

THE STRUCTURE

Despite their unique appearance, most ultralights share the characteristics of conventional aircraft. For instance, if the ultralight doesn't have a tail, it simply means the tail surface has been moved up and out to the wing tips. The designer then must shape these tips to work like a tail during control movements. Most of the parts on an ultralight can be related to those on conventional ships, so the names are the same.

A pilot should be familiar with the parts of his craft so he can speak to others without referring to "what-cha-call-its." The nomenclature of typical structural components is shown in figure 52. The leading edges on any wing is the portion that meets the air first. Similarly, the trailing edge is the rearward portion. Struts are solid braces used to hold the wing rigid. On bipane designs, a number of struts are placed

119

between the wings.

The ribs are solid structures that hold the curve on the wing surfaces to the proper shape. In a flex-wing, these ribs may be removed and are called battens. The undercarriage consists of a cage that supports the pilot and includes wheels, seat, fairings, etc.

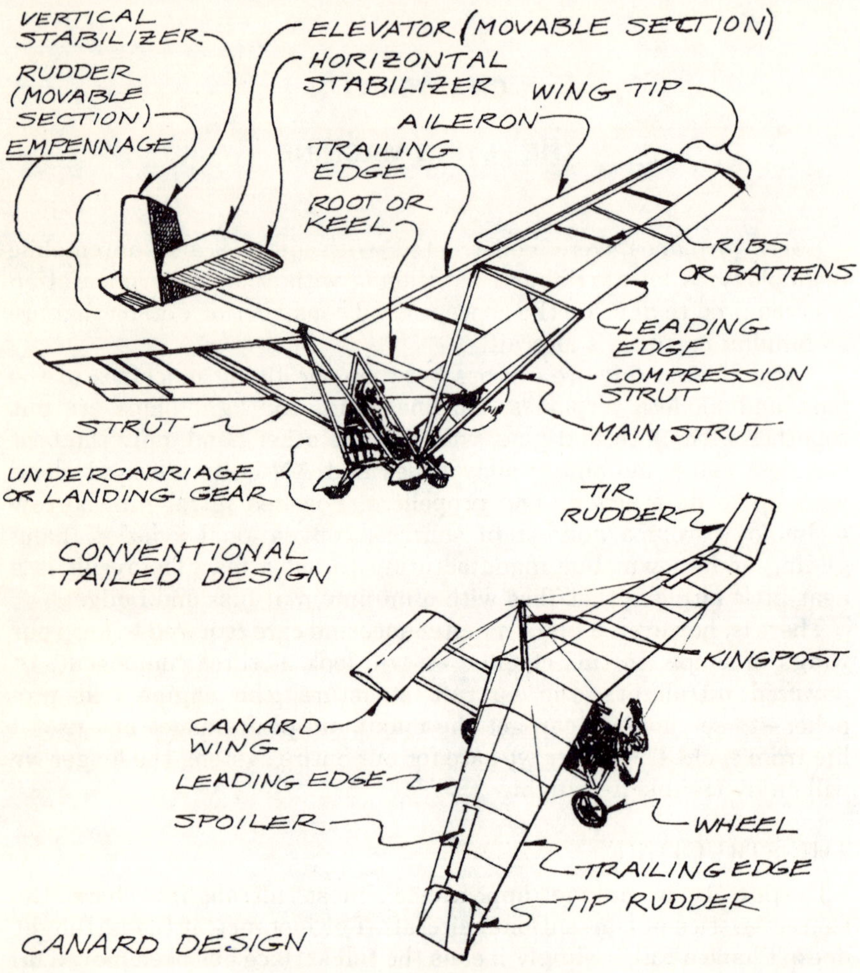

Figure 52 · Nomenclature

The kingpost holds the wings up when the craft is setting on the ground. These usually don't appear with strut-braced ships. The keel is the tube that lies at the center or root of a wing. A flex-wing may possess an additional spar called a cross-bar used to hold the wings apart in flight. Some ultralights dispense with struts or cable bracing and utilize a strong D-shaped tube in the leading edge that is solidly attached to the fuselage or undercarriage. This type of construction is called a cantilever wing.

Many ultralights use stainless steel cable for bracing or control lines. This cable must be of aircraft quality and properly attached. Figure 53 shows the approved method of connecting cable to a bolt. A flat metal blank called a tang goes over the bolt with a hole provided for the cable. A thimble protects the cable from wear, then a NICO swage is pressed on the cable to hold it securely.

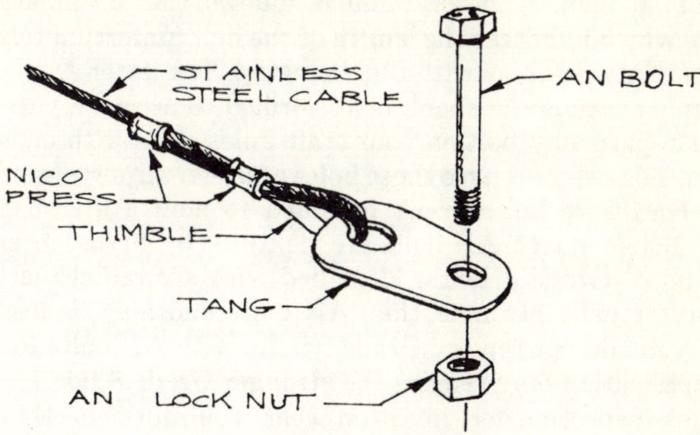

Figure 53 · Cable Connection

The NICO fittings must be pressed in a specific manner to an exact diameter. A special tool is required. Don't attempt to install them yourself until you've had expert instruction. Too much pressure will cause the cable to break and too little pressure will allow it to slip. Also, if the ends of the NICO are pressed, the cable will break under vibration and use. The swage tool must be centered on the NICO. If you have cables with the ends the NICOs pressed, replace them for they will eventually fray. This fraying is hard to detect since it occurs right at the NICO edge.

Vibration is the most harmful villian in powered ultralight flying. The engine vibrates the airframe continuously during powered flight. This vibration can cause nuts to loosen, pins to work out and holes to elongate. The nut pictured in figure 53 is a Nylock nut. This means it has a plastic insert that prevents it from loosening. However, if you remove this nut and replace it several times, the plastic will wear and the nut will no longer lock securely.

Some bolts have holes in them for pins or safety wire. In this case, non-locking nuts may be used. However, if a Nylock nut is used on these bolts, the hole may cut the plastic and again render it useless. The necessary precaution is to be sure to use locking nuts where possible and safety wire on all other fasteners.

The bolts used in aircraft construction are called AN bolts. They are made from extremely hard and tough steel/nickle/chromium/molybdenum alloy with a specific heat treatment. They are cadmium plated and chromate treated to prevent corrosion. When removing bolts, be sure to turn only the nut, not the bolt itself or you will wear the plating off the bolt. AN bolts have a tensile stength of at least 125,000 pounds per square inch.

The most common AN bolts used in ultralights have shanks of 3/16, 1/4 and 5/16 inches. These are identified as AN3, AN4 and AN5 bolts respectively. The number in the designation refers to the diameter in 16ths of an inch. Another number follows this designation (as in AN4-15) which indicates the length of the bolt (unfortunately, it is not a simple relationship as with the diameter). The letter A following the last number means the shank is *not* drilled to accept a pin.

Never replace any bolt on your craft unless it is with an equivalent AN bolt. You can purchase these bolts at larger airports, not hardware stores. Hardware bolts aren't intended to hold a life suspended at several thousand feet. AN bolts are identified by a cross or an asterisk on the head. Grade 8 bolts, identified with six radial marks on the head, are actually stronger than AN bolts and may be used in their stead. (Note: do not replace Grade 8 bolts with AN bolts for the particular application may require the stronger Grade 8 bolt.)

Besides inspecting for vibration wear, you must check for damage incurred in transportation or flying mishaps. Be especially on the lookout for damage to tubes and the undercarriage. The wheels should be maintained in good shape and greased if so required. In passing, we may mention the desirability of covering the sides of your wheels. This will reduce drag and may even look snappy if you color coordinate the covering with your wing. Be sure to leave a port for air and access to the hub, if necessary.

The control surfaces, control lines and handles are most critical in an ultralight. If unseen damage occurs to the control assembly, you may find yourself in the airstream without a rudder. Keep the control surfaces from flopping in wind by tying them to the wing (don't forget to free them before flying). Keep the cables clean and working freely. A bit of light oil on rotating shafts and bearings will keep things working smoothly.

The care of your aircraft's structure should give you the least amount of trouble. However, just because it doesn't squeal for attention doesn't mean you can neglect it. Most manufacturers have a regular schedule for replacing certain airframe components. This is to insure against the deteriorations due to vibration.

Another problem you should be aware of is corrosion, especially if you live near salt water. Inspect tubes carefully for white particles, a sure sign of aluminum corrosion. Places where tubes have been bent will show fine cracking in the anodizing (called crazing) which allows moisture to get to the metal and promotes corrosion. Needless to say, you should replace any tube showing signs of corrosion as they may be greatly weakened by the metal eating action of corrosion.

Bent or dented tubes should also be replaced. Straightening a tube bent more than a few degrees not only cracks the anodizing, but work hardens the tube which makes it more brittle and thus, more apt to snap. Never heat a tube to straighten it for you will ruin its temper and weaken it.

Dents in tubes concentrate stresses as well as greatly weaken compressive and bending stength. The best thing to do with a dented tube is subject it to the water test: drop it in water—if it floats use it again; if it sinks throw it away. Be sure to remove the endcaps before you conduct the test.

A wise pilot will learn as much about his or her ultralight's airframe as soon as possible so that any changes can be detected. A sound structure is the basis for safe operation.

THE ENGINES

An engine suitable for powered ultralight flying must be reliable and reasonably lightweight. The most common engines used are two-cycle snowmobile or motorcycle gasoline engines. The two-cycle engine has a better weight-to-horsepower ratio than a four-cycle engine in sizes of 250cc or less. In addition, the two-cycle is simple in design and easy to work on. There are no valves, camshafts, etc.

The drawbacks of a two-cycle engine are its noisy operation and the requirement of mixing oil with the fuel (a two-cycle is lubricated only by the fuel in the cylinder). But, the availability of two-cycles and their good properties outweigh the drawbacks to the extent that they will probably always be popular for powering ultralights.

The Rotax Engine

In the early days of the sport, powered ultralights were required to foot launch. This meant that power systems had to be light. Little 10 to 15 horsepower engines with no reduction units were the norm. Now, ultralights with landing gear and a 254 pound limit sport engines of 40 horsepower or more with full instrumentation and reduction systems. These engine systems may weigh 60 pounds (27 kg) or more and produce anywhere from 100 to 250 pounds of thrust. The climb rates with such abundance of power is impressive.

Despite all these advances, we still must spend some time and effort taking care of our engines. They are fickle and should be treated like a spoiled child. The more experience we gain, the better we can handle their idiosyncracies.

At this point we should mention icing (ice build-up on aircraft parts). Icing is not as severe a problem with ultralights as it is with conventional airplanes since we don't usually fly in adverse conditions. Ice build-up can deteriorate engine and flying surface performance. Carburetor icing is the only factor we need to consider unless we are foolish enough to fly in a sleet storm. Carburetor icing occurs when the air is cool and damp so that the lower pressures in the carburetor cause ice to form in the carburetor throat. As this ice builds up, it chokes off the air, stalling the engine, or making it run roughly.

Carburetor icing occurs most often in the East (where the air contains more moisture) in temperatures between 40 and 60 degrees farenheit (4.4 °C to 15 °C) although icing may occur from 20 °F to 90 °F (-6.6 °C to 32 °C). The minimum humidity generally necessary for icing to occur is 50% with the hazard increasing with humidity. Icing most often shows up when an engine is cold started. It may run for a bit then die. Once it is heated, the carburetor warms and prevents ice build-up. To prevent icing problems, let your engine run until all parts are warm before attempting to take off on a humid day. Also make all increases of throttle somewhat gradual to avoid sudden drops in carburetor pressure and thus large temperature drops.

ENGINE MOUNTING

If you have purchased an engine separately from the aircraft, you face the problem of mounting it in the proper manner. The amount of caution required when mounting an engine on an ultralight cannot be stressed enough. As mentioned in Chapter IV, the position of the thrust line of a powerplant can have a great effect on the pitch stability of your craft. Performance too is greatly dependent on thrust line angle.

For this reason, you must obtain expert help when mounting your engine. Consult the manufacturer of your ultralight. It is desirable to have the thrust line pass a little above the center of mass, which usually means mounting the engine as low as possible on most designs. In addition, the thrust line should be angled so as to be directed at the flight path when flying at best climb rate angle of attack.

The engine mounting system must consist of rubber shock absorbers to minimize stress and vibration on the airframe. When a two-cycle is dieseling it tends to shake the aircraft like a monkey in a cage. Don't compromise on the mounting platform and shocks—there are several good designs on the market—get one. Of course, all bolts and fasteners on the mount and engine as well must be safety wired or secured with lock nuts to prevent them from working free.

FUEL SYSTEMS

There is only one ideal fuel for powered ultralights—sunshine. However, most of us can't afford solar cells and exotic batteries, so we must rely on fossil fuel, namely gasoline. Alcohol (methanol and ethanol) can be used in place of gasoline with a minor carburetor modification. All the following statements about gasoline apply to alcohol fuels as well.

Placing fuel tanks on an ultralight requires some thought. They must be far enough away from the engine to prevent the possibility of dripping fuel igniting on the hot manifold. In addition, fuel tanks should be located near the center of gravity of the craft so that the balance is not greatly affected as the fuel is used up. Gasoline weighs about six pounds per gallon (.72 kg/1), so a fuel load of one or more gallons can cause a trim problem if the fuel tank is mislocated.

A Unique One Bladed Propeller and Reduction System

The only suitable material to use for fuel tanks is clear plastic. This allows a visual check on the fuel level and reduces the danger from a flying fuel tank in the event of a nose-in. The fuel line opening should be placed a small distance above the bottom of the tank so that water is not drawn into the engine. Water is heavier than gasoline and oil (remember, a gallon of water weights eight pounds), and will accumulate at the bottom of the tank. A drain at the very bottom, or a removeable tank is necessary to rid the tank of collected moisture. Remember the 5 gallon limit in the US. This does not include fuel lines and carbuator bowl.

The right fuel mixture is most important for long life and reliability of the engine. Proper oil mixture must be used to assure good lubrication. Improper lubrication leads to excessive wear and thermal runaway (everything heats up and the engine seizes). The richest oil mixture useable is 20 parts gasoline to one part oil. This 20 to 1 mixture is only used for break-in and would tend to foul plugs if used extensively. The leanest mixture is 100 to 1 for synthetic oil. At this limit the risk of overheating is great. The mixture recommended is about 40 to 1. This is easily produced by mixing 1 quart of oil in 5 gallons of gas (4 quarts make a gallon).

The best fuel to use is aviation gas (avgas) due to its high octane rating. However, most pilots use regular (leaded) gasoline from the local station. This seems to work quite well. When you add oil to your gas, be sure to mix it well by shaking and rocking the can for a spell (one chorus of "off we go into the wild blue yonder" is a good timer).

If your fuel has been standing for days, be sure to remix it for some separation of the oil and gas may occur. This situation will announce itself by the sudden silence of a seized engine. Again, a 5 gallon can is the best storage/mixing container.

The best oil to use is two-cycle motorcycle or snowmobile oil. Take great care in selecting your oil for they vary in quality. The engine manual should be used as a guideline here. Synthetic oils are great lubricants and reduce the chance of plug fouling. However, exercize great care not to use synthetic oils with mineral oils for the two are incompatible. The result will be that same old story: seizure. Also, never use more synthetic oil than called for in a mixture. Too much synthetic oil in a mixture will create problems as well as too little regular oil.

DON'T use outboard motor oil (for boating) as these engines are water cooled and don't require as much from their oil. CAUTION: synthetic oil must not be used for breaking in. Use regular oil in a rich mixture. Consult the owner's manual for proper break-in procedures. Remember, bad gas and oil will result in black deposits on the spark plug and cylinder walls.

When refueling the engine, be sure to keep any open flames (cigarettes, matches, etc.) well away from your operation. It would hurt to see your beautiful ship go up in smoke. Wipe up any fuel spilled on the aircraft immediately. Follow the manufacturer's guidelines and solicit the opinion of your dealer concerning the use of fuel and the fuel system in general.

CARE OF THE ENGINE

A human body gets tired after a long period of exercise. On the other hand, an engine never gets tired but does wear out. For this reason, we have to periodically check the engine. The most common points of wear are the piston rings and cylinder wall. The rings may need replacement after about 20-30 hours of use, although this may be extended to 100 hours with synthetic oils. Use the manfacture's guidelines here.

The piston may need replacement after 50 hours. Replacement kits are available for these jobs and the work is not too difficult. Indications of the need to replace a piston are a scored piston skirt, sloppy wrist pin attachment or carbon build-up (especially in the ring grooves) that cannot be removed.

You can check the cylinder wall for wear with your fingers. A ridge forms at the top of the piston stroke as shown in figure 54. The maximum wear that can be tolerated here is .003 inches. Check this with a gauge and have the cylinder wall reamed out if it is too worn. See your motorcycle dealer for this.

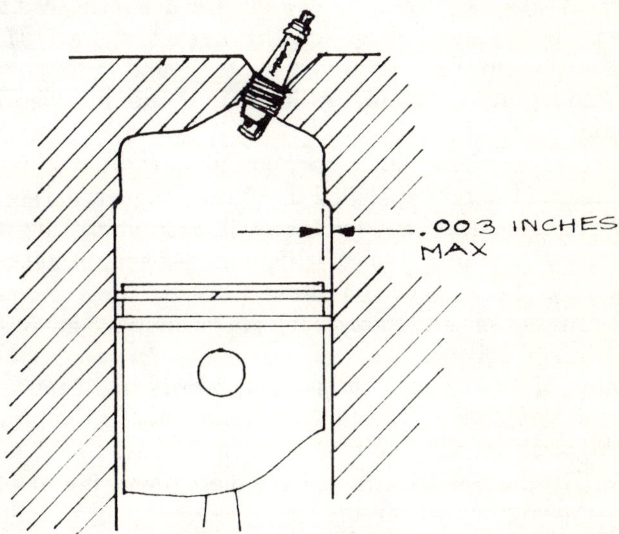

Figure 54 · Cylinder Wear

Spark plugs should also be changed often. Many engine problems can be traced to fouled, improperly gapped or a mismatched plug. Be sure to follow the manufacturer's recommendation on plugs (the owner's manual should provide a code number). The wrong size or heat range plug can damage the piston or seize the engine. Generally a cooler plug should be used in the summer and with a more advanced ignition timing. A cooler plug has more center probe electrical insulation which dissipates heat more readily.

You can tell much about how your engine is running by inspecting the spark plugs. The plugs should appear to be a dry brown or tan color. If they are black or fouled, you are running too rich. As we shall see these problems are taken care of by carburetor adjustment. One point to remember, is that while you can clean spark plug probes (be sure to check the gap when you're done), once the insulation is fouled they should be replaced. Material buildup on the insulation will cause a loss of spark intensity. Plugs are cheap—when in doubt, throw them out.

The bearings in an engine will sometimes wear out due to improper lubrication. If the engine is connected to a direct drive, the bearing receives an end load that it was not designed to take. You can check for wear by wobbling the crankshaft. If there is any play at all, you need a new bearing. Also, the bearing seals can leak if metal particles wear the bearing. Again a replacement is in order. Any leakage in the engine block should be attended to immediately as air can enter at this point and lean the mixture, causing seizure. A sign of leakage is black deposits near a seam or joint in the engine block. These may be at the seals, at the place where the cylinders and heads meet as well as the carburetor and flywheel cover seams. The usual cause of this leaking is an improperly installed or leaking gasket or seal. If your engine displays this problem, get out your tools and trusty owner's manual and produce a fix. Damage will occur if this problem is allowed to continue.

When reassembling an engine, you must tighten all bolts according to the manufacturer's specified torque and sequence. Don't neglect this very important point or your work will be in vain. Talk to other pilots and dealers who use your specific engine for information concerning problems or tricks they may have learned. The experience of others always saves time and money. Keep a clean machine by wiping with a good rag and solvent.

Timing of a two cycle engine is extremely important for maximum power and reliability. Timing consists of setting the proper point gap and the occurance of point opening in relation to the position of the piston. The more spark advance the more power (up to a limit) but the hotter the engine will run and the greater chance of failure.

Each engine has a specific procedure and timing, so the owner's manual must be consulted for the proper steps and settings. However, in general you will need a dial indicator (to measure piston position) and a timing light or voltmeter besides the disassembly tools and a feeler gauge. You usually gain access to the points through the flywheel cover. Then you remove a spark plug and install the dial indicator. Next, connect the timing light between the wire from the points and ground on the block.

Now you rotate the flywheel until you get the desired setting on your dial indicator. At this point the timing light should grow brighter indicating that the points have opened. It they do not open at the precise moment, an adjustment must be made. You must consult the owner's service manual for the correct settings and adjustment procedure. Timing can be a big factor in ease of starting as well as other factors mentioned above. Check your timing regularly for maximum reliability of the engine.

ENGINE ADDITIONS

Certain items are added to the engine block for normal operation. These include the carburetor, fuel pumps, muffler, engine gauges, and reduction drives. The carburetor is treated separately in the next section.

Fuel pumps are required in all but the simplest of installations. These usually work off the pulse of the piston by being connected to a nozzle off the crankcase. The pulses move a diaphram back and forth which operates the pump though a simple valve arrangement. In general, a pump should be used only to move fuel from the main tank to the carburetor. If a pump is connected to more than one tank it will suck air or overload. In the case an auxiliary tank is used, install a separate pump to pump the fuel from the auxiliary to the main tank. The fuel is then pumped from the main tank to the carburetor by the original fuel pump. If you fail to use this arrangement, pump failure may result (usually at the most inopportune time such as during takeoff). Do not connect two pumps to a Y in the line for a reasonance may set up that reduces the pump's output. Also, be sure that the pump itself as well as the lines leading from the block tap to the pump are above the tap hole. This will prevent oil from draining into the lines and blocking pumping action.

Mufflers are a very necessary part of ultralight operations. Not only do they make the noise tolerable but they can increase performance if tuned properly to help the fuel charge cycle properly. The best muffler probably comes with your engine system, but be aware that there are those sold by independant manufacturers that may be an improvement.

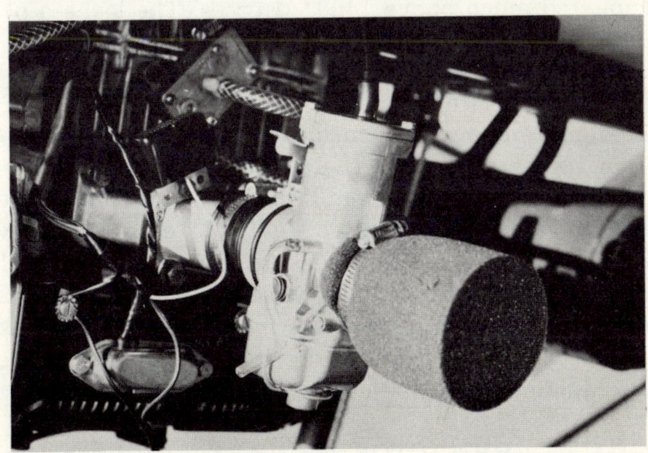

A Typical Ultralight Carburetor

Care should be taken when mounting a muffler. A crack in the exhaust system can allow air to be sucked in the cylinder, leaning the mixture and causing seizure. Both ends of the muffler should be carefully secured, usually with some sort of shock mounting. The muffler undergoes a good deal of vibration so it should be inspected carefully. Springs and muffler interiors have been known to shake loose and end up in the prop—a messy state of affairs. Flat black paint is a good muffler finish as it doesn't discolor as does chrome plating and it radiates heat well.

Engine instruments include tachometers, EGTs (exhaust gas temperture) and CHTs (cylinder head temperature). Tachometers are a nice item for telling how fast your engine is turning over, but not absolutely necessary for safe engine operation. An EGT or an CHT is recommended for tuning or general operation. By monitoring the temperature of your engine, you can shut down before a problem results in an expensive repair.

The opinions vary as to which is better, EGT or CHT. An EGT will tell you much sooner when an engine is overheating. An CHT may not show the temperature rise until too late. However, an EGT is very sensitive to installation position. You must follow the manufacturer's guidelines carefully or your readings will be way off. A CHT simply takes the place of the spark plug seal and is easy to install. Most engine experts recommend using both an EGT and CHT for proper control of temperature.

Here are the general guidelines for temperature ranges, although these may vary somewhat with engine design (again, consult your owner's manual). A safe CHT reading is about 350°F (197°C). Anything above 400° is risking disaster. A safe EGT reading is between 1150° and 1250°F (621° to 677°C). Under extremely hard running, this may increase to 1300 degrees, but remember, aluminum melts at not too much above 1400° degrees. The leaness of the fuel mixture as well as throttle setting (along with timing) is what determines the operating temperature. In the next section we'll look at finding the best mixture settings.

The last engine add-on we'll consider is a reduction system. A reduction system serves to reduce the RPM's of the engine to a more reasonable value for the propeller. Two to one is a common reduction figure (this means the engine drive shaft rotates twice for every one propeller rotation). Common reduction systems consist of belt drives or planetary gears. Great care must be taken to keep these systems in adjustment or lubricated as the case may be. Otherwise, expensive damage will occur. In the section on propellers we discuss the advantages of a reduction system.

TUNING THE CARBURETOR

The carburetor is an essential engine part that serves to mix air with fuel and deliver this mixture to the cylinders. When the piston moves up it creates a vacuum in the crankcase which draws air in through the carburetor. This rushing air picks up fuel metered by the carburetor so that the proper mixture results. Once the fuel is in the crankcase, it lubricates the bearings, crankshaft, connecting rods and wristpins. When the piston moves down, it pushes the mixture up out of the crankcase and into the space opened above the piston. This phase of two-cycle operation is shown in figure 55a. The piston returns, closing the intake and exhaust ports, drawing a new charge into the crankcase and compressing the fresh charge at the top of the cylinder. When the piston is all the way up in the cylinder, the plug fires and the fuel explodes, sending the piston back down and starting the process all over as shown in 55b.

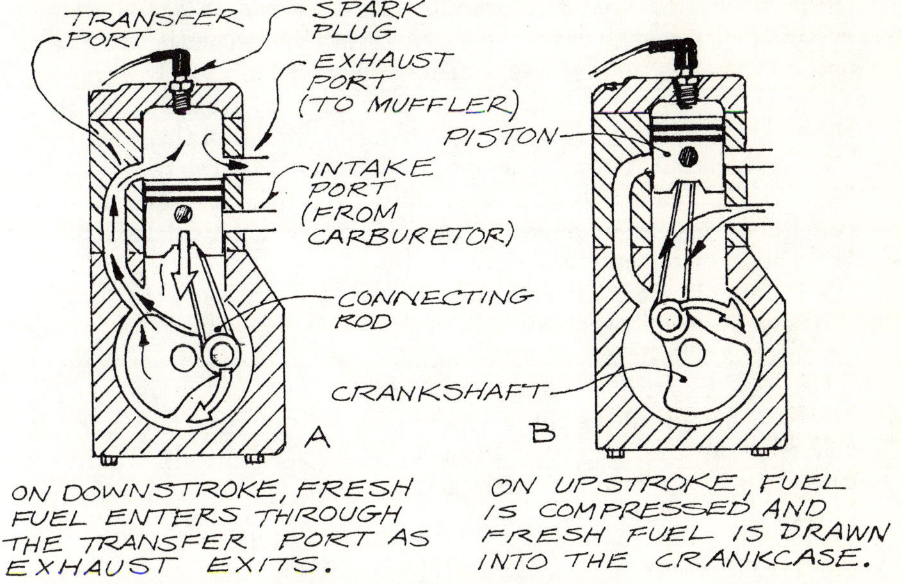

Figure 55 · Two-Cycle Engine

From the above discussion, it should be apparent that a carburetor should be carefully adjusted to provide the proper mixture in order for good lubrication and ignition to take place. If the mixture is too lean, not enough lubricant will be supplied and a hotter explosion will take place, both of which leads to thermal runaway and damage. If the mixture is too rich, the extra oil in the fuel will leave residues that foul the plug.

Now, with this background, let's see how we can control the proper mixture. At this point, it should be noted that carburetors vary just as engines do so we can only speak in general terms. Consult your dealer or manufacturer for the specifics regarding your particular carburetor. Another matter to note is that although a carburetor is a precision instrument, it is not too complex with relatively few moving parts. It behooves every pilot to learn how to dismantle, repair and readjust his or her carburetor, unless, of course, you have more money than time.

The air passes mainly through the throat of a carburetor. Due to the shape of the throat, a vacuum is set up around the fuel vents that causes the fuel to be sucked into the air. There are several circuits or passageways in the carburetor that we should examine.

The first is the enrichment or choke system. This consists of a valve that lets in an extra charge of fuel for cold starting. There's not much to adjust here, but we'll return to this later when we look at the overall picture.

The next circuit is the low-speed system. This controls the engine operation at idle and has a diminishing effect up to about ¼ throttle. The low speed pilot jet determines the amount of fuel available while the pilot air screw sets the amount of air. If this system is too lean (not enough fuel) the engine will show signs of stalling when the throttle is opened from idle. In this case, you may richen the mixture by screwing the pilot air screw in a little at a time. If the pilot system is too rich, the engine may load up or four-stroke (miss) at idle. In this case, turn the air screw out. If the air screw is ineffective in correcting the problem, you will have to replace the pilot jet. A larger jet makes the mixture richer, smaller jet makes it leaner. Pilot jets are available in sizes 15 to 80 in increments of 5.

The next circuit is the midrange system. It consists of the throttle slide and the needle system. The throttle slide takes effect from 1/8 to 1/2 throttle. This is merely a valve that opens or closes the carburetor throat (see figure 56). The angle of the cutaway can be varied. The greater the angle of the cutaway, the leaner the mixture (the more air delivered) at the midrange throttle settings. Generally, the slide cutaway will not need to be changed.

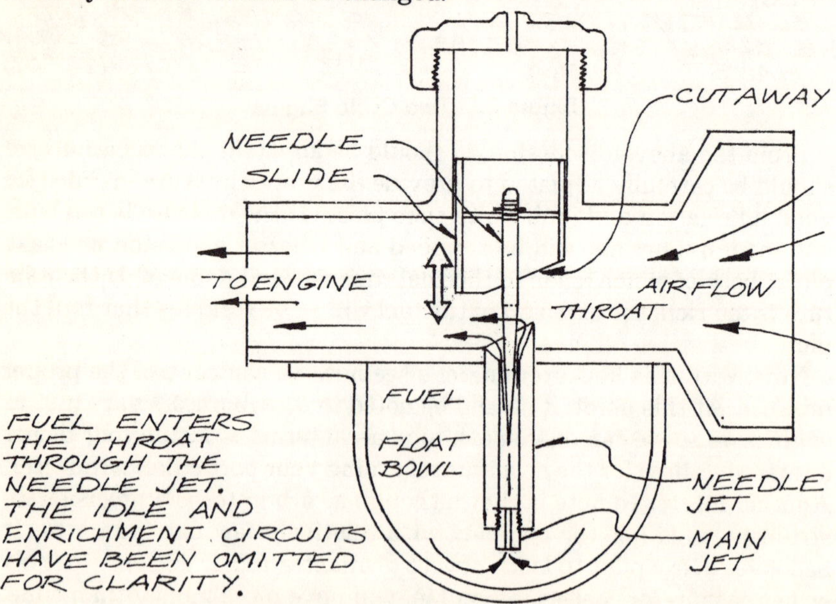

Figure 56 - Carburetor Operation

Most of the midrange adjustment takes place with the needle valve and the needle jet. The needle valve sits inside the needle jet and is drawn up as the throttle slide opens. The needle valve is tapered so that the fuel opening gets larger as the needle is raised. The needle jet takes effect from about 1/8 to 2/3 throttle while the needle valve effects the mixture from about 1/4 to 3/4 throttle.

If the mixture is too lean in these throttle settings, again the engine may stall or be unresponsive to opening the throttle. If it is too rich, it may bog down or miss.

To enrichen the mixture, you must raise the needle. This is accomplished by *lowering* the clip on the top of the needle. The clip holds the needle in the throttle slide. To lean the mixture, raise the clip (there are 5 clip positions on the top of the needle) to lower the needle, thus limiting fuel. If the needle adjustments do not produce the desired effect, use a larger (for richer) or smaller (for leaner) needle jet.

The last circuit we'll consider is the main jet. This is an orifice that lets a certain amount of fuel in when the throttle is from a little under ¾ to full open. A larger main jet enriches the mixture while a smaller main jet richens it. Bogging down or missing are again the signs of too rich or lean a mixture and thus improper jetting.

One system we should mention is the float system. This consists of floats that control a valve that allows fuel in from the tank when the carburetor bowl level is reduced. Do not make an adjustment to the float system—the springs are preset. However, a different float valve is required for a gravity feed (larger) than for a pump feed (smaller). Make sure your system is set up properly. With a proper valve, a slight trickle of fuel will come out the overflow lines on the carburetor at idle.

Now looking at the entire system, we should be able to run the throttle all the way up and down with no surges, misses or hesitations. If this occurs at any point, adjust the proper circuit. Here's a little trick: at each increment of throttle setting (say in 1/8th throttle steps) depress the choke lever. If the engine bogs down and dies or coughs then it is probably set right at that throttle position. If it surges with power before it bogs down, it is probably too lean. (You are adding a blast of fuel when you hit the choke). Remember, it is at higher throttle settings that the engine usually overheats, so take great care to adjust the mixture well from ½ to full throttle.

How about those instruments we recommended in the preceding section? This is where they really come in handy. Use an EGT and CHT when you make carburetor adjustments and you should have few problems. Remember, higher temperatures mean too lean of a mixture. Let the engine run at a given throttle setting until the temperature stabilizes or your readings will be inaccurate.

One more point we should mention is the effects of density altitude (see Chapter V). As the air gets thinner, the mixture gets richer (less air for the same amount of fuel). Thus, we may need to lean the mixtures if we move to a higher altitude or summer heat moves in. Use the test procedures outlined above (and in your owner's manual) to make the necessary adjustments.

Don't forget to keep an air cleaner (foam rubber works best) on your carburetor. Your engine doesn't like breathing dust any more than you do.

THE PROPELLER

Finding the perfect propeller for your ship almost always results in a compromise. The reason this is so is that a specific diameter propeller is required to match your horsepower, RPM and flying speed. Your body weight on your particular aircraft system is probably not duplicated exactly by anyone else. Consequently, the propeller you use will be a compromise unless you choose to carve your own.

A Typical Ultralight Propeller

The duty of a propeller is to push loads of air rearward, thereby thrusting the aircraft forward. The more air the prop moves with the least disturbance, the more efficient it is. What determines this efficiency? Let's look at figure 57. Here we see a schematic of a propeller drawn as if it were two airfoils rotating around an axis. A pro-

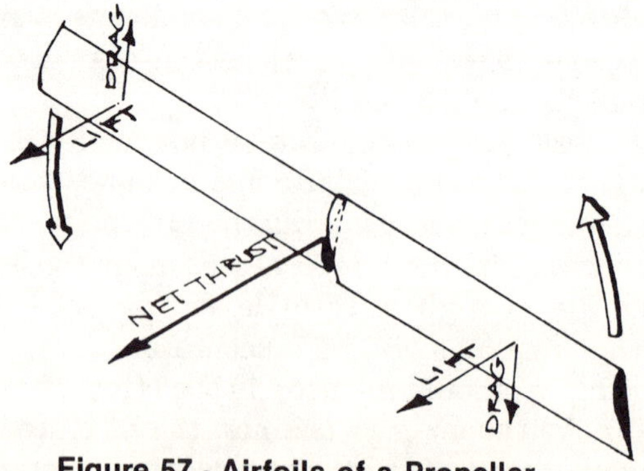

Figure 57 - Airfoils of a Propeller

peller is exactly this: two airfoils tilted to a given angle of attack or pitch. As the prop rotates, lift and drag is produced by the airfoils moving through the air, just like a flying wing. A propeller designer can vary the lift-to-drag ratio of a prop and change its performance by altering its dimensions, airfoil section or pitch.

A very real difference in a propeller and a flying wing is that the propeller rotates. Thus, the velocity through the air of different sections of the prop increases toward the tip. To prevent excessive loading on the tip, the angle of attack is reduced toward the tip. Also, the thickness is reduced considerably at the tip since stresses are greatest near the hub and thinner tips reduce nose. Figure 58 illustrates the varying pitch and thickness in a prop.

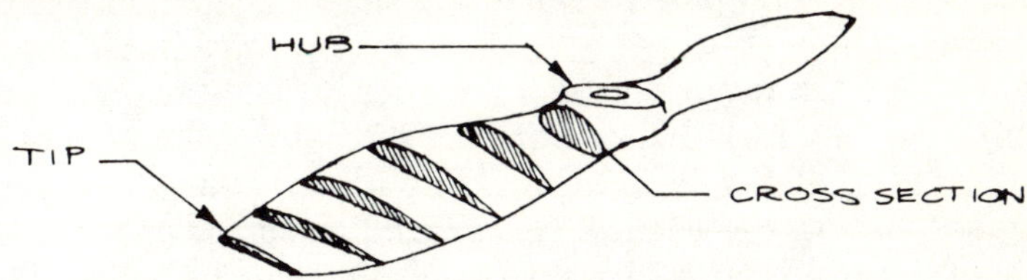

Figure 58 · Propeller Shaping

The principle stresses in a propeller are: (a) Bending due to the lift forces on each side. Figure 59 shows the lift distribution along one side of a prop. For most designs, we can consider the total lift to be centered at a point ¾ of the distance from the hub to the tip. In this case, each blade acts like a beam supported at the hub. (b) Centrifugal forces due to rotation. The high operating RPMs require a strong hub with proper hole placement to prevent the prop from pulling itself apart. (c) Twisting stresses due to the fact that the lift and drag forces at each section do not pass through the neutral axis. (d) Bending resulting from gyroscopic action when the aircraft is in curving flight.

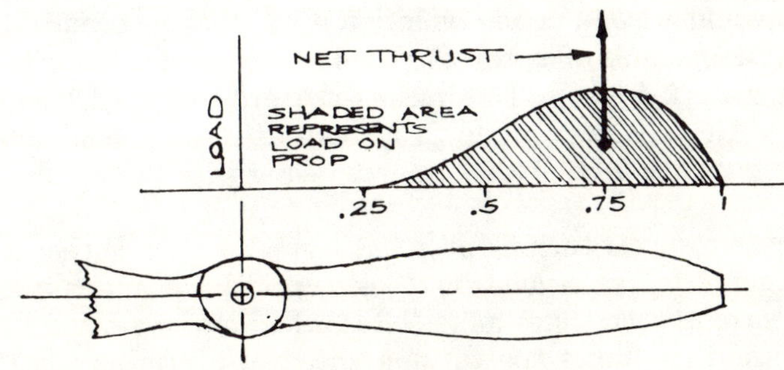

Figure 59 · Load Distribution

From foregoing, it is obvious that a propeller must be constructed to take forces of many types. Props are carved out of close grained birch, maple, mahogany, ash, sitka spruce and other suitable woods. Synthetic materials are also widely used although they tend to increase the price of the propeller. All wood props should be made from six or more laminated pieces glued together. This lamination increases strength and eliminates the possibility of hidden flaws in the wood. The finish should be glass smooth (to minimize drag) clear varnish. This finish allows inspection of the material and prevents moisture from swelling the prop.

Grass clippings, water spray and snow tend to be very hard on propellers, eroding the leading edges. Some pilots put fiberglass edges on their props or use the commercially available props with metal leading edges. Constant attention must be given to this matter in order to avoid weakening the prop and lessening performance.

Various designs of props are available besides the familiar two bladed egg beater. There are three or four bladed props, counter rotating props, variable pitch props and scimitar props. Scimitar props are so named because they look like a sword out of the Arabian Nights. The curve in the prop allows it to bend at high loads, thus changing its angle of pitch for more efficiency. Ask around about the advantages of these items in conjunction with your ultralight/engine set up before you invest needlessly.

The structural stresses on the propeller can be greatly reduced simply by slowing it down. This will also reduce the noise. A further benefit is an increase in efficiency. In general, the slower the aircraft, the slower turning and longer the propeller should be. The drawbacks of a large propeller are increased weight and more drag when the pilot tries to soar with the engine off. The limits to propeller size are usually dictated by the necessary ground or structural clearance, however, not the increased weight and drag.

A propeller is identified by its diameter and the pitch at a distance 75 percent out from the hub (this is where all the thrust can be located). The pitch is given in inches and is identified by how far forward the propeller would travel in one revolution if no slippage occurred, as in figure 60. An example of a propeller used for connecting directly to the engine is a 27 x 8 prop. This means the propeller is 27 inches in diameter with an 8 inch pitch. Propellers used with gear reduction drives are typically 36 to 54 inches in diameter with 10 or more inches of pitch.

The reason a slower turning prop has a greater pitch is that it must take a bigger "bite" per revolution to keep up with a given cruise speed. A faster turning prop takes more "bites" of a smaller size.

The factor that limits the turning speed of a prop is the tip approaching the speed of sound. Above a tip speed of 950 feet per second, cavitation and subsequent energy loss occurs at the tips. Slowing the prop down increases the overall efficiency and reduces the noise.

Most reduction drives consist of a belt or chain system from a small pulley or gear on the engine crankshaft to a larger one on the propeller

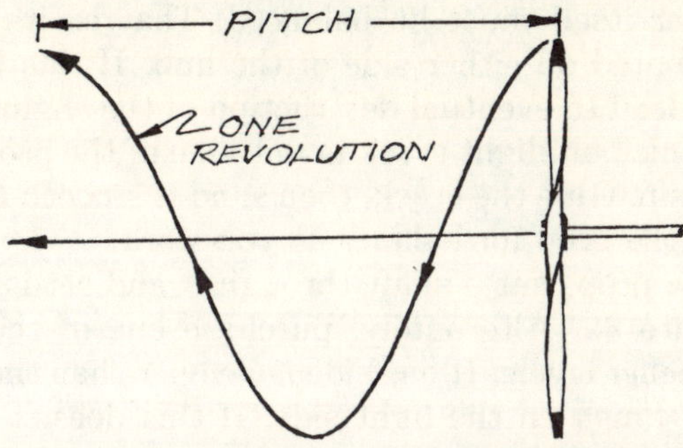

Figure 60 - Propeller Pitch Designation

shaft. Planetary gear systems are also quite popular. Thrust bearings are installed on the propeller shaft. This arrangement greatly relieves the chance of failure since small engines aren't designed to carry a load parallel to the crankshaft. One problem with the reduction drive is that jerky operation of the two-cycle engines at slow speed tends to destroy the drive belt or chain. Oil baths and special belts can help relieve this factor.

PROPELLER MOUNTING

One of the most critical matters concerning a power set up is mounting the propeller properly. A propeller must be almost perfectly aligned when mounted. This means that there should be 1/64 of an inch or less difference in the path of one tip from the other. This is shown in figure 61. To correct the alignment, adjust the bolts on one side as shown. Note the safety wires on the prop bolts.

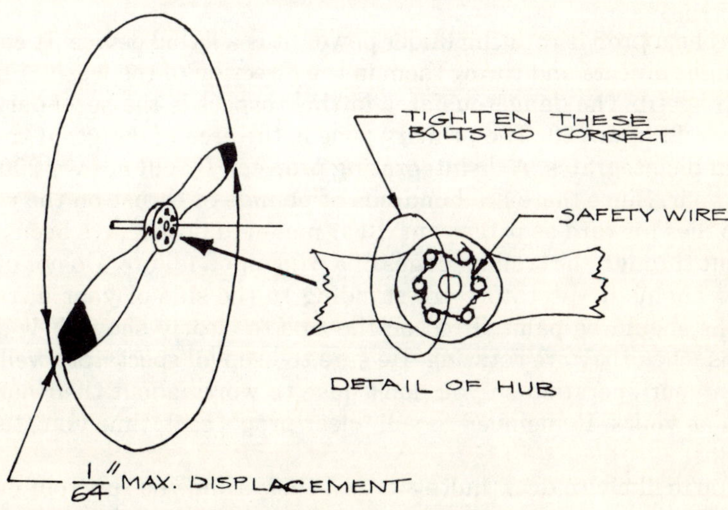

Figure 61 - Propeller Adjustment

The propeller itself must be balanced. That is, its mass must be equally distributed on either side of the hub. If this is not the case, vibration will lead to eventual destruction of the engine or prop itself. If you have a nick or slight crack in one side of the prop, fill it in with sawdust or resin. Glue the crack, then sand it smooth and refinish. Be sure to check the prop for balance as you work.

To balance a prop, put a shaft through it and set it on V blocks as shown in figure 62. Alternately, purchase one of the commercially available propeller levels. If one side is heavier than the other, spray a little paint or finish on the light side. If this doesn't suffice, sand a little wood from the heavy end. Remember to store your prop sideways so that sap doesn't run.

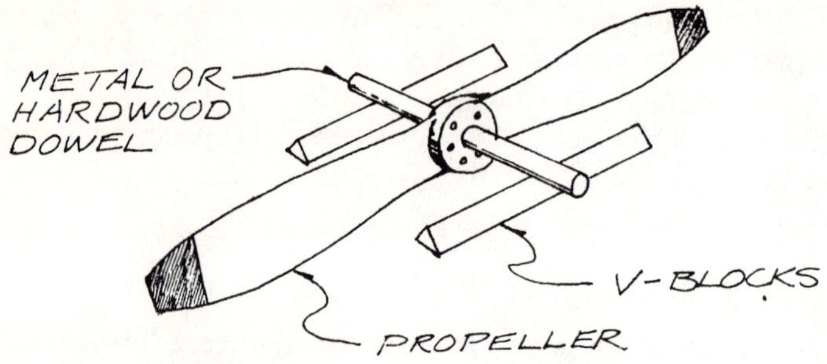

Figure 62 · Balancing A Propeller

While balancing a prop, it's a good idea to check the straightness of your drive shaft with a dial gauge. All that vibration could be due to a bent shaft, not an imbalanced propellor. Replace a drive shaft that is not true.

When a prop is rotating under power, it is a lethal device. It can pick up light objects and throw them in the direction of the wash at quite a high speed. The dangerous area in this respect is the secondary zone shown in figure 63. The primary zone is the area of danger if the prop itself disintegrates. A disintegrating prop can fly out at over 200 miles per hour. Since there are hundreds of pounds of thrust on the prop, it also flies forward as it flies out. Rear mounted props have been known to cut through the trailing edges of a wing upon failure. Do not operate your engine if spectators are standing to the side of your ultralight. Props should be painted red on the tips to clearly show their dimensions when they are rotating. Be sure to keep all spectators well away from your operation so you don't have to worry about their hands as well as yours. Remember to yell "clear prop" each time you start the engine.

You're likely to draw quite a crowd every time you run your engines up. Be sure to keep spectators well out of your danger zone. If necessary, shut your engines down and ask politely. They will eventually realize that you will not fly without their cooperation. They are there to take in the sight of a daredevil defying gravity. Little do they know that you are flying carefully with a well tested and inspected lightweight aircraft. Let the spectators sit on the ground while you reach for the beauty in the sky.

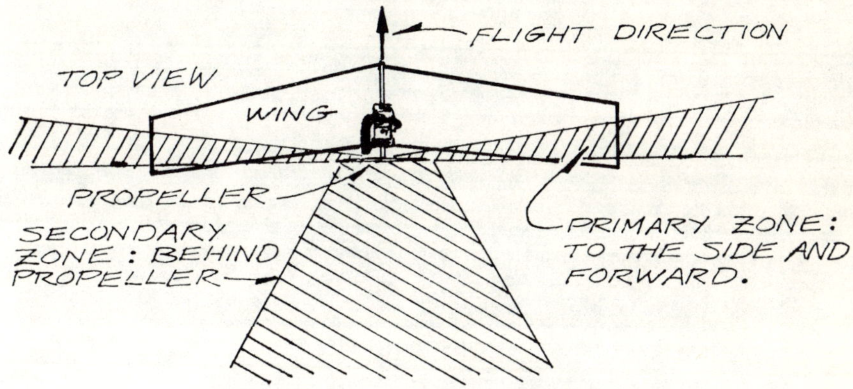

Figure 63 · Propeller Danger Zones

The BI-RD

The Australian Scout

CHAPTER VII

MORE ADVENTURES

Once you become experienced in the many aspects of normal flying in your little aircraft, you may look for new challenges. There are many aspects of ultralight flying left for you to explore. Certainly one of the appealing aspects of ultralights is that they are readily adaptable to each individual's personal style and taste. Not only the many different designs, but the ways of using them offer the ultralight pilot a wide variety of experiences.

In this chapter we discuss some of the directions an ultralight pilot may choose. Obviously, we cannot exhaust each subject nor can we predict all the possible developments that may yet appear. However, we can provide guidelines concerning what to look for in terms of safety and increasing your skill. In the interest of safety, we begin with a review of parachute care and deployment methods.

USING A PARACHUTE

The most important part of using a parachute is to wear it. That may sound obvious, but too many pilots forego the hassle of putting their chute on because they plan to just stay low, buzzing the airport. Ultralight parachutes have saved lives from as low as 70 feet, so don't neglect to wear yours. As implied in that last sentence, we believe all ultralight pilots should own a parachute. The sport is rendered much safer by a good back-up chute.

Ultralight parachutes are basically of two types: hand deployed and ballistically deployed. The former derived from hang gliding parachutes and are cheaper, lighter, less drag producing but slower to deploy than the latter. Prices and other information are given in Chapter I.

Parachutes are constructed mainly of 1.1 oz. ripstop Nylon (some are a lighter material). Nylon shroud lines may go over the canopy or be sewn to the canopy at the bottom (skirt). Nylon tape may be sewn around the circumference at the bottom and other positions to stop a tear from reaching all the way up the canopy. V-tabs are often sewn to the shroud lines at the skirt for added strength. The shroud lines come together about 25 feet below the canopy and attach to a bridle made of Kevlar or steel cable. The general appearance of an ultralight parachute is shown in figure 64.

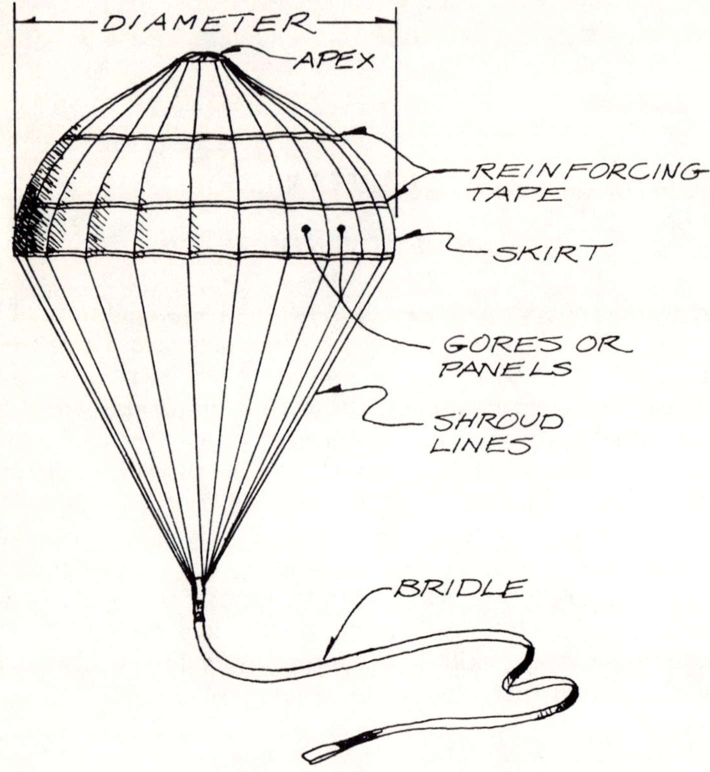

Figure 64 · Parachute Construction

Design factors to consider are the size and shape of the parachute. The canopy size is given according to the diameter when inflated. The larger the inflated diameter, the slower the chute descends or the more weight it can settle at a safe speed. Heavier pilot/aircraft combinations should use a larger chute. Typical sizes are 26 and 28 feet.

Most parachutes are designed to be conical by cutting the gores or panels at various angles along their length. This practice adds stability to the chute. Other designs employ a pulled apex. This consists of a line that pulls down the center of the parachute causing the skirt to flare out. The result is a larger diameter canopy for less material — an asset when trying to save weight. The only problem with "pulled apex" parachute is they tend to open with more of a shock than regular parachutes. Back-up parachutes usually don't have cut outs for stability and control as do sport jumping chutes, because such openings reduce, reliability.

To care for a parachute, keep it dry and out of direct sunlight. Store it in a cool, dry place and never sit or put a heavy weight on it as this will reduce reliability. If your parachute gets wet, air it out to dry thoroughly (float plane operators should be well aware of the damaging effects of water in a parachute). Do not dry it in the sun as ultraviolet rays will deteriorate Nylon rapidly.

Most manufacturers recommend repacking every six months. This airs the chute and keeps the folded material from sticking together. Many large cities have parachute centers that will do this, or you can mail it back to the manufacturer. Unfortunately, many pilots neglect getting their chutes repacked because of the inconvenience. Therefore we believe that a pilot should learn to repack his or her own chute. An experienced parachute rigger can show you the steps and let you practice a few times until he's sure you know what you are doing. Remember, the repacking of an emergency chute is very critical and don't begin to attempt it unless you are well trained.

The parachute exterior should be inspected periodically. During your preflight is a good time. Make sure the Velcro on the pack is secured and the bridle line is well attached and unabraded. The bridle line should be hooked to a secure point on the ultralight (usually the keel) so that both the aircraft and the pilot are lowered to the ground safely. The attachment point should be on top of the aircraft so a steep pitch attitude does not occur after deployment. Tape or Velcro will hold a bridle line in place and rip out if deployment occurs. Route the bridle line from the parachute, up a cable and back to the attachment point.

Ballistic chutes should be repacked by the manufacturer. The charge must be replaced periodically and the whole system should be checked during preflight. Be sure to route the contact switch within easy reach while in flying position.

The use of a parachute in the event of a mishap requires a cool head. In most cases, it is important to act instantly. This usually means deploy the chute without hesitating when low. Looking around to see what happened may put you too low for a successful deployment. When in doubt, "whip it out" is the oft quoted guideline. If you have plenty of altitude you may check out the problem, but many incidences that didn't appear to be too bad were unsafe as the pilot descended to lower level turbulence. If you are going to err, err on the side of safety.

The general procedures for hand-deployment are as follows:

1. Kill the engine. This will prevent damage to the bridle.

2. Look at the parachute handle and grab it firmly. You cannot grab accurately without looking. This is especially true when flying with gloves.

3. Look for the clearest opening. In some cases you may have to pull debris out of the way to get a clear enough space.

4. Pull the parachute out of the bag and fling it through the clear area into the blue as hard as possible. The movement should be one smooth, continuous action. Don't sacrifice accuracy for stength of

throw. If your damaged craft is spinning, throw in the direction of the spin to prevent the chute from wrapping up as it opens.

5. If the chute fails to open, pull on the bridle. Jerk it or pull the chute back in and rethrow it if it still doesn't open.

6. Once the chute is opened, try leveling the wings as much as possible by leaning (weight shift helps here). Your aerodynamic controls will not do much good in controlling the ship's attitude . As you prepare to land, try to position the landing gear or other part of the airframe between you and the ground. Also, move any broken spar away from your area to prevent injury during landing. As soon as you land, unhook and get out of the craft so the wind doesn't pull you into power lines or other nasty ground objects. Needless to say, a good safety belt system is absolutely necessary for the success of any parachute deployment.

For ballistic chutes, about all you need to do is press the deployment button. Because of this simiplicity, ballistic chutes are much faster operating, so more reliable at low altitudes.

CANARDS

A canard aircraft is one with the little wing (tail in conventional designs) up front (see figure 52). This seemingly odd arrangement was the reason for the application of the name "canard" which means duck in French. In truth, canards do not operate much differently than a tailed aircraft. The reason it is included here is to reassure pilots of conventional craft that these designs are very much a viable part of the ultralight experience.

The Ptiger Equipped With A Canard

One of the best assets of the canard design is its very low susceptibility to stalling. The reason for this is that the designer sets the angle of attack of the canard higher than the main wing so that if the pilot raises the nose too high the canard stalls then drops, lowering the angle of attack of the main wing before it reaches stall point. Thus, control is retained around the stall point and the aircraft mushes merrily along. It is this feature that makes the slower canard designs ideal teaching vehicles.

The use of a canard on an ultralight can provide a good horizon reference — something many conventional pilots miss when they start to fly ultralights. A canard set up can be very efficient as well since both wings contribute to the lifting whereas only the main wing does in a tailed design. Takeoffs in a canard are quite easy since the canard lifts once flying speed is achieved and automatically rotates the main wing for liftoff. In turns, the canard tends to pull the nose around once a bank is established, so little or no pitch up pressure is required. The results of an uncoordinated turn are usually not as severe in a canard design since they are resistant to spins. Of course, you can stall the main wing in a canard ship with a radical enough pull up, but this type of flying is dangerous in any type of ultralight. Treat a canard as you would a conventional design and you'll have years of fun.

TRIKE SYSTEMS

A trike system connects to a hang glider and turns it into a powered ultralight. The advantages of these systems are portability (both the hang glider and trike system fold down into a small package) and simplicity of operation. Also, with certain trike designs, the low weight and drag render them very capable of soaring since a hang glider is a very efficient thermal flying craft.

The main disadvantage of trikes is that pilots may be unfamiliar with weight shift control. The problem is that the control directions are backwards. For example, conventional nose up control consists of pulling the stick back while on a trike system you push the control bar forward to raise the nose. Weight shift control can be very effective however. A modern hang glider can handle turbulence much easier and safer than most powered ultralights because their response is quicker.

Mounting A Hang Glider On A Trike

Also, not much can go wrong with weight shift control.

Because of the necessity of keeping the glider's weight forward on the ground for proper balance, the main support tube on the trike must be angled forward. Thus, when the craft lifts off, the pilot, gear and engine swing under the wing putting the pilot's feet high in what originally appears to be an unusual position. This requires some getting used to, but doesn't feel uncomfortable after a few hours of air-time.

In addition, the engine is in pendulum along with the pilot so changes in power change the position of the pilot with respect to the control bar. Besides these two items and the difference of controls, most of the ideas and techniques in this book that apply to regular ultralights also apply to trikes.

Learning to fly a trike can be an interesting experience. Although some pilots have learned to fly exclusively on trikes, we recommend learning to fly on a hang glider and a regular powered ultralight first. The reason for this is that it is very difficult to raise a trike system gently off the ground. Once the wing starts to lift, the undercarriage swings under the wing, the thrust points upward and a climb ensues. The pilot finds himself sudddenly in the air with the necessity for producing the proper controls. With the background indicated above, this is not problem, but it's asking a lot of a beginner to handle all the inputs and come up with the correct output.

Trike Take Off Position

Takeoffs on a trike are fairly straightforward. You simply aim into the wind, lean forward to hold the control bar full out to set the proper angle of attack, then apply full power. The aircraft lifts automatically and fairly leaps into the air. As soon as rotation occurs, you should bring the control bars back to normal flying position (this varies with the set up).

Once in the air, turn control consists of moving the bar to the side (to the right for a left turn) which tilts the wing and initiates the turn. As the wing begins to bank, a certain amount of push out is required to prevent a slip. Once the desired bank angle is established, center the bar while holding the push out. Remember, a steady airspeed is the key to a coordinated turn. Leveling out merely consists of a control movement to the opposite side, then a return to neutral.

Take Off Sequence Of A Trike

Landing requires a special technique. Since the pilot is suspended in pendulum, if he pushes back hard as in a flare, the undercarriage will move back as the glider's nose lifts. This may be confusing and drop the nose wheel to the ground first. For this reason, it is best to fly the ultralight on the runway with ample control speed and a minimum amount of flare. A little practice renders a picture perfect landing.

There are several other matters to consider when flying trikes. When taxiing crosswind, keep the upwind wing low or it will lift and slam the low wing to the ground or against the trike frame. Beware of damage from this quarter. Also, because of the nature of the flexible hookup (usually a universal joint) between the trike and the hang glider, some yawing may occur in flight. The pilot can easily dampen this out by holding the control bar firmly so it isn't too much problem. Be sure to inspect the main juncture carefully, because everything hangs on its integrity.

Finally, we should say a word about the safety of a flexible flying wing. The hang gliders used on a trike system should be certified for strength, stability and control by the Hang Gliding Manufacturer's Assn. (HGMA) in the U.S. They should display a sticker indicating this. As such, these gliders are stronger than the average ultralight, very controllable and just as stable with the trike application. The wing tips on a hang glider are swept back and washed out to act like a tail with negative incidence as on conventional craft. Defined tips and reflex bridles also add to the positive pitch stability of a modern hang glider.

The stability of a flying wing or any aircraft depends on center of gravity location. This is usually a little in front of the normal hang point used when flying without the engine due to the extra weight. Be sure to consult the manufacturer of a particular design to find the exact location for the trike attachment point. Trikes are fun and are a great alternative for the pilot without a hangar available or with the desire to soar.

FLOAT FLYING

Flying off of water is a unique experience in itself. By adding floats to your ultralight you open up many potential flying sites — namely the lakes and rivers that dot our countryside. Imagine taking a trip down the Mississippi or across Lake Michigan on your ultralight.

Before you can embark on such an adventure, some precautions and much learning must take place. Flying with floats is not extremely difficult, but it is more complicated then flying from land. First, you must be aware of the local waterway rules and obey them just as you must obey the airway rules. Check with the Seaplane Pilots Association to find out the federal, state or local laws which apply to the area of water you intend to fly. Their number is 301-695-2083.

Next, you should have some form of pilot flotation and a method of detatching yourself from the aircraft (how are you going to unhook that parachute?) in case you overturn. Some experienced pilots caution that when flying ultralights from floats you should always expect to capsize.

The floats themselves usually consist of a fiberglass (or other composite material) shell with individual compartments (see figure 65). The bulkheads add strength and keep the float floating if a puncture occurs. Other components of a float are shown in the figure. Spray strips may be added along the upper chine to reduce spray on the propellor. More on that later.

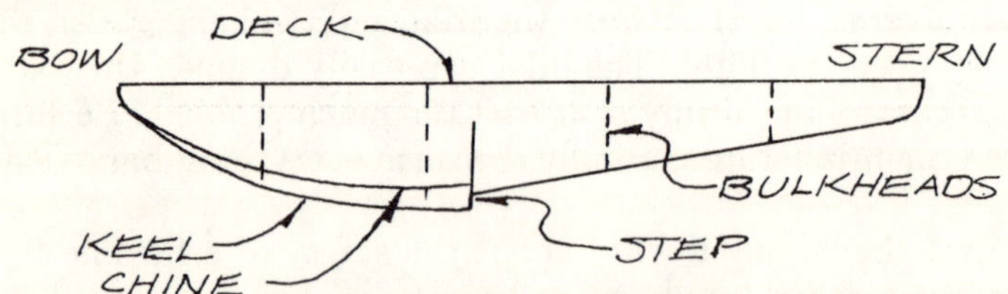

Figure 65 · Float Construction

The step on the bottom of a float is critical. Without this step, the water would create suction on the bottom of the float so that the aircraft couldn't rise. The step causes cavitation of the flow and allows the rear portion to lift off.

Installation of floats on an ultralight deserves some consideration. Floats must be located so that the center of bouyancy of the float is a little in front of or under the center of gravity. If this is not the case, the craft may tilt at the wrong angle when at rest and experience the wrong forces during takeoff and landing. Fortunately, the manufacturers have worked these problems out and have fixed mounting systems for most ultralights.

The problem of operating ultralights from water is that the surface drags much more than with wheels on land. Also, the current in the water must be taken under consideration along with the wind. Finally, since the floats can tip fore-and-aft as well as side-to-side, the center of bouyancy changes, creating different drag forces and balance.

Before we start flying, we must include our floats in the preflight. Look for cracks in the hulls. A crack can allow the float to ship water or cause excessive drag, producing an uncontrollable turn. Be careful of hard landings. Any float can be damaged if bounced hard enough on water or ground. Preflight the attachment pins and make sure they are safetied.

One of the aspects of float flying requiring the most care is getting ready. When launching the ultralight, do it nose first or the rear may sink and capsize since the floats are most bouyant up front. Likewise, when climbing into the ultralight, do not step on the rear of the floats or they may sink. Step on the front and have an assistant steady the craft. You must be very nimble to avoid tipping the ultralight too much, especially in a current.

Taxiing and maneuvering in floats can be challenges in themselves. The ultralight will always drift with the wind and the current as well as with the power applied. A pilot must learn to "sail" the ultralight as well as power it around. With power off, the ultralight will weather-cock into the wind if it has a vertical tail, and drift backwards. You can learn to control this drift with your rudder to alter your course as with a sailboat. If your ultralight has spoilers they can be raised to enhance the sailing effect.

A slow taxi consists of remaining on the entire float and moving slowly through the water. At these speeds you have to consider drift. At higher speeds you should apply nose up control to lift the front of the floats to overcome drag. This action also reduces the spray. A prop will erode very quickly when subjected to water spray. The midrange taxiing speed is called the "hump" or "plowing" since this is where the water drag is the highest.

Once you've reached top speed on the hump, apply more power and lower the nose slightly to free the rear of the float and ride on the forward position. This is called getting up on the step and can be used for fast taxiing.

The three taxiing positions are shown in figure 66. Use only the slow and fast taxi positions for any length of time to minimize prop damage from spray. With experience you can learn to tell your water speed and position by observing the pattern of the spray. The sooner you learn this, the better.

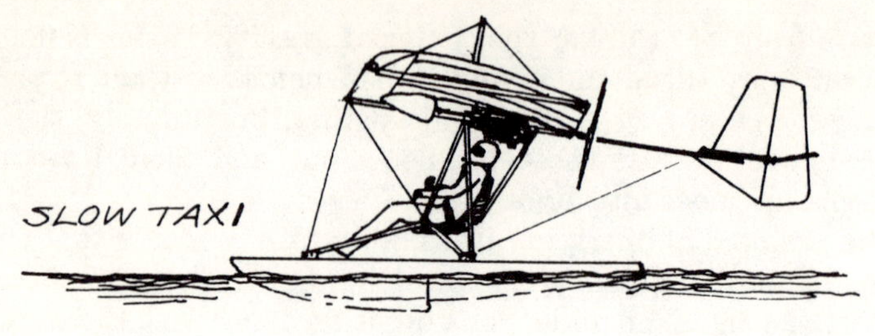

Figure 66 · Taxiing on Floats

Turning while taxiing on floats has its own problems, especially in wind. Centrifugal force combined with the wind makes things interesting. Because the floats are bouyant, the outside float in a turn will be loaded more and possibly dig in. The worse case is when turning from downwind to upwind. In this situation, the wind and centrifugal force may act together to capsize the craft. Downwind turns are much simpler as shown in figure 67.

A strong wind can present similar problems when taxiing straight across the wind. You can try applying up aileron on the upwind wing, just as on land, or take a zig-zag tack to head more into the wind and downwind, watching the upwind turns. It may be necessary to power back and let the craft weathercock into the wind to perform an upwind turn without tipping. Then, add power when the wind drifts you in the proper direction.

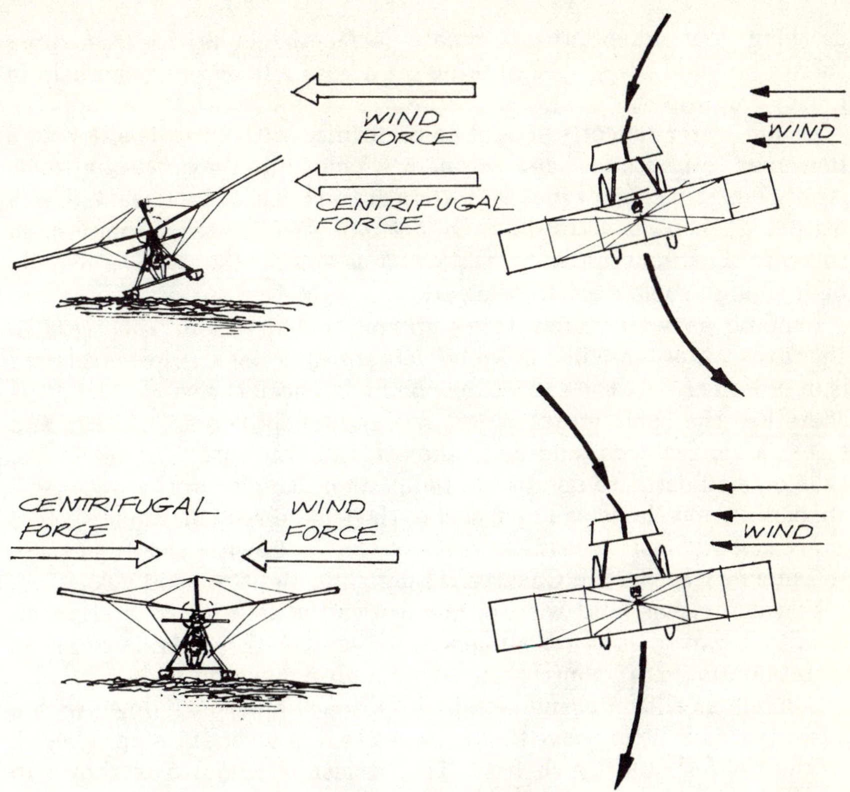

Figure 67 · Turning on Floats

Takeoffs when operating from floats are more complicated than when on land. You must control the position of the floats relative to the water as well as overcome the extra drag. This drag is greatest just before getting up on the step.

First, you should know your area well to avoid any hidden snags or floating debris. If you aren't sure of the area, taxi over your takeoff stretch to make sure it is clear. Also, you are likely to attract boats, so be sure they are well clear before you start out.

The beginning stages of takeoff were described as the taxi and consist of getting up on the step to the fast taxi position. Now, add power and raise the nose smoothly to lift off. Too much nose up control can cause the tail of the floats to enter the water and cause drag. Too little can cause the bow of the floats to remain in the water as the wing lifts. The result can be violent porpoising that can result in nosing over. If this occurs, throttle back and start over. Some minor porpoising may occur which can be controlled with pitch inputs opposite to the pitching action.

Glassy smooth water may be the hardest condition on which to take off. This is because the smooth flow is reluctant to detach from the bottom of the float. A good trick here is to motor around in a big circle crossing your takeoff run to create surface irregularities (remember there's no wind here). Also, taking off across a boat wake can help in glassy conditions.

Rough water takeoffs should be performed with care. The bow of a float may "stub its toe" and go under when it hits the crest of a wave. Apply nose up control just as you meet the crest of each wave. Use a little higher nose attitude than normal, just as with rough field takeoffs. Fortunately, when the water is rough, the wind is usually high enough to shorten the takeoff.

Landing on water again takes special consideration. Take care to check the water for debris or underwater obstructions. A low level pass is in order here. At the same time you must check the wind. Along the shore use the same indicators as on land, such as smoke, flags and trees. Also, seabirds land and take off into the wind. The set of the sails on sailboats are good wind indicators. Streaks on the water will appear in appreciable wind parallel to the wind direction. Finally, there is always a smooth spot near a shore that is upwind (see figure 48). Reexamine the chart in Chapter III detailing signs of wind velocity.

You can either land with power or dead stick when operating on floats. However, it is recommended to land with power in order to maintain maximum control and avoid a nose down position.

Come in as with a normal landing approach and touch down with a nose attitude a little above that required to remain on the step. The tail of the float should touch first. The perfect touchdown is shown in figure 68. As soon as the float contacts the water, begin a slow nose up control. This will prevent the extra drag from digging in the bow and flipping the craft. The faster you come in, the more nose up control necessary since the greater the drag. If you wish to continue taxiing on the step, add power and set the proper attitude.

Figure 68 · Landing on Floats

The most difficult condition to land in is flat, glassy smooth water. This is because it is extremely hard to judge the position of the water surface. Landing near a shoreline helps. You should fly the ultralight on to the water in this condition holding the proper attitude all the way down until contact is made. Don't try to flare, just maintain the slowest descent possible. The situation is especially difficult at dusk as light diminishes. In clear water, the bottom may appear to be the water surface. Use extreme caution!

Rough water landings should be accomplished by flying fairly level until a suitable spot between swells is encountered, then cutting power and settling down. Emergency landings can be made on grass without damage to the floats if done properly. Hold sufficient power to touch down with the floats as level as possible. As soon as they touch, add nose up control to keep from nosing over due to the severe drag. Don't worry about needing brakes.

Crosswind takeoffs and landings can be performed if you know a little trick. Don't try to head directly across the wind or turn upwind once you start. The craft will weathercock into the wind setting up the centrifugal forces described in the discussion on taxiing, leading to a "waterloop" similar to a ground loop on land. The proper technique is to aim a little into the wind and make a gradual downwind turn as you run up or roll out. The right and wrong techniques are shown in figure 69.

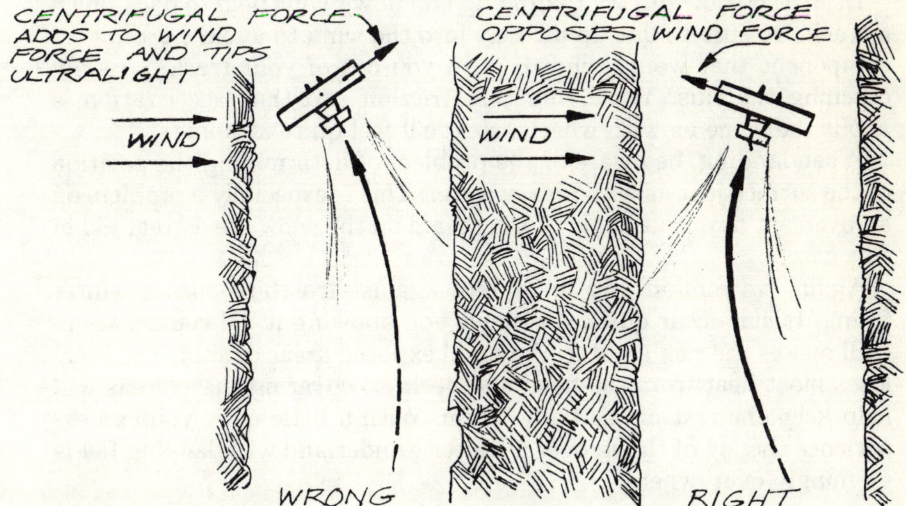

Figure 69 · Crosswind Operations on Water

Obviously, float flying takes a little getting used to but can be learned safely by a careful pilot. Mistakes lead to dunked aircraft more than structural damage, although the latter can occur readily since the water is *hard* when hit at a high velocity. Float hulls vary in strength, but continued hard landings will damage any hull. Perfect your landing on wheels before you try water—floats can be expensive.

If a dunking occurs, retrieve your soaking ultralight as quickly as possible and take things apart to let them dry (remove endplugs from tubes). You are probably in for an engine overhaul or at least a partial dismantling to let the insides dry. Fortunately, most internal items are coated with water repelling oil. Learn from your mistakes and go on to experience this fascinating form of flying.

FLYING ON SKIS

Just because your runway is covered with ten feet of snow doesn't mean you can't enjoy flying over the beautiful white countryside. Dress warmly, check the windchill chart, rig up a set of skis and head for the sky.

Skis are available commercially or you can make your own and attach them to the normal gear positions. Make sure they have a bit of up and down play and are aligned straight ahead. A groove in the bottom of the ski on a steerable nose gear will make steering much more positive.

Flying with skis is about the same as with wheels, except for the varying snow conditions. It is best to avoid light, deep snow as the flying flakes will erode the prop as readily as water spray. Also, slushy and wet snow will present variable drag which is hard to control.

In a fresh snowfall, try taxiing up and down your field to pack down a track. Be sure to line up directly into the wind to avoid a crosswind component that would tend to push you out of your track, possibly catching the skis. You'll find that friction and thus acceleration is about the same as with wheels, so you'll feel quite at home.

When landing, be aware of the problem of determining the position of the surface just as with glassy water. This is especially a problem on an overcast day or at dusk. Markers laid on the snow are a great aid in this case.

Again, we remind you to protect against frostbite during winter flying. It can occur quickly without you knowing it. Of course, windchill makes the risk greater. Cover all exposed areas of skin. The body loses most heat from the head and neck, so covering these areas will help keep the rest of the body warm. With a little care, you can experience the joy of flying over a winter wonderland with landing fields seemingly everywhere.

AEROBATICS

Aerobatics refers to flying manuevers beyond the normal pitch and roll regimes of the aircraft — say 20° up and down and 45° to the side. Ultralights are not necessarily ideal craft for aerobatics for their speed range — from stall speed to top speed — is not too great. On the other hand, ultralights operate at fairly low speeds, so the maneuvers take place relatively slowly. In general, we do not approve of aerobatics on ultralights for there are too many unknown factors. However, we include this information here since some manufacturers are building ultralights capable of doing aerobatics and pilots are attempting them.

Again, we say don't do them, but if you do, here are some matters to consider.

Most pilots start doing extracurricular maneuvers with tight 360s. The problem with these is that you often encounter your own wake at the same time you are increasing the G loading on your airframe (remember, a coordinated 60° banked turn doubles the G loading). Turbulence encountered in a tight turn can compromise the structure's integrity.

Wingovers are another common aerobatic feat. In this case, the pilot does a climbing turn much like a skateboard turning up a curving wall. Wingovers can get quite steep and go well past 90 degrees of bank. The problem with wingovers is the high G loading at the bottom of the pullout and the possibility of stalling at the top of the turn. A stall in such a nose high or inverted position results in severe consequences.

The consequences are the same as with whipstalls. Whipstalls occur when a pilot gathers speed and stalls at a radically nose high attitude. The result is a tail slide of some degree and a rapid fall through of the nose. The ultralight may easily go past vertical and end up on its back in this case. Structural damage most surely will occur. Without a doubt, whipstalls are the most dangerous maneuver on an ultralight. Even experts should avoid them.

Another manuever is spins. Spin entry and control is a reasonable skill to learn, but a prolonged spin can be impossible to stop with certain controls, or may end up in a steep spiral. As mentioned earlier, spirals may overstress the aircraft readily. Some pilots have entered spins and continued to spin until they hit the ground. Approach spins with caution.

Loops and barrel rolls have been accomplished on ultralights. Needless to say, the pilots doing them are expert aerobatic pilots (usually having learned in regular airplanes) and know the risks they are taking. There isn't much margin for error in such antics. The rewards are rarely worth the risk. Powered ultralights are such fun little craft that you don't have to get radical to be satisfied.

SOARING ULTRALIGHTS

Several times earlier in this book we have mentioned soaring. This refers to using the rising air currents to maintain altitude or to climb. This is some fun and presents a continued challenge long after you tire of circling around your home airfield or making the mail run to town and back. Soaring takes place in an everchanging environment and invites the pilot to achieve new heights and greater distances.

Before we look at the specifics of soaring with ultralights, remember two points. First, you can learn to soar simply by cutting the engine back—you don't have to chop power entirely. The less power you carry, the more sensitive the craft will be to the texture in the air. This helps when detecting patches of lift. Secondly, your performance will be much better when the power is cut totally than when the prop is idling. Make sure you can stop the prop totally with the engine off, for a still prop will produce less drag than an idling or autorotating one. Learn the difference in performance with the engine off, for you must set up a dead stick landing if you can't restart the engine. Remember, ultralights originated as hang gliders and hang glider pilots perform hundreds of thousands of powerless flights annually.

To learn to soar with an ultralight, it is a good idea to get a variometer or vertical speed indicator. You may have to strap this to your leg to eliminate the vibration on such a sensitive instrument or use a rubber instrument mount.

There are a number of sources of lift that soaring pilots exploit. These are ridge lift, thermal lift, convergence lift and wave lift. We will start with ridge lift since that is the easiest to detect and learn to utilize.

Ridge lift occurs when winds are blocked by a hill or mountain and get deflected upwards. The lift will appear above and in front of the ridge as shown in figure 70. Downwind from the ridge will be turbulence and rotors, so the pilot flies a path that will keep him or her in the area in front of the ridge or mountain. As you have probably guessed, if the ridge is of any length, you must parallel the ridge to stay in the lift. This is shown as a top view in figure 71.

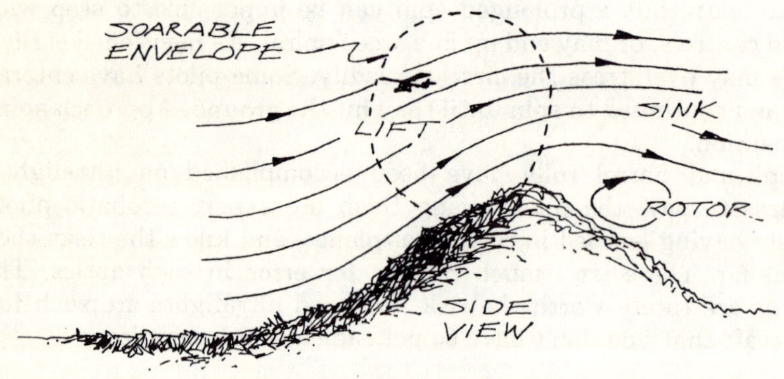

Figure 70 · Using Ridge Lift

Note that the ultralights in the figure are pointing slightly into the wind to offset the drift and stay in front of the mountain. This is our familiar crabbing angle. The stronger the wind, the more we must point away from the mountain and the slower our progress along the ridge. If the wind is slightly cross, the crab angle is the same, but the progress up or down the ridge will be quite different (slower into the wind).

The best ridge soaring conditions occur when the air is quite bouyant and rises readily once the ridge starts it lifting. This often happens at the end of a hot day. Hang glider pilots call this magic air or wonder winds. Strong winds may produce good lift, but often can

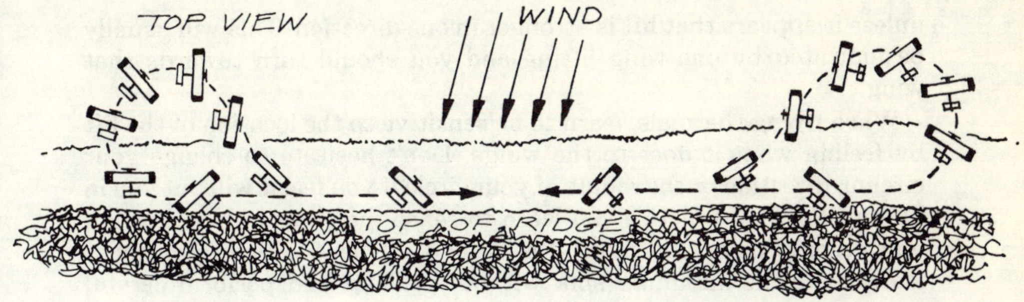

TURNS AT BOTH ENDS REQUIRE THE SAME HEADING CHANGE, EVEN WHEN WIND IS CROSSING. HOWEVER, A TURN AT THE DOWNWIND END (IN A CROSSING CONDITION) WILL DRIFT MORE THAN THE UPWIND TURN. ALL TURNS SHOULD BE AWAY FROM THE RIDGE (INTO THE WIND) AS SHOWN. WATCH YOUR POSITION CAREFULLY DURING EACH TURN TO END UP CRABBING ALONG THE RIDGE AS SHOWN.

Figure 71 · Soaring Along a Ridge

exhibit little vertical air if they are very stable. An ultralight is most suitable for soaring in light conditions.

When learning to fly ridge lift, power back tentatively and check your instruments to see your progress. You may have to get fairly close to the hill in light winds, but don't risk getting too close in turbulence. Make all turns away from the mountain and let your turn continue until you drift back right above the top of the slope. Do not drift behind the mountain. Needless to say, you should fly your minimum sink speed which is close to stall. Take great care to avoid a stall, especially in turns. Turns should be gentle so to lose a minimum amount of altitude. Be sure to look for other air traffic before turning—clear your turns always.

Common mistakes that beginners make are to fly too far away from the hill and to turn too often. Use as much ridge as you can to minimize turning. Remember, your sink rate increases in all turns. Practice makes perfect.

Thermal soaring consists of finding an ample thermal and staying within its confines. Thermal flying is very rewarding, for you can reach great heights irregardless of the terrain. Some turbulence accompanies thermals, so learn to handle turbulence before working thermals.

A thermal will usually announce itself with a bump and a raising of the ultralight's nose. Your variometer should indicate up if you're really in a good thermal. An ultralight probably needs at least a 100 foot per minute indication in order to use the lift. Once you have detected lift, count 3 to 4 seconds to make sure the thermal is large enough, then begin circling. Which direction do you turn? The choice is yours unless it appears that lift is stronger in one direction. This will usually be indicated by one wing lifting and you should turn towards that wing.

When flying thermals, learn to be sensitive to the location of the lift by feeling what it does to the wings. Don't hesitate to change your circling direction or the radius of your circle if you feel it will put you in better lift. With practice you learn to sense the areas of best lift and you become more and more precise and efficient. Again, you must learn to fly at minimum sink without stalling and perform careful turns. Most of your turns should employ bank angles below 30 degrees. Learn to judge your bank angle by viewing the horizon as shown in figure 72.

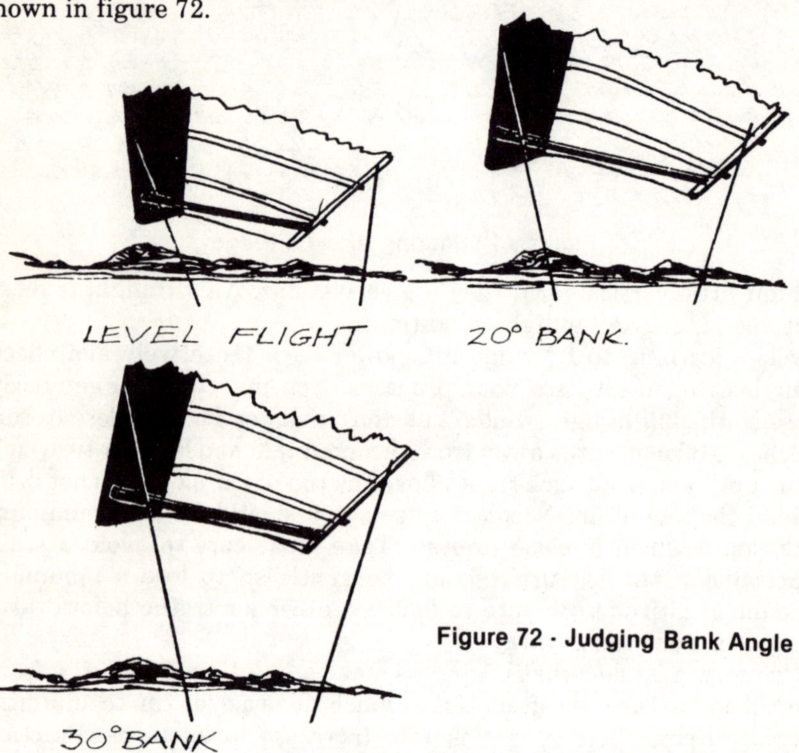

Figure 72 · Judging Bank Angle

Thermals are where you find them, but an experienced pilot knows where to look. Firstly, learn the ground sources for thermals. These are areas that heat readily with the sun such as plowed fields, dry crops, rocky areas, beaches and parking lots. Also note that thermals drift with the wind so they will be downwind from their source—the higher they are, the more downwind. This is shown in figure 73. Birds, cumulus clouds and other pilots can indicate the position of thermals. Thermals may appear as bubbles or columns, so you may or may not be able to ultilize a thermal that a pilot at another level is using. If you are above the other pilot, search downwind from him, but be aware that the thermal may not have reached your level.

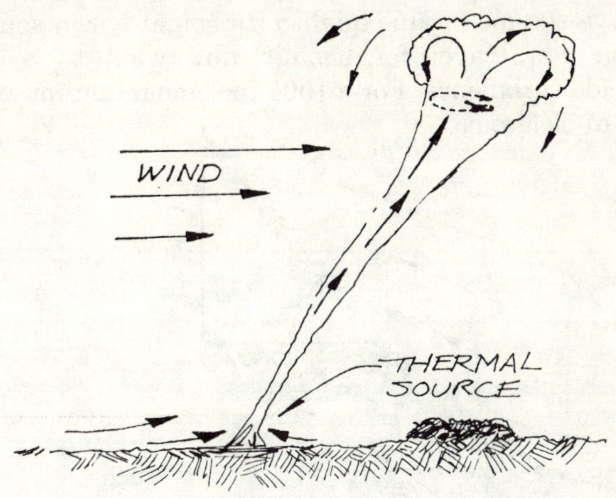

Figure 73 · Thermal Drift

Thermals may be abundent on a sunny day, or may be quite rare. In any case, the best place to look is above a hill or mountain, for these irregularities collect thermals. If you find a thermal in front of a ridge, perform S turns in it until you have enough clearance to 360 (see figure 74). Be cautious of hitting the ridge on the downwind portion of your turn, especially if you are low. Remember your drift!

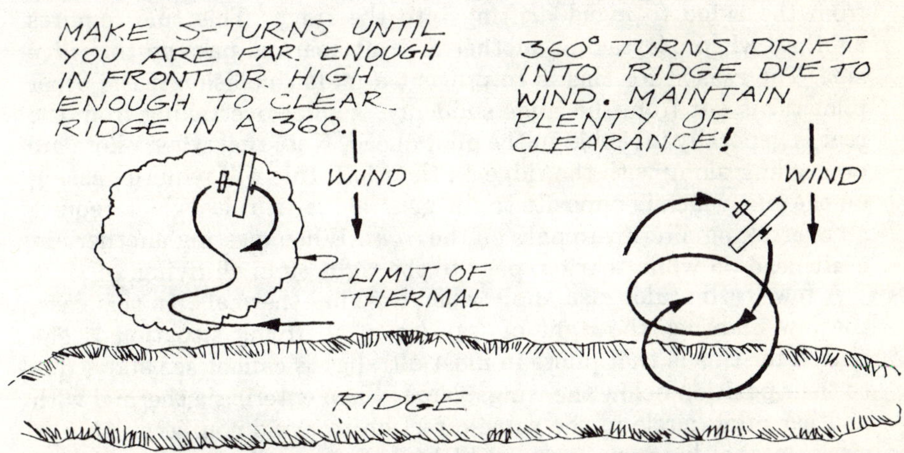

Figure 74 · Using Thermals on a Ridge

You can work thermals up and back behind the ridge as long as your thermal is strong enough so that your rise equals your drift back. This will keep you at better than a 45° angle with the mountain as shown in figure 75. This is important, for once you exit the thermal you'll probably encounter sink and a headwind that prevents you from reaching the front of the ridge if you get too low. If you choose to continue over top the ridge, do so with great care, for turbulence and downdrafts lurk for the unwary. Cross a ridge or mountain only with an altitude above the mountain equal to its height (when soaring) to make sure you can travel far enough downwind to avoid the mountain's leeside turbulence. For a 1000 foot mountain for example, have 1000 feet of clearance.

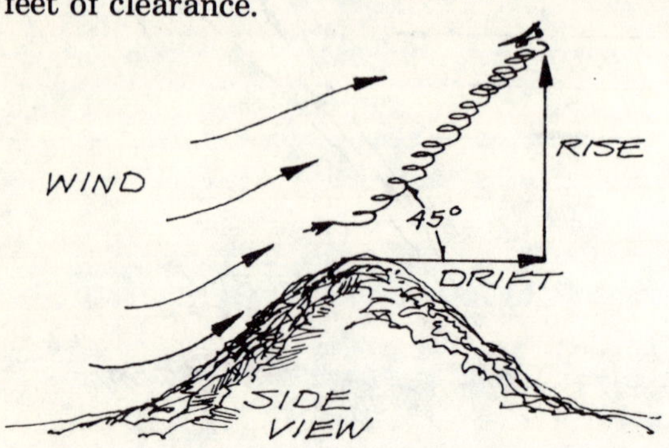

Figure 75 - Thermaling Behind A Ridge

Thermal soaring takes some practice, but in no time at all you can learn the techniques. For more information on the nature of thermals, read the book *Flying Conditions* by this author. Your efforts will be well rewarded.

Here we should note a few special rules related to ridge and thermal soaring. Remember we cautioned that all turns should be made away from the ridge to avoid drifting into the ridge? This rule requires another: when overtaking another aircraft soaring, pass on the *ridge* side. The reason for this is to prevent a midair collision if the other pilot turns out from the ridge suddenly. A pilot overtaking from the rear is generally invisible to the pilot ahead. Note that when pilots are proceeding along with the ridge on their left, this will require passing on the *left,* which is opposite to the general traffic rules which require an overtaking aircraft to pass on the *right.* When meeting another aircraft head on while soaring, pass to the right as in all flying.

A few traffic rules also apply when working thermals. In this case, the low man has the right of way (as in all flying situations). The reason for this is that pilots in most ultralights cannot see above due to their position below the wings. Next, when entering a thermal with another pilot, circle in the same direction to avoid conflicts. *Always* circle in the direction established by the first pilot in the thermal whether he is above or below you. Be sure to look around for traffic continuously when thermaling. Don't stare at your variometer or the ground — be aware of your copilots' positions.

Convergence zones and waves are not exploited regularly by powered ultralight pilots. This is because they are less predictable than the above two forms of lift and they may be accompanied with strong turbulence (or they may be glassy smooth).

Convergence lift occurs when two airflows come together. This is most common in the middle of a valley at night, or above a mountain during the day. Also a seabreeze meeting the land wind often displays convergence. Use this lift if it suits you and proves smooth enough.

Waves are formed downwind of mountains or ridges as shown in figure 9 of Chapter III. Waves generally require a wind velocity of 15 mph (24 kph) or more and may display strong turbulence at an inversion layer. Also, rotors may occur under the waves downwind that are very dangerous to a powered ultralight. Fly in waves with great caution. Stay in the lift by running parallel with the forming ridge just as with ridge lift. Waves extend to great altitudes, so dress warmly.

The most common (and safest) conditions in which to encounter waves in an ultralight is when a soarable ridge is in phase with a wave produced by the terrain upwind. This means that the upward moving part of the wave is located approximately where the normal ridge lift would occur. The difference is, the wave lift extends much higher than the ridge lift and usually is located in front (upwind) of the ridge as shown in figure 76.

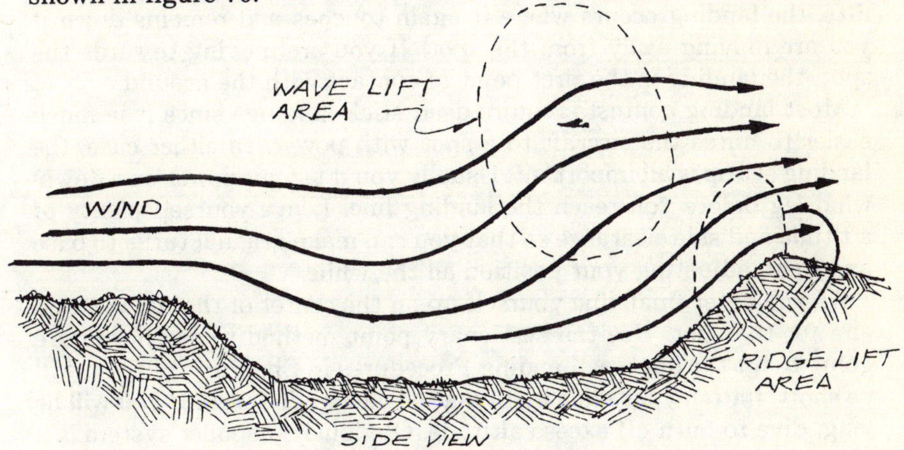

Figure 76 - Wave Soaring

Explore for this type of wave lift by flying out from the ridge as you get higher. Conditions of this sort may be encountered most often at the end of a good soaring day as the stability changes. Waves of this sort strong enough to lift ultralights are not that common, so don't expect to gain a lot of wave experience in a short time. Again we caution all pilots that waves can harbor fierce turbulence and ultralights in general are not suited to explore the air in strong wave conditions.

COMPETITION FLYING

Competition in any sport is a great way to test your skills, learn new techniques and meet other enthusiasts. Powered ultralight competition is still evolving, but by combining the background of other sports and the unique ultralight experience, we are in for some spectacular events indeed. Every pilot will benefit from competition whether it is in terms of a competitor, spectator, judge or by virtue of the advancements in design that competition fosters.

There are a number of events used in ultralight competition. Some of these such as bomb drops, ralleys and climb competitions do not really measure piloting skills so we will leave these events to the fly-ins. A competition choosing a champion pilot should pick the winner on the basis of skill required to fly precisely and safely. No contest should reward a pilot that risks safety to win.

Some of the skills worth testing are landing precision, control precision, fuel efficiency, use of air currents, proper use of airspeed and altitude judgement. Some events that measure these items are spot landings (with and without power), duration events, pylon courses and limited fuel cross-country flights.

Spot landings usually are actually line landings. In this event, the pilot must land as closely to a line as possible. A landing consists of a touchdown in which the main wheels do not lift off again. If a wheel lifts, the landing occurs where it again touches and remains down if you are moving away from the spot. If you are moving towards the spot, the landing is the first point of contact with the ground.

Most landing contests require dead stick landings since it is much easier to nurse the aircraft to a spot with power. In either case, the landing set up is all important. Usually you must cut power on a downwind leg before you reach the landing line. Leave yourself plenty of altitude and side clearance so that you can make gradual turns to base and final, adjusting your position all the while.

As you enter final, line yourself up on the center of the runway and aim for the spot. Use the stationary point method to see if you are going to hit the line (see Landing Procedures in Chapter V). If you will be short, flatten your glide by flying the best glide speed. If you will be long, dive to burn off excess altitude. Obviously a spoiler system is a great asset here. Also, it is easier to shorten your glide then lengthen it, so allow plenty of altitude.

When it comes to actual touchdown, you can come in slow and flare hard if you are going to be long. If you are going to be short, maintain your best glide attitude and "grease" it on to land as close as possible. As soon as you touch down, apply down elevator and brakes to prevent bouncing back into the air and thus lengthening your distance. Obviously, much practice is in order here. Your home field is an ideal place to begin.

Duration events usually consist of supplying pilots with a limited amount of fuel and seeing who can stay up the longest. Usually the best method consists of climbing as high as possible until fuel is exhausted then working evey bit of lift on the way down. Use your best rate of climb speed on the way up. Throttle setting will vary with the aircraft and power system, but is rarely full power. Try experimenting on your own to find the setting that gets you the highest on a given amount of fuel. If you encounter a thermal on the way up, power back and thermal up if possible.

On the way down, fly minimum sink speed to descend as slowly as possible. Look for thermals downwind from ground sources. Watch other ultralights in the air for signs of lift. At the very least, avoid sink areas like the plague. Most directors usually run these events in midday when some lift is present. Obviously, practicing your soaring skills is important here.

Pylon courses require a pilot to round a series of pylons as fast as possible or in an exact time. Much skill is involved, for the pilot must know when and how to turn, especially in wind. For example, if the pylons are set a proper distance apart, flying with the engine at a full scream isn't the fastest way to complete the course. The reason for this is that fast turns require a much greater turning radius and thus a much longer track. The course is a matter of finesse, not power.

Pylon turning is a skill important to a number of sports including auto and ski racing. The secret is to enter the turn wide and slow and come out tight and fast. In wind you must take into consideration the wind drift and turn accordingly. In a tailwind, begin your turn earlier. Delay the initiation of your turn in a headwind. In a crosswind, you must be aware of the drift and crab. If given a choice, make the turns on the outside of the pylons into the wind as shown in figure 77. This will minimize the change in heading required and thus the amount of altitude lost in the turn. When turning in a pylon course, don't get too high or you can't run the pylons precisely. Likewise, don't get too low or you won't be able to bank properly. Add your power between the pylons but slow the turns down.

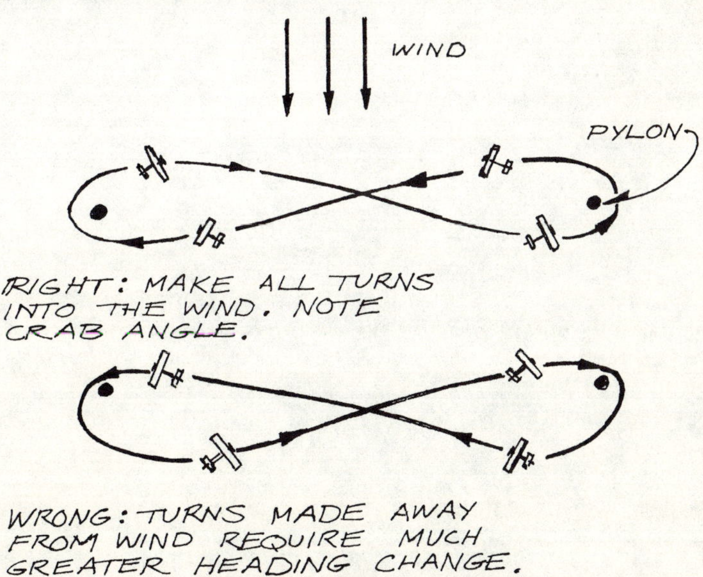

Figure 77 - Pylon Turns in Wind

Cross-country events are great fun and call on all your reserves of skill and artifice. They are flown very similar to the duration events except the quest is to go as far as possible on a limited amount of fuel. The technique is to climb only as high as necessary on power, hook some lift and work it up as far as possible. Once you top out, glide along looking for another thermal or ridge lift. Use the engine only as a "save" to conserve fuel. Again, all your soaring skills are at a premium here. There is nothing like a long distance flight accomplished on a minimum amount of fuel.

The Birdman TL-1A

CHAPTER VIII

MEDICAL CONSIDERATIONS

A pilot may master all the material in this book, develop his flying skills to the expert level, fly the safest powered ultralight design and still may be taking risks if he neglects one last component of the flying system—his body. As human beings, we are designed to operate in a fairly limited range of temperatures and pressures. It is easy to exceed these limits when flying. The wise pilot will take precautions to keep his body functioning well within the safety zone.

In this chapter we will cover the medical considerations that you may encounter at some time or other in your flying career. Study them well to keep flying as it should be: enjoyable and relaxing, not dangerous.

VISION

Our eyes are the principle sensory organs used in flying. It is imperative that our vision, be acute and unobstructed. Sunglasses or goggles are recommended for those pilots who don't wear prescription glasses. Remember, you are in an air flow of 25 mph or more. Good depth perception is necessary at all times in the air. Make sure both eyes are corrected for proper vision.

The human eye has a blind spot where the optic nerve passes through the retina. We can see this by closing the left eye and staring at the left dot (with the right eye) in figure 78. Now, move the paper forward or back until the middle dot disappears. The figure will be about seven inches from your eyeball. Now, move a little further away and the middle dot will reappear while the right hand dot will disappear. This is due to your blind spot.

By looking a little to the side of the dot you are staring at, it is possible to get an idea of the extent of your blind spot. It is surprisingly large. With both eyes open, the blind spot in one eye is taken care of by the other eye. However, one-eyed pilots and those who wear certain types of glasses may have the inside vision of each eye blocked so the blind spot is indeed blind. The blind spot is located approximately 16° to the outside of each eye's line of sight. Obviously, being aware of your blind spot is important so that you know to double check for traffic when other aircraft are in the vicinity.

●   ●   ●

Figure 78 - Finding Your Blind Spot

Flying at dusk has its own vision problems. It takes over 30 minutes for the eyes to acquire their maximum night vision capacity. Also, depth perception is seriously hampered as the light fails. At 5,000 ft. (1,600m), there is a 6% loss in image sharpness over that at sea level, even on a bright day. Also at this altitude, night vision becomes hampered due to lower oxygen supply to the retina. On top of a very high mountain, stars actually appear dimmer due to this effect. Cigarettes, alcohol and other drugs also reduce night vision dramatically. An ultralight pilot should not attempt to fly at night.

One of the important functions of vision during flight is avoiding other air traffic. Anything that adversely affects our vision compromises our safety when other air traffic is around. Some of these factors are: dust, fatigue, emotion, germs, age, optical illusions, oxygen supply, accelerations, glare, heat, drugs and psychological effects. The eyes only see what our mind lets us see. A daydreaming pilot is a prime candidate for an in-flight collision.

One problem that occurs when looking for other air traffic is that of focusing. It takes one or two seconds for the eye to change focus from far to near and this may be a significant delay if a collision is imminent. Furthermore, if there is little or nothing to focus on at infinity (such as above a haze), our eyes do not focus at all. We stare but see nothing, even if other aircraft enter our field of vision. Backlighting and the effects of another aircraft moving over cluttered ground can also prevent detection of that aircraft. Also, we have previously mentioned the fact that an aircraft on a collision course with you will appear to remain stationary (whether you are converging head on or from the side) without growing significantly in size. A fast moving aircraft will suddenly loom larger as it gets near – this is known as the blossom effect.

Obviously, we need some technique for using our eyes effectively. The following scan method is suggested as being perhaps the most effective.

In normal flight, scan from 90° to either side and 30° up and down. Also, clear the area behind and to the side of you before making a turn. Be sure to perform clearing turns to scout out an entire area before performing a series of extended maneuvers.

To scan the area outlined above, divide the area into vertical segments of 10 to 15° wide. This corresponds to the normal focusing field of vision. Now you have 12 or more segments from one side to the other. Start in the middle segment and scan it for about 3 seconds (up and down). Move left to the next segment and repeat. Follow this procedure until you have cleared all the way to the left, then return to center and scan to the right.

Obviously, this takes a bit of time to cover the entire area, so repeat this scan procedure often and keep track of any air traffic you see. Occassionally, check behind you (a bit of heading change is helpful) for airplanes can sneak up from the rear and your size may make you nearly invisible. Keep your eyes in good shape, remain alert, scan carefully and avoid other traffic.

VERTIGO

Another hazard is flying in clouds. Not only do you risk a midair collision in congested areas, but the danger of vertigo is great. Vertigo is spatial disorientation caused by the senses reporting something different from what your body is feeling. For example, you can be in a coordinated turn within a cloud so your body feels as if you were flying level (gravity and certrifugal force combine to give an illusion of level flight). When the wisps of cloud clear away and you suddenly see the ground, the effect can be very confusing.

One of the worse cases of vertigo occurs when you are in a tight turn then suddenly turn your head to the side. The result is often confusion, nausea and vision impairment. The cause of this is the semicircular canals in the inner ear that are used for balance. If you are in a turn, two of the canals are activated. The sudden turning of the head causes the third canal to react violently and send a confused input to the brain. To avoid this type of vertigo, avoid quick head movements when in a turn, especially if ground reference is not good. Also avoid looking to the outside wing in a turn (look to the inside of a turn) and don't try multiple 360s at a high bank angle until you have experienced many turns. You can gradually build up resistance to disorientation through practice.

HYPOXIA

The term hypoxia simply means low oxygen. As we climb higher, the oxygen we take in for each breath is less since the air is thinner. At 15,000 ft. ASL we get about half the amount of oxygen with each breath that we get at sea level. The reduced oxygen in our blood results in lower efficiency of all our body's vital organs.

Hypoxia is particularly dangerous since there are no overt signs of its onset. In fact, the brain center that would normally warn of subtle signs of danger is one of the first areas to be affected. One of the signs of hypoxia is euphoria and a disregard of danger. The affects of hypoxia vary with the individual. If you are older, physically unfit, smoke, use drugs, drink or are improperly rested, you will be more susceptable to hypoxia.

The following is the average response to hypoxia: At 10,000 ft. (3,000m) there is a definite effect of hypoxia. This is the highest altitude a pilot should consider himself competent without oxygen.

At 14,000 ft. (4,500m) the vision becomes blurred and blue discolouring of the fingernails occurs. Clouding of memory and judgement as well as lack of concentration are appreciable. The pilot will not necessarily recognize these symptoms.

At 16,000 ft. (5,300m) euphoria and complete lack of judgement sets in.

Powered ultralights have climbed well into the hypoxia danger zone, so every pilot should be aware of these symptoms. To avoid hypoxia, simply employ supplemental oxygen above 10,000 ft. Also, stay in shape and keep your vices to a minimum (note: there is no evidence that sex exacerbates hypoxia). One test for hypoxia is to add a couple two digit numbers together in your mind. If you find this becomes increasingly more difficult, get yourself down.

Another test is to try "grunt" breathing. To do this, take a breath, hold your mouth closed, and create pressure in your lungs by bearing down. If you suddenly hear better and your vision clears around the edges, then you are probably suffering some of the effects of hypoxia. Again, the smart thing is to descend immediately.

Remember, once hypoxia sets in it takes hours for the faculties to return to normal. Also, judgement is one of the first things impaired by hypoxia so you will not necessarily make the right decision concerning when to come down. For this reason, make all necessary flight decisions and plans while you are still low and thinking clearly — and stick to them.

At high altitudes you may find yourself breathing fast or hyperventilating due to anxiety or lack of oxygen. This activity upsets the normal carbon dioxide/oxygen balance in the blood and can worsen the effects of hypoxia and cause dizziness. The remedy is to force yourself to breath at a normal rate at all times.

PHYSICAL FITNESS

The better shape you are in the better you will be able to avoid the effects of fatigue, hypoxia and anxiety. It goes without saying that you must have a good working heart and mind when engaged in an active sport such as ultralighting. Emotional stresses are very common causes of aircraft accidents. If you are upset by a job situation, family problem or any other psychological stress, you are probably not operating at 100% and should not be flying. Anger and anxiety impairs a pilot's ability to make judgements and controls. Good physical health can contribute greatly to good mental health. Keep emotionally and physically fit for flying.

FATIGUE

Physical fitness goes a long way in preventing fatigue. However, there are other factors that must be considered. Obviously sleep must be ample or mental fatigue is unavoidable.

Fatigue lowers the resistance to stress and hypoxia, leading to impairment of judgement and concentration. One of the factors leading to fatigue is constant noise and vibration. It goes without saying that our powered ultralights are quite noisy and vibrate a bit. The cure is to always wear earplugs when flying. Fortunately, we are usually not called upon to fly many hours cross-country, but if we are fatigued before we fly the result can be dangerous since many decisions are required when motoring at low altitudes. In any case, the ears must be protected to prevent hearing loss. Ear damage can occur with as little as 85 decibels of continuous sound (a decibel is a measure of sound intensity — normal conversation is 60 to 70 decibels). Most ultralights are well above this level in the pilot's seat. Protect your ears so your friends won't tire of hearing you respond with "what?" to everything they say.

The Teratorn

Eating and drinking habits are a factor in fatigue. If you skip meals, your energy reserve will be low which can bring on fatigue with the attending impairment of reactions. Overeating is equally unwise since it can lead to drowsiness and lack of alertness.

Not enough is said about dehydration. If you spend a day flying in the hot sun your body's water supply may be drastically lowered. This can lead to fatigue-like symptoms with the same results. Keep plenty of fresh water or fruit juices on hand to prevent dehydration. Some pilots strap a handy plastic water bottle on their frame for use in flight.

HYPOTHERMIA

When the body temperature drops below its normal level the result is hypothermia. This condition is particularly of concern to powered ultralight pilots, since even on a warm summer day temperatures can be freezing cold aloft. Most powered ultralight pilots fly exposed to the wind. For this reason, all bare body parts should be covered during high or long flights. If you find yourself getting cold, come down to a warmer altitude, or land, dress warmer and motor back up. The body is designed to protect the vital organs at the expense of other parts in dire situations. In the case of lowered body temperature, the capillaries in the hands and feet will constrict so as to reserve more blood and warmth to the brain. Thus, the best way to keep your hands and feet warm is to keep your head and neck warm. This is especially pertinent since a large part of the body's heat loss is from the head and neck in windy conditions. The silk scarf, leather helmet and goggles worn by the open cockpit pilots of yesterday were for a very good reason. They knew that hypothermia results in reduced efficiency.

DECOMPRESSION

Under normal conditions, nitrogen is always present in the blood and other body fluids. At high altitudes this nitrogen comes out of solution and forms little bubbles that can block blood vessels and cause headache, pain, and other more serve symptoms including death. Other gases in the body may expand at altitude and cause pain in the ear, sinus, teeth or intestines. In general, powered ultralight pilots don't climb high enough to suffer decompression effects. However, if a scuba diver attempts to fly soon after diving below 30 ft. (10m), the ceiling for the onset of decompression sickness is lowered dramatically. Since scuba diving introduces more nitrogen into the blood stream, the simple rule to follow is wait for 24 hours after diving before flying.

MISCELLANEOUS FACTORS

Carbon monoxide from a poorly placed exhaust system can be deadly. Carbon monoxide will cause disorientation and eventually death. The effects of carbon monoxide poisoning can last for days, so make sure you aren't breathing exhaust fumes at any time. Although carbon monoxide is odorless, it is usually accompanied by other exhaust fumes. If you smell exhaust, make some corrections.

Ear discomfort or pain can occur when changing altitudes. Usually this results from congestion in the sinus passages. Chewing gum and swallowing are the standard ways to clear the ears. What you are trying to do is equalize pressure on both sides of the eardrum. Note that pressure effects can upset the inner ear balancing system, so do not fly if ear pain persists. In addition, consult a physician if ear pain does not go away soon after landing. Beware of flying when suffering from a cold.

Blood donation can affect a pilot adversely by causing weakness or dizzyness. Other factors such as diabetes or excessive fear can have debilitating effects on decision making or clearheadedness. Be sure of your steadiness before you fly. If you feel excessively fearful when flying, go back to work on the basics or have an instructor watch your technique to correct possible mistakes and teach you confidence building procedures.

The Results Of A Hard Landing

DRUGS AND ALCOHOL

Since flying any aircraft requires so much judgement and motor coordination, any substance that impairs these items is dangerous. The case against alcohol is well documented. The loss of flying ability goes up with the amount of alcohol consumed. The more drinks under the belt, the longer the effects last. For example, it takes about three hours for one ounce of alcohol to wear off. Only time will reduce alcohol's effects, not coffee, exercise or sleep. In addition, altitude worsens the effect of alcohol since lowering oxygen supply to the brain is exactly how alcohol works. For example, if you have ever had a drink on a commerical airline you may notice its strong effect since the cabins are pressurized for 9,000 feet. Then, when you return to sea level you sober right up.

Drugs are extremely dangerous since they can blur the senses, cause confusion and act in unpredicatable ways at altitude. This includes seemingly harmless non-prescription drugs. Antibiotics, antihistamines, tranquilizers, barbituates, anaesthetics, sulfa drugs, reducing drugs and even aspirin have been implicated in flying accidents. Each of these drugs requires a 12 to 48 hour waiting period before flying can be considered safe.

Remember, you are flying for enjoyment, so don't risk ruining your fun permanently by using questionable substances before your flights. There is plenty of time to fly tomorrow if your system is not in shape today. If you enjoy flying in the present, fly with the utmost caution and you will enjoy flying far into the future.

The Mirage

APPENDIX I

FEDERAL AVIATION REGULATION PART 103
FOR OPERATION IN THE UNITED STATES

This regulation contains the current regulations pertaining to ultralights. Besides the "rules of the road" given in Chapter V, an ultralight pilot should learn the rules of Part 103 and obey them carefully. Most of the rules are quite simple, but we include some explanatory notes here for clarity. The numbers refer to the sections as listed in the regulation.

103.3 (b) – Satisfactory evidence usually consists of a statement from the manufacturer that your ultralight complies with Part 103 definitions.

103.7 – All these programs (airworthiness certification; airman certification, vehicle registration) are in existance on a voluntary basis. In the future, the FAA may make these programs mandatory (probably as a result of the lack of participation in the voluntary programs).

103.11 (a) – The official hours of sunrise and sunset are posted in many newspapers. Note that when operating with a light you must remain out of controlled airspace. (103.11(b) (2)).

103.15 – A congested area has been taken to be a single house by the FAA. You will probably only run into this strict of a definition if you are annoying someone and they complain. However, avoiding houses and inhabited areas is the best way to avoid problems.

103.17 – These areas are designated on a sectional chart. The only areas you should consider operating in are airport traffic areas and control zones if you are operating out of an airport. In this case, the airport director is the proper authority. Do not fly into an airport without first receiving permission to do so.

103.21 – This item means do not fly in or above widespread clouds.

103.23 – Since most of the U.S. is in controlled airspace above 1,200 ft. above the surface, the best policy is to only fly with over 3 miles visibility and 500 ft. below, 1,000 ft. above and 2,000 feet to the side of clouds.

PART 103

103.1 Applicability.

This part prescribes rules governing the operation of ultralight vehicles in the United States. For the purpose of this part, an ultralight vehicle is a vehicle that:

(a) is used or intended to be used for manned operation in the air by a single occupant;

(b) is used or intended to be used for recreation or sport purposes only;

(c) does not have any U.S. or foreign airworthiness certificate; and,

173

(d) if unpowered, weights less than 155 pounds; or
(e) if powered:
    (1) weighs less than 254 pounds empty weight, excluding floats and safety devices which are intended for deployment in a potentially catastrophic situation;
    (2) has a fuel capacity not exceeding 5 U.S. gallons;
    (3) is not capable of more than 55 knots calibrated air-speed at full power in level flight; and
    (4) has a power-off stall speed which does not exceed 24 knots calibrated airspeed.

103.3 Inspection requirements.

(a) Any person operating an ultralight vehicle under this part shall, upon request, allow the Administrator, or his designee, to inspect the vehicle to determine the applicability of this part.
(b) The pilot or operator of an ultralight vehicle must, upon request of the Administrator, furnish satisfactory evidence that the vehicle is subject only to the provisions of this part.

103.5 Waivers.

No person may conduct operations that require a deviation from this part except under a written waiver issued by the Administrator.

103.7 Certification and registration.

(a) Notwithstanding any other section pertaining to certification of aircraft or their parts or equipment, ultralight vehicles and their component parts and equipment are not required to meet the airworthiness certification standards specified for aircraft or to have certificates of airworthiness.
(b) Notwithstanding any other section pertaining to airman certification, operators of ultralight vehicles are not required to meet any aeronautical knowledge, age, or experience requirements to operate those vehicles or to have airman or medical certificates.
(c) Notwithstanding any other section pertaining to registration and marking of aircraft, ultralight vehicles are not required to be registered or to bear markings of any type.

Subpart B — Operating Rules

103.9 Hazardous operation.

(a) No person may operate any ultralight vehicle in a manner that creates a hazard to other persons or property.
(b) No person may allow an object to be dropped from an ultralight vehicle if such action creates a hazard to other persons or property.

103.11 Daylight operations.

(a) No person may operate an ultralight vehicle except between the hours of sunrise and sunset.
(b) Notwithstanding paragraph (a) of this section, ultralight vehicles may be operated during the twilight periods 30 minutes before official sunrise and 30 minutes after official sunset or, in Alaska, during the period of civil twilight as defined in the Air Almanac, if:
  (1) the vehicle is equipped with an operating anti-collision light visible for at least 3 statute miles; and
  (2) all operations are conducted in uncontrolled airspace.

103.13 Operation near aircraft; Right-of-way rules.
(a) Each person operating an ultralight vehicle shall maintain vigilance so as to see and avoid aircraft and shall yield the right-of-way to all aircraft.
(b) No person may operate an ultralight vehicle in a manner that creates a collision hazard with respect to any aircraft.
(c) Powered ultralights shall yield the right-of-way to unpowered ultralights.

103.15 Operations over congested areas.
No person may operate an ultralight vehicle over any congested area of a city, town, or settlement, or over any open air assembly of persons.

103.17 Operations in certain airspace.
No person may operate an ultralight vehicle within an airport traffic area, control zone, terminal control area, or positive control area unless that person has prior authorization from the air traffic control facility having jurisdiction over that airspace.

103.19 Operations in prohibited or restricted areas.
No person may operate an ultralight vehicle in prohibited or restricted areas unless that person has permission from the using or controlling agency, as appropriate.

103.21 Visual reference with the surface.
No person may operate an ultralight vehicle except by visual reference with the surface.

103.23 Flight visibility and cloud clearance requirements.

No person may operate an ultralight vehicle when the flight visibility or distance from clouds is less than that in the following table, as appropriate:

Flight Altitudes	Minimum Flight Visibility	Minimum Distance from Clouds
1,200 feet or less above the surface regardless of MSL altitude:		
(1) Within controlled airspace—	3 statute miles	500 feet below 1,000 feet above 2,000 feet horizontal
(2) Outside controlled	1 statute mile	Clear of clouds
More than 1,200 feet above the surface but less than 10,000 feet MSL:		
(1) Within controlled airspace	3 statute miles	500 feet below 1,000 feet above 2,000 feet horizontal
(2) Outside controlled airspace	1 statute mile	500 feet below 1,000 feet above 2,000 horizontal
More than 1,200 feet above the surface and at or above 10,000 feet MSL:	5 statute miles	1,000 feet below 1,000 feet above 1 statute mile horizontal

APPENDIX II

ULTRALIGHT SAFETY

Here are some of the guidelines for safe flying. Learn them well and continue to practice safety throughout your long and enjoyable flying experience.

NEVER
- Fly in strong or gusty winds. The strength of the wind and its effect on control increases with the square of the velocity. Doubling the wind velocity produces four times the force.
- Fly when thunderstorms are present. These are some of the most dangerous and unpredictable conditions.
- Fly over buildings or crowds.
- Fly close to ground obstructions downwind. The general rule of thumb is to remain a distance downwind 7 times the height of the object.
- Fly under the influence of drugs or alcohol.
- Fly when emotionally upset. Many accidents can be attributed to the pilot's distracted state of mind.
- Fly above 12,000 feet MSL without oxygen.

ALWAYS
- Fly with a parachute and helmet.
- Preflight your ultralight before flying.
- Maintain your engine and airframe on a regular basis.
- Yell "clear prop" when starting the engine. Wait for the "prop clear" response when others are present.
- Obey all air traffic rules and FAA regulations.
- Have a landing area available within easy glide in case of an engine failure.
- Maintain extra airspeed when descending for a landing.
- Cross mountains or ridges at an angle with a clearance equal to their height.
- Fly conservatively when spectators, family or friends are watching. The most dangerous pilot is the one flying to impress others. Gain your reward in flying from the joy of being airborne and free to explore the sky, not from the adulation of others. With these simple guidelines, your flying should be safe and fun for years to come.

GLOSSARY

AERODYNAMIC (EFFECTS) – Factors caused by the flowing of the air.

ADVERSE YAW – Yawing towards the outside of a turn (in the wrong direction) when a roll is induced.

AILERONS – Surfaces at the rear outboard area of the main wing used to deflect air and create a roll force.

AIRSPEED – The speed of the aircraft in relation to the air.

AIRSPEED INDICATOR – An instrument for detecting airspeed.

AN BOLT – Airforce/Navy designated bolt with very high strength. Three marks on the head identify an AN bolt.

ANGLE OF ATTACK – The angle at which a wing meets the air or relative wind.

ATTITUDE – The angle the chord of a wing makes with the horizon.

BEST ANGLE OF CLIMB – The angle of attack that provides the steepest climbing flight path.

BEST GLIDE – The angle of attack that allows the aircraft to fly the farthest with the engine off.

BEST RATE OF CLIMB – The angle of attack that achieves the most altitude in the least amount of time.

BIPLANE – An aircraft with two main wings, one atop the other.

CANARD – A small wing in front of an aircraft's main wing.

CARBURETOR – A device on an engine used for mixing air and fuel.

CENTER OF GRAVITY – The point where the total mass of the pilot and aircraft balances.

CENTRIFUGAL FORCE – An apparent force that tends to move a mass to the outside of a turn.

CHOKE – A carburetor control that enriches the air/fuel mixture for starting.

CHORD – A measurement on a wing at each point along the wing from the leading edge to the trailing edge.

CHT – Cylinder head temperature gauge. An instrument for monitoring the engine's cylinder temperatures.

COLD FRONT – An advancing mass of cold air.

CONTROL STICK – A vertical tube that the pilot moves to effect roll and pitch control.

COORDINATED TURN – A turn in which a slip or skid does not occur.

CORIOLIS EFFECT – The apparent turning of the air to the right (left is the Southern hemisphere) as it moves over a period of time.

CORROSION – The eating away of a metal through chemical action.

CRABBING – Moving somewhat to the side during flight due to a crosswind component.

CROSS-COUNTRY – Flying to some point not visible from the takeoff point.

CROSSWIND – A wind not meeting an aircraft directly head on.

CUMULUS CLOUDS – Puffy clouds caused by small areas of lifting air.

DACRON — A synthetic material made by Dupont and used to cover most ultralight wings.

DENSITY ALTITUDE — The apparent altitude at which you are flying due to pressure, humidity and temperature effects.

DIHEDRAL — An upward angling of a wing from the root outward when viewed from in front.

DRAG — Rearward acting aerodynamic forces tending to slow an aircraft down.

DRAGELONS — Control surfaces that slow one side of a wing down by creating more drag, and thus turn the wing.

DRAG STRUT — A spar from the keel to the leading edge used to prevent the wing from folding back.

DUST DEVIL — Swirling air that picks up dust caused by a thermal lifting rapidly in unstable conditions.

EDDY — See VORTEX.

EGT — Exhaust gas temperature gauge. An instrument for monitoring the engine temperature at the exhaust port.

ELEVATOR — A control surface used to effect pitch control.

ELEVONS — Control surfaces on flying wings used to effect both roll and pitch control.

EMPENAGE — The tail of an aircraft consisting of stabilizors, elevator and rudder.

FLEX WING — An aircraft in which the wing surface may change shape in flight.

FLOATS — Small, boat-like floating devices for operating aircraft on water.

FUSELAGE — The main body of an aircraft to which the wings and gear are attached.

GEAR — See LANDING GEAR.

GRADIENT — See WIND GRADIENT.

GROUND EFFECT — The apparent floating of an aircraft near the earth's surface due to a suppression in tip vorticies.

GROUND HANDLING — Moving an aircraft around on the ground.

GROUND SPEED — The speed of an aircraft with respect to the ground. Airspeed combined with windspeed equals groundspeed.

GUST FRONT — A miniature cold front caused by fallout (cold descending air) from a thunderstorm that hits the ground and spreads rapidly.

GYROSCOPIC EFFECT — The tendency for a rotating mass such as propeller to turn on an axis 90° from that at which it is turned.

HANG GLIDER — A non-powered ultralight weighing less than 155 lbs.

HEADWIND — A wind directly into the nose of an aircraft.

HULL — The exterior surface of a float.

KEEL — The center tube of an ultralight wing.

KING POST — A vertical tube on some ultralights used to support the wing (with cables) on the ground.

LAND BREEZE — A breeze, usually occurring in the evening, that blows from land to sea.

L/D — Lift to drag ratio of a wing used as a measure of performance.

LEADING EDGE — The first part of a wing that meets the air.

LIFT — The upward directed aerodynamic forces produced as a wing moves through the air.

MINIMUM SINK — An aircraft's slowest vertical sinking speed with engine off.

MOUNTAIN WINDS (DOWNSLOPE) — Winds that blow from the mountain to the valley (usually at night).

MUSH — The action of descending in a semi-stalled mode.

NAVIGATION — Determining one's position during flight and the heading necessary to reach a given destination.

P-FACTOR — The tendency for an aircraft to yaw when a pitch   control is made due to different angles of attack on the propeller.

PITCH (CONTROL) – A nose up or down control. Motion about the lateral axis.

PITCH (PROPELLER) – A propeller designation determined by how far a propeller would advance if no slippage occurred.

PITCH STABILITY – The tendency for an aircraft to resume level flight if disturbed by a gust or a control input.

PRE-FLIGHT – A thorough check of the aircraft prior to flight.

PRESSURE ALTITUDE – The apparent altitude which varies as air pressure (and thus density) varies.

PROPELLER – A device (usually wooden) spun by the engine with blades angled so as to puch air backwards and create thrust.

PYLON – A marker used to mark a vertical reference point.

RELATIVE WIND – The wind a wing "sees." Relative wind is exactly opposite the flight path in a steady flow.

RIGID WING – An aircraft whose wing is fixed in a given shape.

ROLL – A control in which one wing moves up or down. Motion about the longitudinal axis.

ROLL STABILITY – The tendency for a wing to level out if one wing is lifted by a gust or a control action.

ROOT – The center or kee; of a wing.

RUDDER – A vertical moveable surface used to yaw an aircraft.

SEABREEZE – A wind from sea to land that sets up during the day near large bodies of water.

SECTIONAL – A chart or map showing airports, airways, terrain features and airspace limitations.

SHEAR TURBULENCE – Rough air caused by adjacent layers of air moving with different velocities.

SIMULATOR – A device set up to simulate flight. A flight simulator may be static or may actually move on a trailer.

SKID – A sliding motion to the outside of a turn as a result of too much rudder control applied.

SLIP – A sliding motion to the inside of a turn as a result of too little rudder or elevator control applied.

SOARING – Remaining aloft by using vertical air currents.

SPIN – A continuous uncontrolled turn caused by a stalled inside wing during a turn.

SPIRAL – A steep nose-down continuous uncontrolled turn usually resulting from a worsening spin.

SPOILERS – Control surfaces on top of a wing used to "spoil" lift and produce a turn (when used on one side) or degrade performance (when used on both sides).

STABILITY – See PITCH, ROLL AND YAW STABILITY.

STABILIZOR – A fixed horizontal or vertical surface at an aircraft's tail used to maintain straight and level flight. An elevator and rudder attached to the stabilizors deflect air during maneuvers.

STALL – A sudden increase in drag and loss of lift that occurs on a wing when the angle of attack is raised too high and the airflow separates from the wing.

STANDARD PRESSURE – The average pressure normal for a given height above sea level.

STEP – The notch on the bottom of a float. "Getting up on the step" means taxiing on the front part of the float.

STRATUS CLOUDS – Widespread layer clouds formed when a layer of air rises slowly. Usually smooth conditions are associated with stratus clouds.

STROBE – A blinking light mounted on an aircraft to improve visibility.

STRUT – A brace that runs from a wing to another portion of an aircraft.

SWEEP – An angling back of the wings when viewed from above.

TAIL – The area of an aircraft behind the main wing consisting of stabilizors, elevator and rudder. The empenage.

TAIL DRAGGER – An aircraft with a wheel at the tail and two main gear up front.

TAIL WIND – A wind directly from the rear of the aircraft.

TAXI – To run along the ground under power.

THERMAL – A warm bubble or column of rising air.

THREE-AXIS CONTROL – A control system consisting of rudder, elevator and ailerons or spoilers.

THROTTLE – The fuel control on an engine which makes it speed up or slow down.

THRUST – The forward force produced by the propeller.

THUNDERSTORM – A local violent storm caused by large volumes of rapidly rising moist air.

TIP RUDDERS – Rudders at the tips (outside ends) of a wing. Also called dragelons.

TIP VORTICIES – See VORTICIES.

TORQUE – Rotational force applied to the propeller.

TORQUE EFFECT – The tendency for an aircraft to roll the opposite way the propeller is rotating due to drag on the propeller.

TRAILING EDGE – The rearward most part of a wing.

TRICYCLE GEAR – Landing gear arranged with one wheel up front and two main gear further back.

TRIKE – A landing gear/seat/engine unit that attaches to a hang glider to convert it to a powered ultralight.

TRIM SPEED – The speed at which an aircraft flies with no input from the pilot.

TURBULENCE – Random swirling of the air felt as gusts and bumps in flight.

TWIST – See WASHOUT.

TWO-AXIS CONTROL – A control system consisting of only rudder and elevator or weight-shift and rudder.

ULTRALIGHT – A small single place aircraft weighing less than 155 pounds if unpowered or 254 pounds if powered (U.S. regulations).

VALLEY WINDS (UPSLOPE) – Winds that blow from a valley up a mountain during the day.

VARIOMETER – An instrument indicating how fast an aircraft is rising or descending. A vertical speed indicator.

VORTEX – A swirl or eddy in a fluid (such as air).

VORTICIES – Organized swirls produced at the tips of an aircraft's wings.

WASHOUT – Twist held in a wing so that the angle of attack of the wing tip is always less than at the root to help avoid stalling of the wing tip.

WARM FRONT – An advancing mass of warm air.

WIND GRADIENT – A slowing of the wind near the earth's surface due to surface roughness drag.

WINDSPEED – The speed of the air in relation to the ground. See also airspeed and groundspeed.

WING – The lifting surface of an aircraft.

WINGLET – A small wing (usually a vertical surface at the tips of the main wing).

WING LOADING – The number of pounds per square foot of wing area (or kg. per square meter).

YAW – A control in which one wing moves forward or back. Motion about a vertical axis.

YAW STABILITY – The tendency for an aircraft to resume a given heading when disturbed by a gust or control. Sweepback or a vertical stabilizor effect yaw stability.

ABOUT THE AUTHOR

Dennis Pagen was born and raised in Port Huron, Michigan where he became a devotee of swimming, water skiing, scuba diving, sailing and lying on the beach. He attended Michigan State University and graduated with honors in Electrical Engineering. While in college he participated in cross-country and rugby as well as two expeditions climbing an 18,000 foot peak in Mexico.

After college he moved to Boulder, Colorado then Leysin, Switzerland. Dennis spent three years in Leysin, a climbing and ski resort high above the Rhone valley in the French speaking portion of Switzerland. During this time he taught mathematics at an American High School for two years and skiing for one. He traveled extensively throughout Europe and toured North Africa and Russia. Upon leaving Switzerland, he headed east and spent a year visiting numerous Asian countries before crossing the Pacific to the U.S.

Dennis first saw hang gliding in 1973 and quickly became an avid flyer. His first book—Flying Conditions—was written in 1975 when he discerned a distinct lack of knowledge of small-scale weather effects. The libraries of Penn State University near his current home and the active sailplane community were an ideal source of information on this subject. After the success of this book, he has written a number of others covering sport aviation and outdoor recreation.

Dennis has served on the United States Hang Gliding Assn. (USHGA) Board of Directors since its inception in 1975 and wrote the USHGA's Instructors Manual as well as the certification guidelines. He was the 1978 National Hang Gliding Champion, twice member of the American Cup team and has won numerous meets, including four Regional Championships (1977, 1978, 1982, 1983). He is a Master rated hang gliding pilot.

Dennis began flying powered ultralights in 1979 with a Gemini system attached to a hang glider. Since then he has owned three different ultralights and has flown many other designs. He served two years as vice president of the Experimental Aircraft Assn. Ultralight Division and currently serves as advisor to the Aircraft Owners and Pilots Assn. Ultralight Division and is an instructor for the Air Safety Foundation's Ultralight Examiner program. He authored the original powered ultralight instructor standards for the USHGA which was subsequently used as a model for other organizations.

In 1980, Dennis wrote the first book on the sport of powered ultralight flying (it has since then been replaced by his newer books). Later, his training course appeared which was the first use of the gradual accomodation method now standard in the sport.

Music, Art and outdoor activities are Dennis' hobbies while flying over the Pennsylvania mountains is his favorite pastime.